A SONG
FOR JENNY

A SONG FOR JENNY

A Mother's Story of
Love and Loss

JULIE NICHOLSON

HarperCollins*Publishers*

HarperCollins*Publishers*
77–85 Fulham Palace Road,
Hammersmith, London W6 8JB

www.harpercollins.co.uk

First published by HarperCollins*Publishers* 2010

1 3 5 7 9 10 8 6 4 2

A catalogue record of this book is
available from the British Library

ISBN 978-0-00-725079-0 (hardback)

Printed and bound in Great Britain by
Clays Ltd, St Ives plc

This book is dedicated to Jenny's family.

The writing of it is dedicated to Lizzie and Thomas.

Contents

CHAPTER 1

Overture

Time is constant, life changes

Traeth Bychan, Anglesey, Thursday 7 July 2005

I awake to a tap on my bedroom door and the rattle of china as my uncle comes into the room with a cup of tea. 'It's going to be a lovely day' he says as he puts the cup and saucer down on my bedside table.

I mutter a sleepy 'thank you', watching through half-closed lids as he leaves the room, a dressing-gowned form capped with a head of snowy white hair. I lie still, becoming aware of the early-morning sun pouring in through the curtains and the gentle chirping of birds outside the window confirming the lovely day. The room is bathed in a warm and creamy glow. I watch the curtains for movement, for sign of a breeze; there's not a flicker in their long creamy folds. As I laze in a half-asleep, half-wakeful state, the sound of a distant kettle boiling reminds me of my waiting cup of tea. Propping myself up on one elbow, I lean over to drink some, narrowly missing banging my head on the frame of the bunk bed. I take a couple of sips, replace the cup in its saucer and pick up my watch to check the time before lying back on the pillows: 7.40 a.m. No rush to get up. Looking above I contemplate the strips of pine in the base of the top bunk, crossing from side to side, supporting the mattress, bedding tucked neatly around; even the underside made up with care and precision, no crinkles or creases. I smile, remembering countless arguments and negotiations between children over who got the top bunk.

Voices and noises merge from other parts of the house: a teapot being filled; cupboard door opening and closing; bathroom door locking; a cough. Still I lie, cocooned in the bottom bunk while sounds, sun and domestic activity wash over me. Holiday mode!

An image of the church where I am Priest-in-Charge intrudes briefly. With a blink it is gone. There is no one to call me vicar here and I can relax in the knowledge that I am what I have always been with these people in this place, daughter and niece. For a week; no clerical collar or ministerial responsibility, bliss!

This holiday is a bonus for me. My parents planned to visit my uncle and aunt and I was in a position to take some time away from work at short notice in order to drive them, leaving Greg, my husband, at home in charge of the dog and other household delights. While I'm languishing under the covers, enjoying a lazy start to the day, Greg will already have left for his office, avoiding the worst of Bristol's morning rush-hour traffic and be getting ready to begin a day's work.

I close my eyes, not sleeping but thinking, daydreaming, and roaming back over years of visits to the island. I try to work out how long it is since my Uncle Jimmie first came here to work; it seems like a lifetime ago. It is. I was in my teens. Had it not been for that move I may never have ventured far enough into North Wales to discover this small Isle of Anglesey, and a whole chunk of family history would have been different. Is that fate or serendipity or maybe just plain old chance? One action leads to another. My uncle, aunt and cousins moving to Anglesey from Gloucestershire set in motion a whole other sequence of meetings and relationships. There's a thought and not yet eight o'clock in the morning! I consider writing the thought down, it may come in useful for a sermon, but decide the effort of getting out of bed and looking for a pen is too great. I ponder instead a rapidly moving montage of memories – adventurous, ambivalent – spanning thirty-plus years of visiting Anglesey. After a few moments I yawn and stretch, returning to the present. One thing at least remains constant: the warmth and close affinity with this household.

Martyn and Sharon; Julie and Vanda: two sets of siblings; four cousins with a close bond from childhood which has not diminished over age or distance and which has extended to our children and partners. In theory our children are a mixture of nieces, nephews, first cousins and second cousins. In practice they are all simply cousins and their parents a collective of aunts and uncles.

It gets better. Two cousins then married two brothers. My cousin Sharon met Mike, whose family had a holiday home on the island. Later, I was introduced to Mike's elder brother Greg at a party and the rest as they say is history. Sharon and I are first cousins who became sisters-in-law through marriage. Our respective children are our cousins but also our nieces and nephews. To each other the children are second or third cousins through their mothers and first cousins through their fathers.

It is impossible not to smile at memories of when Sharon and I have referred to each other interchangeably as cousin and sister-in-law. The children have always been close cousins whether they are one, two or three times removed and Sharon and I have always been 'auntie' more than cousins to each other's offspring.

To people who meet us en masse, as it were, this can appear a complicated set of family relationships. I prefer to see us a wonderfully diverse group of individuals who look, sound and act differently but who all come together as something akin to a pseudo Greek chorus. This doesn't mean to say we are always in perfect harmony. Quite the contrary. Over the years there have been fallouts, hurts and disagreements as I imagine there are in most families. Somehow we all muddle through and keep reforming in solidarity and unity.

Fully awake now, I make no effort to leap out of bed, reaching instead for my book. I spot a pencil and write down the earlier thought in the inside cover. My uncle pops his head around the door. 'More tea?'

'Yes please,' I answer, draining the cup of now cold tea before handing it over for a refill. I hear my mother and aunt discussing the merits of showering first or last. Decision made, my aunt comes into my room and asks how I slept, tells me my mother is currently taking a shower. We talk briefly about the change in weather and the fact that the washing machine is about to go on if I need anything washed. I nip out of bed and hand over a small pile of light washing before retreating back under the covers, book in hand, turning resolutely away from the room to immerse myself in a tale of subterfuge and deceit.

After a second cup of tea and short but satisfying read, the bustle of household activity finally coaxes me out of bed; that, and my mother pointedly informing me that the bathroom is now free!

Showered, dressed for a day at the beach, bed made and curtains pulled back, I join the kitchen throng and offer to help with breakfast, handing my used cup and saucer to my uncle washing up at the sink after the early morning round of teas. I glance at the kitchen clock: the time is just coming up to 8.45 a.m. My aunt is preparing a pan to cook bacon for the men and taking orders for breakfast as she places plates in the oven to warm. A partly cut loaf of bread and bread knife are laid out on the bread board. Toast in waiting. I decide to leave the bread-slicing task to my mother. Instead I open a cutlery drawer, count out five sets of breakfast cutlery, and gather side plates, jar of marmalade and other breakfast paraphernalia and head for the dining room. As I walk down the hallway I pass my father coming out of the bathroom, clutching his toilet bag and upbeat about the sunny start to the day. His hair is standing up in little white tufts, not yet brushed. 'Not dressed yet dad?' I joke. 'No,' he quips back indignantly. 'I've been waiting to get in the bathroom. You lot have taken so long!'

I go about the ritual of setting the table for breakfast, placing my armful of cutlery and crockery temporarily on the sideboard while I pull out the gate-leg table and position the chairs. Sunlight filtering through trees casts patterns across the carpet, like little scatterings of popcorn. Drawn by the sunlight I go over to the window and look out at the garden; my eyes are attracted by greenfinches feeding greedily from tubes of nuts and seeds suspended from the bird table, hanging on by clawed feet, their heads bobbing up and down as they peck busily. Every now and then one lifts its stout head, seeming to look around, proudly displaying distinctive flecks of lime green on its breast and wings. I watch, unobserved, before looking beyond the bird table to the hedge of shrubs by the stone wall that borders the property: dark green leaves mingling with bright red drooping fuchsia heads. My eyes skip over the road to trees standing tall and partly obscuring the sun, then on to an empty car park adjacent to the local pub, fields rolling away into the distance, grazing sheep dotted about the landscape, the edge of a golf course; beyond it all, towering vast and magnificent in the distance, the Snowdonia mountain range. Hands cupped around my chin, elbows resting on the window sill, I lean for a while and gaze out at the glorious picture, embraced in the stillness. A movement to my right draws my attention as my uncle moves into the frame and scatters crumbs on to the bird table; part of his morning ritual. I straighten up and turn back into the room.

I move contentedly from table to cupboard, counting out place mats and arranging them around the open table, completely engaged in my task. My aunt comes in with some glasses and orange juice, saying she and my mother would just have toast so wouldn't need forks. She's freshly showered, hair still damp. My mother comes in and the three of us continue a conversation started the previous evening as to how we should spend the day. We talk about driving to a cove further around the island, or going across the Menai Straits and driving down to Criccieth where we can have a walk along the coast and buy some home-made ice cream. I mention going to visit my husband's aunt in a local nursing home later in the day.

My mother and aunt are alike and easily recognisable as sisters although they are slightly different shapes. My mother is the taller and more slender younger sister and my aunt is shorter and slightly more rounded. Both now have grey hair, my mother's slightly more steel grey than my aunt's, but both with modern short cuts which, without any shadow of doubt, will soon be transformed from their current slightly springy post-shower state into stylish coiffures.

Alone again I get on with setting the table. A ray of sun streams in through the window illuminating particles of dust floating in the air. Pictures of children and grandchildren mounted on the wall are caught in the line of sunlight. Distracted, I lift my face for a moment and gaze at the pictures, each telling their own story of time passing. How lazy I feel. The ray passes and the room is cast in shadow as the sun is hidden momentarily behind some clouds. The sound of a toaster popping up reminds me to get a move on as the irresistible aroma of bacon cooking wafts along the hallway from the kitchen. A voice calling out from the kitchen instructs everyone to sit down, breakfast is almost ready. I speed up my task, leaning across the table to set the last few bits and pieces and just as I retrieve two surplus forks the telephone rings on the sideboard behind me.

Transferring the cutlery into one hand I lift the receiver to my ear, expecting to pass it over to my aunt Karina. It's my younger daughter Lizzie. I can hardly take in what she's saying; she sounds urgent and is speaking too fast to make sense. Words leap out: explosions ... underground ... mobile ... not able to reach Jenny. The words are confused but the fear in her voice is clear.

'It's all over the news,' she says firmly and with absolute clarity. 'Haven't you heard?'

'No,' I say. 'Calm down, tell me again.'

Lizzie speaks slower this time but with no less urgency. 'I think something's happened to Jenny, Mum.' She sounds upset.

'Calm down,' I repeat. 'Don't panic. There's no reason to think anything has happened to her.'

A small crowd gathers in the doorway as my parents, uncle and aunt make their way in for breakfast, the latter laden with plates.

'Who is it?'

'What's the matter?'

Voices overlapping; I try to shush them, waving my cutlery-laden hand, indicating for someone to turn the television on and speaking over the mouthpiece: 'It's Lizzie; there's been some kind of explosion on the London Underground.'

A small portable TV is switched on in the corner of the room and the space is suddenly full of excitable voices and transmitted confusion. I try to concentrate on what my daughter is saying, keeping an eye on the television screen.

Lizzie tells me she had woken to her radio alarm and the 9 a.m. news reporting explosions on the London Underground. She had tried to call Jenny's mobile but wasn't getting any response. 'Something's happened to Jenny, I know it has' – more insistent this time – 'I've tried her mobile over and over but she's not answering.'

'What time is it now?' I ask. Someone says 9.15.

'She's probably at work already and has her phone switched off.' My voice is calm, more concerned with reassuring my younger daughter than troubled over the whereabouts of my elder daughter.

'As soon as Jenny realizes what's happened she'll call to let us know she's OK.' Of this I am certain.

My father and Uncle Jimmie are heartily tucking into a plate of bacon and egg.

'We're about to have breakfast,' I tell Lizzie. 'I'll speak to Dad and James then call you back.'

'OK, Mum, thanks, but promise you'll call me as soon as you find out anything.'

'I will, don't worry.'

I replace the receiver and relay Lizzie's call to the others as I simultaneously dial my husband's office number. Greg answers immediately. I ask if he's heard the news. He hasn't. I tell him about Lizzie's phone call. He says he'll listen to the news and try Jenny at work. Then I try James, Jenny's partner, on his mobile. He's in the lab and probably hasn't heard any news either. James's phone goes on to voicemail. I leave a message for him and then send a text to Jenny, tapping out the words 'are you ok? call me as soon as you can. Mx'.

I join the others at the table and start to eat breakfast, quite calmly, despite the drama of the phone conversation with Lizzie. The television remains on in the background. A report that the explosion could be a collision between two trains is debated. I drink a glass of orange juice and eat a slice of bacon. I ask my mother to pass the toast.

'White or brown?' she asks.

'I don't mind.' There are coffee cups on the table, filled with coffee, Poole pottery, white, with a brown rim – no mismatched crockery in this house! I don't remember putting the cups there; someone else must have. My father asks what the plans are for today and what time we are going out. 'Later this morning,' I suggest, 'about eleven?' I spread my toast with some butter and marmalade as the others discuss the day's itinerary.

The landline rings; my cousin's daughter calling to speak with my aunt. Delighted, my aunt replaces the receiver, a proud grandmother. 'Joanne has her results, a 2:1.'

Joanne asked if we had heard from Jenny. Apparently she had sent a text as soon as she saw the news but hadn't heard back yet. Jo had also sent a text to her other cousin working in London, Michelle, who had replied saying she was fine and in work.

I take a bite of toast and wash it down with a mouthful of coffee, freshly brewed, savouring the aroma. Replacing my cup in the saucer, I pick up the slice of toast to take another bite and stop, feeling suddenly that it is imperative I speak to Jenny. I drop the toast on my plate and get up from the table, picking up my mobile and searching for Jenny's name in my contacts list. I press call. Ringing out; no reply. I send another text urging her to call a.s.a.p. I don't panic; there's still no real cause for alarm. I just need to hear her voice and then we can all get on with the day.

We switch the television on in the sitting room; listen to reports of power surges, speculation over the cause, explosions at three underground sites, one is Edgware Road, Circle and District line. The camera shows a slanted angle of the entrance down a side road. 'That's the tube station I used when I lived in London,' I comment to no one in particular. We all watch, aghast, as the horror unfolds. I didn't think Jenny's route took her on that line. 'Something has to cause a power surge,' my father's voice cuts across the voices on the TV.

I track down Jenny's work number and call her office. She hasn't arrived yet but her colleague assures me they'll get her to contact me as soon as she walks through the door. I ask if anyone else has failed to turn up. There's a moment's pause before the person on the other end of the phone says, 'No, only Jenny,' and then hastily explains that London is in complete chaos and lots of people must be delayed getting to work. I phone my husband Greg who has also called Jenny's office and left messages on her mobile. We don't linger talking in case Jenny is trying to get through.

Loud sirens blare out from the television, filling the air across London, piercing the already frenzied atmosphere and spilling over into the Anglesey household. Breakfast is being cleared away in the next room and for a few minutes the rhythmic chink of crockery and cupboard doors and drawers opening and closing mingles with the jarring sounds on the screen. Strips of distinctive blue and white police tape begin to appear, criss-crossing the screen, defining scenes of crime. My mother sits beside me saying there's more coffee if anyone would like it.

Confused-looking commuters emerge from the underground, immediately set upon by reporters asking questions, eager for news and information. I listen intently, my senses alert to what is happening on the screen hundreds of miles away, yet immediate here. People seem muddled; most don't have any clear idea of what has happened; some talk of bangs, smoke, darkness; some nurse minor wounds and are being helped away. One person says they heard a bang and describes how the train just suddenly stopped. Another passenger, at Edgware Road, describes seeing bodies in the wreckage. Oh God!

My aunt stands watching in the doorway for a while, a cloth in her hand. 'Terrible, isn't it,' she says, more of a statement than a question.

My mother asks again if anyone would like coffee. I say, 'Yes, please,' and she follows my aunt out into the kitchen, needing to be active more than drink coffee.

My father, uncle and I are left alone in the room, watching, not speaking; Dad in an armchair, sitting back, legs crossed, neglecting the newspaper open on his lap; my uncle leaning forward, intent on the screen, arms resting on his knees; me on the sofa; all three of us bask-ing in sunlight flooding through picture windows on two sides of the room. There's a calm silence between us, in contrast to the tension and barrage of sounds and images currently being transmitted from London. As we watch, reports flood in of another explosion, a bus. 'That's not a power surge,' I hear my father say.

Shocked, we wait for further news, more details. My uncle calls out, 'There's been another explosion,' and my mother and aunt rush back in and sit down wondering out loud, as we all do, how many more? Where will it end? Five of us gaze at the screen in horrified awe as the minutes tick by with barely a movement or a sound between us.

My mobile rings; I snatch it from the sofa and grasp it to my ear. Automatically I move out of earshot of the television and into another room. It's Jenny's partner James; his phone has been switched off as he was doing a radiation test in the lab, he's only now picking up messages. I tell him what I know, or don't know. He says he'll call back when he's checked out news reports. I report back to the others whose looks of resignation mirror my own.

I try to assimilate all the information streaming from the television, beginning to feel uneasy at Jenny's silence and non-appearance at work. It doesn't make sense; she can't be anywhere near any of the explosion sites, so where is she? Why aren't we hearing from her? My eyes are fixed on the screen but my mind wanders. Come on Jenny, call. Maybe networks are blocked; everyone must be using mobile phones. She'll call one of us as soon as she can. Probably she's walking to work – hence the delay in getting to the office. Jenny's never one to hang about waiting for public transport. If anything, she'll be caught up in the crowds somewhere, part of the general throng and exodus spilling out from the underground. Still, it's slightly unsettling that she hasn't put in an appearance at work. I look at my phone, willing the familiar tune. I send another text: 'hope yr ok call me. Mx'.

The TV screen is displaying charts and computerized maps of the underground; coloured dots represent the movement of trains. There's more speculation and repetition of news for people recently tuned in. References to the G8 Summit – of course, that's going on in Scotland, peace talks, poverty, world issues with heads of state. Scotland Yard reports a major incident, multiple explosions but confusion over how many. From time to time I check my mobile, which is resting close beside me on the sofa, close at hand.

The household is quietly functioning, in limbo while we wait for news. Through the side window I see my aunt is now talking to her neighbour, across a stone wall and expanse of garden. The conversation is predictable. Occasional hand movements and a turn of the head in my direction tell their own story. My uncle gets out of his seat, muttering irritably over a journalist's inane comment. A few moments later he appears in the garden and walks around for a bit, before going over to my aunt, saying something to her and then disappearing out of view around the side of the house.

On the television there's still confusion over whether there have been four or six explosions and the official line is they're 'still unsure' as to the cause. The bus explosion was in Tavistock Square, outside the British Medical Association.

My mother comes back in with cups of coffee, followed by my aunt who pulls some small tables out. The tension emanating from the television is eased by routine conversation, reasoning and reassurance as to Jenny's whereabouts. For the moment everyone seems to have given themselves up to following events as they transpire in London; all talk of driving to Criccieth and idly meandering and eating ice cream temporarily suspended. I realize I've slipped from the sofa on to the floor, kneeling closer to the screen. Behind me someone says we're sure to have heard from Jenny by lunchtime so maybe we could have a sandwich here then drive to a cove further around the island for the afternoon.

I pop into the bathroom, clean my teeth and wonder whether to put on a bit of make-up. Staring at my reflection in the mirror, I decide it's hardly worth it as we'll be going to the beach later.

Lizzie calls again; I tell her there's no news and we're waiting for James to call back. I ask about her brother Thomas. She's woken him up and they're sitting together, glued to the television. I call my sister Vanda but she's at work so I leave a message.

Almost immediately my phone goes off again. It's James saying he's received an email from one of Jenny's work colleagues, Michaela. Apparently Jenny sent her a text at 8.30 a.m. saying 'Bakerloo line screwed arse!' We try to fathom out her cryptic text, does it mean Bakerloo line wasn't working, overcrowded, delayed? James is convinced that if there was a problem with the Bakerloo line Jenny wouldn't have hung around waiting but would have found an alternative route to work and confirms she is most likely caught up in the general chaos of it all as her route wouldn't take her near any of the explosion sites. He seems confident and I relax a little. We agree to keep in touch though.

'Was that James?'

'What did he say?'

'Has he spoken to Jenny?'

'No.'

I turn and look into the faces of my family who have gathered in the doorway and relay the conversation with James. My mother moves further into the room and sits on a dining-room chair. My father, frustrated at not being able to hear properly, interrupts; wanting confirmation of what's being said, bending his head in the direction of my voice, deafness causing him to frown in concentration.

As promised, I call and speak to Lizzie, who sounds less fraught, though no less anxious. She and Thomas are regularly leaving messages on Jenny's mobile: 'At least when she checks her phone, she'll know that we've all been looking out for her.' I agree and bring her up to date with what James has said. Bemoaning the fact that I'm so far away, but glad that Lizzie and Thomas are home in Bristol together, I end the call and go back to the television. All we can do is wait and watch.

Over and over again, we watch scene after scene of emerging commuters, visibly shaken. I dare not take my eyes from the screen, scanning for a face with shoulder-length blond hair. Would she be wearing it loose or tied back? What was she wearing? Why am I looking for her? I peer deeper into the screen, tutting with frustration as the camera moves away before I have a chance to properly scan a group of bystanders near Edgware Road tube. A stretcher is brought out and borne towards a waiting ambulance; a girl walks alongside, with long fair hair and a denim skirt. I hold my breath for a second. More passengers emerge. Some turn away from cameras; others speak to reporters. I pick up my phone, press to contacts … search … Jenny … call …

Official voices emerge; the Home Secretary makes a statement from Downing Street, speaking of a dreadful incident and terrible injuries, his face, solemn and worried, communicating more than the careful words being spoken. The Police Commissioner Sir Ian Blair states there have been about six explosions and suggests this is probably a major terrorist attack. Nothing clear; nothing confirmed.

I feel a sudden need to break up the atmosphere in the room and make something happen; all at once I feel uneasy and unable to sit still any longer watching more and more of the same barely changing scenes. I move over to the window and stare out over the panorama of garden, fields and mountains. All so tranquil, no passing cars or even a breeze to sway the leaves in the trees, motionless except for the birds busy and unconcerned, flitting from shrub to tree then away to somewhere beyond my sight. Where are you, Jenny?

A robin lands on the bird table, ignoring the scattering of crumbs, and seems to look directly at me, not moving, its red breast shimmering in the sunlight. We hold the stillness; I gaze back unblinking and scarcely breathe, afraid to break the connection. Moments tick by until unconsciously I raise a finger to my eye and wipe away a tear. The robin captures the movement and flies away. A shiver goes through my body. Why a tear: the beauty of the moment? Or something else, unspeakable, unthinkable?

With sudden determination I turn from the window and move purposefully out of the room, away from the television, calling out to my aunt, asking if I can use the telephone. I dial a number and wait while it rings. Taking a deep breath and keeping my voice steady I say for the first time: 'Hello, it's Julie. We can't get hold of Jenny.'

Silence at the other end of the phone, then a voice, quiet, tentative.

I only pick up fragments of what's being said: watching television; questions; concern.

I respond calmly, hearing only my voice going round and round in my head: *We can't get hold of Jenny*.

'I'll let you know. As soon as we hear, I'll let you know.'

Then again, another number, another silence, more questions – more or less the same questions and replies as before, everyone is watching the television and each time I repeat the words: *We can't get hold of Jenny*.

The morning takes on the quality of a vigil. Watching and waiting. There's very little conversation, all of us focused on events in London. Physically we're gathered together yet each of us is sitting quietly and isolated in our own thoughts and hanging unspoken between us is the hope that we will hear from Jenny soon. If we talk, we talk about what we see, leaving anything else unsaid. Sitting around waiting for a call and watching developments is about all any of us can do, apart from the odd household chore or necessary trip to the loo. Telephone calls are hastily dealt with to keep the lines free for that all-important voice.

I can't bear to leave the television screen, can't bear to watch and can't bear not to. It's the only way of keeping in touch. I look at my watch; it's just turned mid-day.

The scene moves to Scotland, Gleneagles; we're told the Prime Minister is about to make a statement. He steps forward, flanked by other world leaders; there's an ominous air of solidarity, suits and ties, a sea of grey and white against a stone backdrop and blue sky. Tony Blair looks grave and, wringing his hands, begins to speak, telling us what we've already worked out for ourselves: London has been subjected to a terrorist attack. There have been serious injuries and people killed. The PM is returning to London, leaving the summit to carry on without him.

Cameras take us back to London. The Home Secretary confirms four explosions and announces the underground will be closed all day. Never mind that, my mind screams, what about the people, what about Jenny. I don't care if the underground is closed, I don't care if the summit continues or not, I want to know where my daughter is. But I stay calm and don't say anything, just keep watching.

Some of the time I watch from my position on the sofa, a ring-side perspective, not wanting to miss a possible sighting, recognition of a precious face glancing at the camera as it passes by, like the girl in the denim skirt who, for a moment, could have been Jenny. Or, when the screen is taken up by politicians, maps, police, reporters, I move over to the window and spend the time gazing into the distance, listening as the myriad voices behind me assess, explain and attempt to reassure. Voices fade in and fade out as my mind wanders, lost in thought, picturing Jenny, wondering where she is, wishing I could speak to her and hoping she's far away from the places of terror and harm. I imagine her half walking, half running along Shaftesbury Avenue, preparing to burst through the doors of Rhinegold Publishing, full of loud and exuberant explanations for her late arrival at work and being told to phone home, someone saying hastily, 'James, your father, your mother, your sister and your brother are waiting to hear from you, they need to know you're OK.' And I hear her voice as I have so many times on the past from friends' houses after school, teenage jaunts, late trains back to university, almost singing down the phone: *Hi, it's me, I'm here, I'm fine, there's no need to worry*.

Standing at the window, my back to the room, I become aware of other voices.

'I thought we might as well have some lunch.'

'Can you pull that table out, Jimmie?'

'Alf, would you like ham or cheese?'

'Do you want tea or coffee, Julie?'

I turn back to the room. 'Tea please.'

Plates of sandwiches appear: cheese, ham and English mustard, cherry tomatoes halved on each plate. Questions easily answered dart backwards and forwards as lunch temporarily takes priority over television.

'Any salt for the tomatoes?'

'It's already on.'

'Be careful you don't get tomato juice down your shirt.'

'What time is it?'

'Quarter past one.'

New voices speak and voices already heard are repeated. I listen to the Mayor of London describing the attack as a cowardly act and praising Londoners for the way they've responded, with calm and courage. President Bush tells us the War on Terror must continue and the

17

Archbishop of Canterbury urges all religious leaders to stand and work together for the wellbeing of the nation. I listen and I listen and I listen, nibbling at my ham and mustard sandwich and sipping tea from a white china cup.

The phone rings and all our attention is jerked away from the television. I jump to my feet, spilling tea in the saucer as I replace the cup before rushing into the dining room and grabbing the receiver to my ear. I listen to my sister's voice, calling from work in her lunch hour, and hear myself say, 'I'm not overly worried.' Neither of us speaks for a moment – Vanda knows it isn't true and in my heart I know it isn't true. I feel suddenly I have to get out of Anglesey and in a moment I make my decision. 'I'm going to look at train times.'

There's another pause in which I picture Vanda in the blue uniform she wears as a theatre nurse in a Hampshire hospital. 'I'll call as soon as I get home.' Home being a village on the outskirts of Reading which, like Bristol, seems far away from Anglesey.

After replacing the receiver, I stand for a moment looking at it, knowing I've made the right decision, the only decision, and I tell myself not to panic. Then I go back to the others waiting with half-eaten sandwiches, a television with the sound turned down, the sun pouring through the windows and say to their expectant faces, 'I'm going to London.' No one is surprised, no one tries to dissuade me. My mother wants to come with me but is worried about slowing me down. There's also my father to consider. I think it would be better if they stay in Anglesey with my aunt and uncle as I don't know where I'm going when I get to London, how I'm going to get around or how much walking there's likely to be. My mother understands and, hard as it is for her, agrees I should go without her. It's all very gentle and considerate, both of us trying to do what's best. As I leave the room to phone Greg I hear my father say, 'It's just as well she isn't going to drive,' or something like that.

Greg is still at work, keeping occupied but listening to the news and in touch with Lizzie and Thomas.

'I'm going to London.'

'When?'

'As soon as I can make arrangements. This evening probably. I feel too far away from everything here and want to be on hand, just in case.'

He doesn't ask me in case of what, which is just as well as I don't think I could answer.

'Are you driving?'

'No, I'm going by train.'

'Good. Do you want me to come with you?'

We talk about practicalities for a while and settle on Greg staying in Bristol with Lizzie and Thomas so they have one parent with them at least.

I come off the phone and think what to do next; find out about train times, I suppose. I don't do anything straight away but sit on the dining chair next to the sideboard, thinking about the conversation with Greg. I'm not sure the full significance of Jenny's continued non-contact and non-appearance at work has quite sunk in with him yet. Has it with me? I lean my head back against the wall and close my eyes for a minute, feeling the warmth of the sun on my face. *Please be all right, Jenny, please don't be hurt.*

I think about Lizzie and Thomas, alone at home. Anyone would think they were 12 and 7, not young adults of 22 and 17. Still, when the pressure's on, they're my babies and I'm their mother; and the pressure is on. I think of them huddled together on the sofa, frightened and waiting for news. The reality is they're spending the day in the same way as me, watching, waiting and feeling helpless, calling someone when they need to and keeping vigil for their sister. Even so I can't help but worry about them. Which is perhaps why, when my sister-in-law calls from Dorset a few minutes later asking if there's anything she can do, I ask, without hesitation, 'Can you go to Bristol and be with Greg and Lizzie and Thomas?'

Jenny's route takes her from Reading into Paddington, then the Bakerloo line tube from there via Edgware Road to Oxford Circus, change to the Central line for Tottenham Court Road and walk from there to Shaftesbury Avenue. I've checked with James; he's certain of the route. Nevertheless, I call him and ask about the route again, repeating it back for confirmation. We talk about what we should do, how we can get information. James tells me what he knows, which isn't much more than I do, just a few details. The police will be issuing a number for people to call if they're worried about someone – I must have missed that – which will be released through the media. Meanwhile people are being urged not to travel into London.

I can't believe we're having this conversation.

James has decided to go to London as well and is working out the best way to get there if we still haven't heard from Jenny by late afternoon. He thinks there isn't much point in trying to get into London yet, owing to the transport situation. If Jenny hasn't contacted any of us by the time the police release the helpline number we'll phone in with her details and decide what to do from then.

We talk more about where Jenny could be and why we haven't heard from her, staying rational, calm and focused on the positives. She could be trying to find a way to work on foot, there's still such chaos with commuters trying to get places, the underground at a standstill, mobile phone networks down, people trying to get out of London. We talk about the cryptic 'Bakerloo line screwed' message to Michaela and how she may have been forced to find an alternative route. We explore all the possibilities we can think of. James also believes she would walk, not hang about. If by any chance she is caught up in the mayhem, she would be helping others in some way; if someone was hurt Jenny wouldn't leave them. Maybe she's standing on the sidelines somewhere, in the crowds, watching from a distance? All sorts of things could have happened in the mass exodus, people falling over each other, incidents that wouldn't be noticed or reported, minor road traffic accidents. She might have dropped her bag, be searching for it. *But it's several hours now since the blasts,* a little voice in my head niggles. I drive the thought back. I tell James I'm going to phone my friend Bruce, a police inspector, to see if there's any other way we can get information.

When I call Bruce he's shocked and concerned, says it's best to go with the system at the moment, frustrating as it is. He's going to keep in touch and asks if there's anything he can do, or anyone he can call. I don't know. I don't want it to become a big thing, maybe let one or two mutual friends know.

There's a passenger talking to a reporter outside Edgware Road, sounding shaken and describing what he can remember. As the tube pulled out of the station his eye was caught by a girl at the opposite end of the carriage who was standing by the doors reading a book. He was looking at her immersed in her book; he said she glanced up for a moment and smiled, he noticed her big eyes and how attractive she was, then the next moment there was a blast and he watched her fly backwards out through the window or door.

I can only stare at the screen in horror and disbelief. He could be describing Jenny. *Don't be so ridiculous,* I tell myself. *It's not Jenny. It couldn't be Jenny.* The train was going in the wrong direction; he said it was going to Paddington. Jenny would be travelling away from Paddington, not towards it. But it sounded so like her, head buried in a book, everything he described. The reporter and camera have gone to another passenger. *No,* I want to scream at the television, *come back to him; I want to find out more.* I look around the room to say something and find I'm alone, no one to share it with. The moment has gone. When my mother and aunt come back into the room, I tell them about the interview and they watch with me for a while in the hope that it will be repeated. A number of eye-witness accounts are retold or rerun, but not this one and I wonder if I imagined it.

No one has mentioned going out since lunchtime. We all know the possibility has long gone.

I've looked at train times but connections are not good at this time of day, I wouldn't arrive in London until late tonight and there'd be lots of hanging about on station platforms. My mother and aunt ponder the alternatives with me as we sit in front of the television.

Police release the promised casualty hotline number for people to call. It's just after 4 p.m. I copy the number down from the screen and go into the dining room to call from the landline but when I dial the number nothing connects. Perhaps it isn't activated yet? I go back into the sitting room and double check I've taken the number down correctly and try again. Nothing!

I keep trying, and finally get an engaged tone. Over and over again I try to get through and all I get is engaged, engaged, and engaged.

'Can't you get through?' my mother asks.

'No,' I answer, slightly impatiently.

Vanda calls again; she's spoken to James and had much the same conversation as I had earlier. It doesn't make any logistical sense that Jenny could be caught up in the explosions. We keep telling each other the same thing. She's also spoken to a friend whose husband works in London. He doesn't know whether he'll be able to get home because of the transport situation. Vanda said she's been trying the casualty hotline number also, as has James. Apparently operators can't deal with the level of calls.

I keep trying and finally get through. Someone takes down Jenny's name and details plus some details from me. I'm given a reference to quote. As soon as there's any news someone will be in touch;

meanwhile if I hear from Jenny can I call and let them know, quoting the reference? End of call. I don't know what I expected but, after the ardours of getting through, it seemed so matter of fact and all too brief.

My cousin Sharon calls from Manchester and I tell her about wanting to go to London and the difficulty with connections. She's back on the line a few moments later saying her husband Mike and middle daughter Joanne were looking up train details on the computer, and then asks if I'd like her to come with me to London. There's a pause, I can't speak and nod my head before getting out an emotional 'yes'. In that second's pause time rolls back to another phone call, in the middle of the night, when I picked up the phone to hear my cousin's voice telling me her baby Matthew had died. That time it was me asking 'Do you want me to come?' Simply that, and Sharon answering, 'Yes.'

I stop off to tell the others that Sharon is coming with me to London and then head for the bathroom, locking the door and sitting on the side of the bath. I feel the tears rising up and spilling over and I don't know who or what I'm crying for: Matthew, Sharon, or myself. I wash my face and go back to the sitting room to answer what seems like twenty questions about the whys and wherefores of meeting up with Sharon and getting to London. 'I've decided not to travel tonight but to leave as early as possible in the morning.'

'I'm glad Sharon's going with you.'

'Is she coming here?'

'Are you going to meet her?'

'What will Sharon do about Megan?' Megan is Sharon's youngest daughter.

They ponder the questions between them while I fetch a notebook and pen from the bedroom to begin making a list of numbers and things to take with me.

My friend Yvette gave me a small leather-bound notebook for my birthday. I carry it around with me and use it for jotting down thoughts or names of authors and 'must read' book titles, music, CDs, things like that. Leafing through the pages looking for a clear sheet I come across a note to myself: '*The Shadow of the Wind* Carlos Ruiz Zafón', followed by some hastily scrawled notes and publication details, then finally at the bottom of the page: 'Destiny doesn't do home visits!' I stare at the words, remembering.

It was a phone conversation, telling Jenny what I was reading and about my determined efforts to get *Shadow* included in the book list of a reading group I belong to – there's often a fierce contest! Jenny said she'd bought the book but hadn't started reading it yet, she was in the middle of something else. I was telling her about a passage I'd just read about destiny. 'Don't tell me any more,' she said, 'you'll spoil it.' About a week and a half later I was in the kitchen, cooking, when the phone rang.

As I lifted the receiver Jenny's voice rang out, no preamble, proclaiming loudly and delightedly, 'I've just got to that bit about destiny, profound or what!' I can hear her laughing voice as though it was a moment ago, not months.

Time has no meaning in memory.

I slowly turn over to a new page and carefully flatten the spine with the palm of my hand, almost reverently, before taking a deep breath, picking up the pen and writing: 'Casualty Hotline 0870 1566344 Ref: N75 Met Police Hendon.'

However tentative, having a task to focus on helps; it provides a purpose and eases the tension. There are practicalities to attend to and a new set of activities to occupy the mind. My mother and aunt sit beside me while I make a list of London hospitals and telephone numbers, details of friends and contacts in London; together we check and double-check relevant family numbers stored on my phone. It's methodical, doing what has to be done. Television becomes part of the background, reporters have nothing new to offer and so the news goes round and round in circles, with more time spent on commentary and analysis of the situation. The web of reporting is wider, advising the public that the Union Flag is flying at half mast over Buckingham Palace, productions in the West End have been cancelled, something that hasn't happened since the end of the Second World War, apparently. We all pause, collectively, when something – or someone – specific and relevant catches our attention; moments of possibility that we cling to with hardly a breath between us.

My mother asks whether I have enough cash on me. There's about thirty pounds in my purse so there's a general emptying of purses and wallets to ensure I have enough ready money for the journey and don't need to worry about looking for cashpoints. Practicalities! My purse is bulging with bits of paper and rubbish, receipts mostly, the odd paperclip and safety pin, a stub of pencil even. I sift through it all on the sofa, coming across a couple of stray five-pound notes folded amongst a distinctive green M&S receipt. Supermarket receipt after supermarket receipt is torn up and discarded, relieving the purse of the non-monetary litter of months. With a newly ordered purse I turn my attention to my bag and go through the same ritual, getting rid of screwed-up tissues, more receipts, bits of paper relating to work, empty chewing-gum wrappers and an assortment of pens which are sorted into those that work and those that join the pile of torn-up paper scattered beside me.

Somewhere in all of this a cup of tea appears but I don't notice until a voice reminds me to drink before it gets cold. I replace all that's relevant in the decluttered bag and gather up debris and discarded contents into a plastic carrier, which my aunt takes to put in the rubbish bin, leaving me to my cup of tepid tea.

The light is not so bright now; early evening shadows start to creep across the lawn. The day is losing its lustre. Patterns of leaves are cast against the grass and I trace the shapes with my eyes. Even though the sun is still warm in the sky the mountains in the distance have lost their earlier heat-haze shimmer; they seem darker and more intimidating as they stand rigid, outlined against the still blue sky.

Where are you Jenny? Are you helping someone, sitting with them and soothing them with your voice, holding their hand? If you're hurt, be brave, we'll be with you as soon as we can. Know that we're all thinking about you and trying to find you. Keep her safe, God, don't let her be hurt or frightened or alone.

The mountains are shimmering again, glistening, though the cause is not heat haze. *Stay positive. Believe she's all right.* I listen to the voice of reason inside my head, saying over and over again that no harm will have come to her; she'll be out there somewhere waiting for us. I turn from the window as I have so many times throughout the day and call her mobile, sending words of love and reassurance.

The last few hours have brought waves of callers and then periods of stillness and silence. Now there are flurries of activity and fewer gaps between calls. We've all found our purpose. I announce my intention to pack a bag and go into the bedroom dragging an overnight bag from the top of the wardrobe. I go through the sparse amount of holiday wear unpacked from the same bag a few days ago, now spread around a couple of drawers, and throw some underwear into the base, not bothering with my usual packing ritual of counting out pairs of knickers or matching sets and colours. My hand shuffles tops around, while my mind tries to decide what will be functional. The two won't co-ordinate and suddenly the simple task is beyond me. A voice from the doorway asks, 'Do you want any help?'

'I don't know what to take!' The voice of a frustrated and frightened child cries out and fills the space as I feel all my composure slipping from me. My aunt takes over and begins packing while I sit and watch. The rhythm of watching item after item being removed from drawers and cupboards, folded neatly and placed in the case has a calming effect. The overwhelming task and inner turbulence of moments ago settles into a gentle, comforting intimacy, *'the still point of the turning world'*.

Somewhere a clock is ticking, the sound regular and hollow, marking out time.

If we speak we speak about the ordinary, the job in hand. My aunt takes a pair of dark red linen trousers from a hanger and begins to fold them, commenting on how badly linen creases. My mother brings a small pile of freshly laundered clothes into the room enquiring if any are needed – she's been ironing, a safe and comforting ritual in times of uncertainty. The two sisters go through the items as I look on. The air is weighted with what is not being said.

'Humankind cannot bear very much reality.'

I think about my father and uncle keeping watch over the television further along the hallway, saying little and feeling much. These four people growing old are still youthful in my memory. Even though time has cast its shadow on their years they are to me as they have always been: constant, reliable, practical, a stoic generation, showing love in action and solidarity. I want to hug them all but don't quite know how.

Job done, we lay out on the bed the clothes that I will travel in and can't help smiling at the denim jacket that Jenny and Lizzie coveted after it was bought for me by the now infamous gurus of style Trinny and Susannah. For a moment I hold the jacket to me like a comfort blanket, breathing in the faint residue of last week's perfume and last year's memory, before hanging it over the bedpost and following my aunt out of the bedroom.

In the sitting room my uncle has poured a drink for himself and my father. There's an absence of the usual banter in the activity and nobody mentions the hilarity of the previous evening when he paid such attention to the ice and lemon that he left the gin out of our gin and tonics. A triumph of style over content! Then the mood was rich with joking and laughter, now the men sit in contemplative silence with their glass of whisky and hardly notice we've come back into the room.

As the evening wears on there's a quiet, fearful limbo about the house. Evening shadows turn to dim light and darkness before curtains are drawn and lamps switched on. *News 24* remains our constant companion and link to London. Number of confirmed dead is now thirty-seven. Earlier news reports are constantly repeated: the attack has all the hallmarks of al-Qaeda ... security services and police had no warning ... Queen is to visit some of those affected on Friday ... Prime Minister says it is a very sad day for British people but we will hold true to the British way of life. As I get up to answer the phone for the umpteenth time I wonder what the British way of life is.

'Julie, it's Martyn.'

'Hi.'

Hearing Martyn's voice is like a piece of an essential form slotting into place. The eldest, the tallest and now, on the end of the phone, the most authoritative.

'I've been talking with Vanda and Sharon. We're not going to let you do this alone.'

Pause.

'It's not looking good, is it?'

'No.'

Although my elder cousin and I speak for the best part of five minutes, that's all I really hear.

The distant brrrr of a replaced receiver at the other end of the line barely registers as I continue to clutch the phone tight against my ear long moments after the conversation ends. It feels like an invisible and sacred line has been crossed.

It's not looking good, is it?

With those words Martyn becomes the first person bold enough to articulate what we're all feeling. The truth, when we hear it, is hard to bear. With the echo of his sombre and resigned voice still resounding in my ear I replace the phone and go back to the others, saying, 'Martyn is coming with us to London,' leaving the rest unsaid.

Humankind cannot bear very much reality.

People are beginning to settle down for the night and family and friends who have been in contact throughout the day now want reassurance that if there's any news of Jenny I'll let them know, regardless of time. I promise to call even if it's the middle of the night. Here, bed and sleep is far from everyone's mind. My sister-in-law Chris has arrived in Bristol and Greg, Lizzie and Thomas are now all at home together. Lizzie tries to muster up a light-hearted comment about Auntie Chris arriving laden with enough food for an army. Thomas sounds very quiet and says he and Lizzie are going to drag the duvets downstairs and sleep on the sofa so they can keep the television on and be close to the phone if it rings. I tell him I'm going to find Jenny and bring her home. Greg speaks with a forced cheerfulness and we both collude with the pretence.

James is getting ready to go into London with a friend now that some of the access routes are reopened. He says he's going to head for hospitals – it's impossible to stay home and do nothing. He's been talking to Vanda and the suggestion is that we all meet up at his and Jenny's house in Reading in the morning and decide what to do if he doesn't find Jenny overnight and we need to resume a search.

Sharon and I talk about logistics of travel. There are no direct trains from Bangor so we'll either have to meet up en route or I could go to Manchester and we'd get a direct train from there. We talk about the possibility of me going to Manchester overnight; Mike, Sharon's husband, would come and collect me, and then we could get a train at 6 a.m. together. My head can't cope with the detail. I want to leave Anglesey and get to London as quickly and directly as I can. I'm aware that Sharon and Mike are trying to help but I can feel myself getting agitated working it all through. Finally we make a decision to travel independently from Anglesey and Manchester and meet up at Crewe station. I'm relieved. It means I'll have a bit of a wait for Sharon's train to arrive but that's OK. I suspect they don't want me to be alone, even for half an hour. 'I'll be fine,' I say.

I call out and ask my aunt if she has a taxi number and there's a scurry of activity while she searches for the number and I go through the saga of train times and connections with my mother who then relates it all to my father in the next room. My aunt comes up with details of a local lady she and my uncle have used for doctor's appointments in the past. She's reliable. That's what's important. The taxi is booked for 5 a.m.

A few minutes later Sharon calls again to say that Martyn wants to meet the train at Rugby and drive us the rest of the way. I sense myself being slowly enfolded in a protective shield. I don't question the motive. I can't go there yet.

Vanda has been calling hospitals, needing to be occupied and do something positive and pro-active towards finding Jenny. I take down a list of hospital numbers from her, adding them to the gathering contact information in my notebook: St Mary's, Royal Free, Charing Cross, Barts, Guys, Royal London.

It is long past midnight and the men are looking tired, wanting to keep watch but needing to sleep. They can hardly keep their eyes open. Television has a mesmerizing effect; reactions to the attacks from around the world fill the late-night airwaves. We leave it switched on because we can't bear to turn it off. My uncle is the first to give in and go to bed. My father stays, focused on the news, until age and the night stretching endlessly ahead get the better of him. My mother suggests he goes to bed. Significantly, he lies on top of the bed not under the covers – resting not sleeping.

The grandfather and the great-uncle drift in and out of sleep while the grandmother and great-aunt sit in companionable quiet with the mother, waiting and hoping and passing the long night together.

My aunt is knitting, filling time rather than enjoying the occupation, fingers on autopilot, eyes on the television. The sound has been turned off. The rhythmic clicking of needles taps into the silence. My mother is sitting very still, gazing at the screen but seeming miles away. There's a book lying unopened beside her on the settee. I wonder what she's thinking or trying not to think.

One of my aunt's sandals has fallen off exposing a strip of pale flesh on an otherwise suntanned foot. We're all wearing flip flops – exposing three sets of painted toenails, shades of red and deep pink – a frivolous sight which already belongs to yesterday.

The click-click of metallic knitting needles has a hypnotic effect. I close my eyes, listening, lulled by the repetitive sound. The distant drone of an electrical appliance, a fridge motor, emphasizes the silence. Minute after minute; needle against needle.

In my head I go over something James said earlier, about Jenny leaving for work, how she took him a cup of tea and teased him about being a sleepyhead; she told him not to stay in bed all morning but to get up and do his research. Then she gave him a kiss and dashed out of the house for the twenty-minute walk to the station. James said he was so sleepy he barely opened his eyes as he responded to her goodbye kiss. I try to visualize the scene; its warmth and intimacy is reassuringly real. I imagine the clothes she is wearing – for some reason I see her dressed in sky blue – and wonder if her hair was tied back or hanging loose, picturing it first one way and then the other. I smile at the exuberance in her voice calling out 'bye' as she slams the door behind her, not waiting for a reply, and inhale deeply at the faint echo of J'adore, her current favourite perfume, recently sprayed and lingering in the air as she hurries down the street. I watch her retreating back and then all I can see is her laughing face.

I wish I was in Bristol; I could be on my way to London now not waiting for morning.

The spell is broken.

My aunt asks if anyone would like coffee. My mother says she'll make it and gets to her feet, probably glad of something to do.

As we drink our coffee we go over the events of the day, recounting every detail from the moment Lizzie called. We go through checklists of people, family and friends called, people yet to be informed. Informed of what? What do we say? Jenny's missing? No! I don't want to say that. It sounds too formal, too meaningful. Say we can't get through to her; we don't know where she is and think she may be caught up in the chaos. Hopefully we'll know more in the morning. Hopefully.

I suddenly remember someone, a close family friend who would want to know and I'm relieved when my mother says she called her earlier.

We drift in and out of conversation, sometimes turning the sound up on the television, sometimes just sitting, lost in thought or watching the silent screen. Every now and then my mother picks up her mobile phone and checks for a message that isn't there, sending yet another to Jenny. My aunt has given up on the knitting for a while and has closed her eyes, drowsing; the partly made sweater lies in her lap, needles shoved into a fresh ball of wool. The waiting is interminable and we're all starting to feel exhausted, time is passing so slowly.

I close my eyes again. Muddled thoughts and anxieties play with my psyche. A tune repeats itself in my head and refuses to go away. I can't remember the passage, only the tune, from a musical setting of the Crucifixion. I concentrate hard, trying to recall the words, but they elude me. Instead, I find my own words, 'Stay awake, stay awake; do not sleep'.

The concentration becomes too much and I can't sit still any longer. 'I'm going to have a shower.'

My mother looks up as I speak. 'What time is it?'

We both look at our watches: – 3 a.m.

'Shall I make you a sandwich?'

'I don't feel like eating.'

'Take something for the journey then.'

'All right.'

When a Hambleton voice speaks, it's easier to assent than to argue! Hambleton is my maternal grandmother's family name. The Hambleton siblings were renowned for strong views and stubborn personalities, often resulting in family fallouts. Although all but one is now deceased, the legacy lives on. Within the current generation there's a lot of teasing as to who inherited the 'Hambleton' streak.

Before going into the bathroom, I sit on the edge of the bed and leave one more message on Jenny's phone, whispering into the mouthpiece as if it was her ear, then repeat the message in a text: 'Wherever you are, Jenny, be safe, we're all thinking about you. I'm coming to find you sweetheart. I'll be with you soon. Everything's going to be all right … be brave … I love you … Mumsie'.

It's a relief to get under the shower, refreshing. For a few minutes I stand motionless, giving myself up to the sensation, finding release in the powerful torrents of water gushing from the shower head, before reaching for the shower gel.

Carefully I step from the shower and pick up a couple of towels, wrapping the fluffy greenness around my head and then my body, drying my face on a corner and tucking it in, sarong style. Then I take a cleaning cloth and wipe down the shower cubicle – force of habit – before padding into the bedroom and drying myself. I bend over to dry my toes before straightening up to towel my hair, when I catch my reflection in the mirror. I freeze, staring in the glass, and like a bolt out of the blue have a sudden recollection of a dream, a nightmare, involving Jenny, that I had a couple of weeks ago, and with the memory comes an overwhelming sense of separation. Why remember that now? A terrible feeling, as if something immense has gone, sweeps over me. All I can do is stare at my reflection, my heart pounding.

For a moment I can't move, and then I start to shake, dreadfully, unable to control my limbs. My hands are trembling as I reach down and retrieve the towel from the floor, folding it around my body like a blanket and sitting on the edge of the bed, forcing myself to breathe steadily, deep breaths, choking back tears and screams. *I don't want this to mean anything*. I shake my head firmly, fighting down the feeling. *I will not allow this to happen; I will not abandon my child to death*. I cry out *No!* again and again but there's no sound, only inside my head.

It's shock, that's all, reaction to the day. I keep trying to breathe normally and start rubbing my body hard with the towel, even though I'm long since dry. The vigorous action stems the shaking. Calmer, I apply moisture cream, deodorant, put on fresh underwear then massage cream into my face before stepping into waiting trousers and top laid out on the bed. Every move is measured, like some kind of strange ritual. With every item I put on, I feel I'm adding another layer of strength, courage somehow, armour for whatever lies ahead.

Composure regained, I pick up the discarded towels, hang them over a towel rail to dry, and go in search of a hairdryer. It was a moment, I tell myself, a terrible moment, but now it's past. Then as I'm drying my hair in the hallway, head upside down, blowing hot air into the roots, it happens again, an extraordinary, stop-you-in-your-tracks, wrenching sense of separation. This time I don't stand shaking,

I drop the hairdryer and go into the sitting room, blurting out to my mother and aunt, 'I've just had a terrible feeling. I remember a dream I had.'

They listen as I relate the experience. I need to speak about it, let it out, be reassured, but there's nothing they can say except 'Oh' while their faces express shock and dismay.

The television is turned off at last, relief from the awful static image of the bus and the constant round of headline text. 'We thought we'd have a break from it,' my aunt explains.

I nod my head in assent, not really minding at this stage, and go back to the bathroom to apply some make-up — make-up or mask, I'm not sure which. Foundation, mascara, blusher and lipstick: normal daily ritual, but this is 4 a.m. and normal belongs to yesterday. Even so, I spray perfume before zipping up the toilet bag and squeezing it down the side of the case, which I fasten and carry out to the hallway, my denim jacket draped over the top.

Vanda calls, asks how everyone is and what we're doing.

'Waiting, watching the clock; everyone's calm but the strain and tiredness is beginning to show.'

'What time is the taxi due?'

'Five a.m., not long to wait, thank goodness, the final hour. I just want to get going.'

It's getting light; I've hardly noticed the darkness, everything's an extension of yesterday. We've come full circle, the birds are singing, yet it doesn't feel like a new day.

'See you in a few hours. Keep your phone on.'

'I will. Bye.'

I don't know who is keeping watch with whom; with me, with each other, with Jenny, for Jenny. Family and friends connected all across the country; our hearts, thoughts, actions and prayers, all for Jenny; our watching, waiting and hoping, all for Jenny.

At 4.50 we're alert for the sound of an engine. When it arrives there's no drama, no tears, just gentle kisses and a fleeting embrace with a mountain of thoughts and feelings left unsaid.

As the taxi pulls away, I turn and look out of the window, watching my mother and aunt standing by the gate, not waving, and retreating into the distance.

The last thing I remember of Anglesey is the look on my mother's face. It is a look of loneliness and forlorn acceptance. Through the day and through the night we have kept watch together, now I am leaving her behind and she must watch me go.

CHAPTER 2

Prelude

Tears, idle tears, I know not what they mean,
Tears from the depth of some divine despair
Rise in the heart, and gather to the eyes,
In looking at the happy autumn-fields,
And thinking of the days that are no more.

TENNYSON

Bangor station is more or less deserted; there's only a smattering of people, holidaymakers I guess from the chatter and clothing and luggage. One or two faces glance at me as I pass along the platform: another holidaymaker in her linen trousers, summer top and flip flops. People smile and nod good morning. I half smile back. There's a family group with three young children, slightly old-fashioned looking, carrying buckets and spades and dressed in knitted cardigans over shorts and T-shirts. I listen to their sing-song chatter, parents, grandparents and children, light-hearted and joyous. The smallest child is wearing red wellington boots and jumping up and down in excitement as the train approaches. The granny takes her hand as the men pick up the luggage and my mobile phone bleeps in my pocket.

A text from Vanda: 'are you on the train yet?'

I wait until I'm settled in a seat – plenty to choose from – before replying and also sending a text to Sharon letting her know I'm on my way. She sends one back almost immediately saying 'see you soon'. People have stopped asking if there's any news.

As the train trundles out of Bangor station I notice the happy holiday family have settled themselves further down the carriage. I'm glad of the distance and the peace and quiet.

It's a fairly grotty train, old bucket-type seats, upholstery worn thin and shiny, windows darkened by dust and grime. Still, I can see out. The train picks up speed and soon we're speeding along the North Wales coast. The sun is rising in the sky, bathing the mountains in early morning glow and causing the sea to shimmer – so beautiful, so tranquil, and so perfect. We pass through one seaside town after another, Conwy, Llandudno, Colwyn Bay, Rhyl, and I watch, hypnotized, as other passengers come and go. The train carries me along, eyes unwavering, fixed on the distance, staring out at the horizon, on and on through mile upon mile of early-morning glistening coastline.

When the train stops at Llandudno Junction a young couple laden down with climbing gear pass by my window. Laughingly they heave rucksacks on to their backs and set off in a joyous mood, hand in hand.

Leaving Anglesey behind exposes a trail of memories of other summers spent watching the happy, laughing faces of my children and nieces and nephews as they scrambled over rocks and enjoyed the freedom of the beach. Memories of wonderful, fun-filled times and of fallouts when family gathered together and inhabited the same small space; of my mother-in-law shouting at careless boat-handlers who leave trailers lying on the beach for little feet to trip over; of endless days spent waiting for the rain to cease and games of Trivial Pursuit with laughter-filled accusations of cheating and red-herring clues; impressive thunder and lightning storms over the bay; a star-filled midnight sky; quiet, tranquil out-of-season days; and noisy, crowded peak-season weekends with a bay full of motor boats and jet skis jamming the approach lane with four-wheel drives and trailers.

I remember the moment I first felt Jenny's life within me. Of course I didn't know it was Jenny then; it could have been Isabel or Christopher or one of my favourite Shakespearean heroines Hermione.

I am in the tiny bay of Traeth Bychan on the island of Anglesey where the Nicholson clan has gathered for the spring bank holiday weekend. Some of us are braving the still wintry temperature of the sea for the first swim of the season. Greg has plunged straight in, strong front crawl strokes taking him away from the shore without a backward glance until he is far out and then he turns, calling to the shore, 'Come on'. My arms are raised in the brace position as the ice cold water laps over my feet, knees and up to my thighs. Counting one, two, three I plunge into the sea, teeth chattering, breathless with cold. After a few strokes I'm used to the water and shout encouragingly at someone still tentatively wading through the shallows, 'It's wonderful once you're in'.

Wonderful it may be, but too cold for more than a quick swim. Before long, I'm picking my way carefully back over the stones and pebbles that separate the sea from the low prom wall surrounding the bungalow and old smithy, two buildings which form the family holiday home. My mother-in-law, already changed from her swim into shorts and a top, is waiting with a mug of coffee as I step over the wall onto the prom. Wet springy curls frame her face as she settles into a deckchair with her own coffee and takes a furtive puff from the cigarette that she thinks no one can see her smoking. Her perpetually bronzed limbs glisten with newly applied olive oil as she raises her feet to the wall for another coating of sun. This place has been her holiday home since she was a child, the place where year after year, at every opportunity, she has brought her own children and now an emerging new generation of grandchildren. Already there are three,

Lucy and Andrew and baby Katie, with the next baby on the way as I am pregnant, barely five months.

Wrapping a towel around my wet and shivering body I drink from the mug of coffee before donning sunglasses, spreading the towel on the ground and settling down to dry off in the sun with a book at the ready. Other members of the family return from their swim and are soon scattered around the prom lazing, like me, on towels reading or dozing or sitting in chairs gazing out to sea. A few small sailing dinghies bob about in the bay and other larger sailing boats are dotted around further out to sea. It is quiet and peaceful in the early season and the entire bay seems to belong to us. As I turn page after page, words fade in and out of focus and I soon give in to warmth-induced sleepiness, resting my head on the open book and closing my eyes. There is barely a sound other than the distant passing whir of a speed boat, an occasional call of a child and the gentle afternoon drone of the corporate Nicholson snore. All is still and in the stillness I feel a tiny move-ment in my womb, like a flutter of butterfly wings. I hold my breath and wait; there it is again, another butterfly movement. For a few minutes I lie secretly revelling in the new sensation before lifting my head and saying, 'I just felt the baby move'.

Turning over onto my back, placing my hands on the spot where I felt the tiny flutters of movement, an instinctive gesture of protection for the life within that has begun to make its pres-ence felt.

Anglesey holds so much of the past, times to treasure and times lost. As the island recedes into the distance of the coast and into the distance of memory I'm surprised by an overwhelming feeling of sorrow and by the idea that I never want to return. My hands feel damp; I look down at them resting in my lap and notice a damp patch on my trousers. For one awful and embarrassing moment I think I've wet myself before realizing that my face is also moist. Instinctively, almost absently, I lift a hand to wipe away tears streaming down my face.

I don't know how long I've been crying, yet not crying. No sound, just tears. How could I not have realized? Instinctively I glance around at the few people dotted around the carriage; no one is looking or taking any notice of the lone traveller staring through the window, lost in thought and crying her silent tears. Wiping my hands on a dry patch of trouser leg, I lean my head against the coolness of the glass window pane, aware but not caring about the sodden patch on my lap. Tears continue to flow and I let them fall, unchecked, on to the spreading wetness of darkening red linen, looking more like blood than water and feeling like the broken waters of impending child-birth. *'Tears, idle tears, I know not what they mean.'* Is this the difference between crying and weeping – sorrow rising from the heart, word-lessly and soundlessly?

Now I can't bear my thoughts; they tumble out with my tears, images of Jenny lying hurt and afraid and alone. I screw my eyes up tight and lament with all my heart: *Please God please God please God.* Please God what? *Keep her safe, keep her safe:* words going round and round my head, picking up the age-old rhythm of the speeding train. I jump to my feet in a rising tide of panic, searching through my bag for a pack of tissues and blowing my nose fiercely to rid my head of wild unwanted thoughts and unuttered prayers. Groping for the sunglasses perched on top of my head I pull them down to shield my eyes, protection against more than the glare of the sun.

I try not to think of the last twenty hours or the implications of my journey but it's impossible not to think of Jenny and I tell myself over and over again *she's going to be all right, she's going to be all right,* keep-ing my mind focused on that one positive thought.

The motion of the train is soothing and must have rocked me into a light doze. When I open my eyes we've left the coast behind, the landscape is duller, industrial and functional, more in keeping with my mood. The guard announces the approach to Crewe. Shrugging on my denim jacket and checking for the ticket in the pocket, I grab my bag, take a quick look around in case I've left anything, then walk along the carriage towards the nearest door, relieved that the first step of the journey is almost over.

I stand with my legs astride my bag and rocking from side to side with the motion of the train. Wales has merged into England and the past into the present. I try not to see the future looming darkly like the shadow currently spreading along the carriage as the train pulls into Crewe station.

I have to lean out of the window to manoeuvre the handle that opens the door, which jams and then swings open with such a force that I almost fall out. I head straight for the Ladies and check the pitiful state of my face. I repair the damage and then contemplate going to the buffet and having a cup of coffee but decide against it and sit on a bench to wait the half-hour or so for Sharon's train.

More waiting! I sit very still, feeling quite composed, looking straight ahead and listening to station announcements, doors slamming and whistles being blown, sharp and piercing. A guard walks by and asks if I'm all right. Instead of answering I ask if this is the platform for the Manchester train.

'You're all right, love, about another twelve minutes now.'

'Thank you.'

I smile to myself. Maybe he wasn't asking after my wellbeing, merely enquiring if I needed any information.

A couple more trains pull in and pull out before the tannoy announces the arrival of the Manchester train. As the train pulls in I get to my feet, scanning the windows for a sign of my cousin; then as it stops I see her at the door directly in front of me. Dark brown hair frames her face on the other side of the window. She doesn't see me at first. All her attention is on heaving down the window to lean out and open the door. Then just as I lift my hand to wave and attract her attention, she lifts her head, catches sight of me and smiles in recognition. My cousin Sharon, tall as I am short, colour co-ordinated and elegant even at this hour of the day, steps down from the train and we move towards each other, embracing, holding each other for a moment. No words are spoken, the hug says everything. As we move apart we both have tears in our eyes. There's a while to wait for the connection so we sit in the buffet with a cup of coffee and catch up, talking calmly and concentrating on details and logistics and what we'll do when we get to Reading.

There's a man, smart, good-looking, youngish, in a seat across the aisle, travelling alone. He has a warm smile and confirms we're on the London train as Sharon and I settle into our seats and dither about a bit, making sure we're on the right train and that it stops at Rugby. He's trying to get back to his family in London. He left home early yesterday, before the explosions, for a meeting in the North and because of the disruption of trains was unable to travel back yesterday evening. He has a wife and two little girls. We talk generally about the horrors of yesterday and then tell him the reason for our journey. He's very concerned and attentive and kind. Talking to him helps; it gives us a sense of purpose and solidarity; it's energizing somehow. We can be positive and say determinedly that Jenny appears to be missing, probably caught up in the chaos and we're on our way to London to search for her. In less than an hour the train pulls into Rugby station and as we prepare to leave our travelling companion gives us his business card and asks if we can give him a quick call when we've found Jenny, to let him know how things are. As he hands me the card he says, 'I'll be thinking about you and hope you find your daughter safe and well. If there's anything I can do, anything, please call.' I want to hold the moment, give myself up to the reassurance of his caring presence and kind words, but we must be on our way and he must be on his.

Stepping down from the train we spot Martyn further along the platform, waiting and looking out for us. After quick hugs and greetings he takes our bags and we head towards the exit. Behind us carriage doors slam and a whistle blows before the train slowly starts to pull out of the station. As we reach the exit I catch a glimpse of the man inside a carriage, standing and looking out, his face no longer smiling but full of concern. He passes before my eyes, his arm raised in farewell.

Martyn and Sharon are talking. I turn my attention deliberately away from the departing train and follow my cousins to the car. Any awkwardness and emotion is alleviated through the chatter relaying details of the journey and the concern and kindness of the stranger who through a chance encounter did us a great service and, in doing so, made all the difference.

Time drags as we motor south. There are hold-ups on the motorway so we find an alternative route which takes us through villages and small towns. I can feel myself growing increasingly agitated as we hit one hold-up or roadwork after another. In distance we're close to Reading yet in time so far away. Martyn estimates we'll be an hour or so, later arriving than anticipated. It's frustrating for all of us and all sorts of useless berating goes on in my head: *We should have taken the train to Reading ... We still have to get to London ... I should have left Anglesey yesterday and ignored police advice ... I should have travelled to Reading last night ... I should be in London finding Jenny not held up by roadworks ... I'm letting her down.* Then I hear my grandfather's voice piercing my memory: *Don't waste your time worrying about what you should have done — things are as they are.*

At last we're on the approach to Reading. We drive past the university and Elmhurst Road where Jenny spent her first undergraduate year in halls; then I phone James for directions to the house. James and Vanda come out as we pull up outside. As we pass through the front door I catch sight of Jenny's black high-heel shoes, kicked off and lying abandoned. The sight of them is almost my undoing.

There isn't time or opportunity to stop and ponder as we move on into the sitting room where my oldest friend Dendy, Jenny's godmother, is sitting with a mug of tea, having travelled from Bristol by train earlier to help with the search. Over mugs of tea we talk about what to do. My sister Vanda is speaking, saying her husband Stefan has stayed home with their children but is concerned that we must have a plan and not wildly rush into London going randomly from place to place. I had thought we could split up into pairs and cover as many hospitals as possible in a short time but James, having been in London the night before, thought we should head straight for the Royal London Hospital as apparently that is where all survivors have been taken who were not yet accounted for. James has printed off a large picture of Jenny, taken outside the Albert Hall. It's not one I've seen before; she looks beautiful, happy and laughing. He's saying how people in London last night were handing out pictures of missing friends and family and thought it would be a good idea to take one of Jenny; someone may recognize her.

Should we go by train or car? Martyn volunteers to drive but there isn't enough room for all of us and it doesn't make sense to take more than one car. Stefan, practically, had thought there should be someone at the end of a phone, providing a kind of base camp and keeping in touch with Greg, Lizzie and Thomas. My sister makes a reluctant suggestion that she should withdraw from the search party and return home to be with Stefan, where they can be the conduit for news. I really want her to come with me but the fact is there isn't room in the car for more than five people and someone has to stay behind. Vanda also has two young children to take care of. All things considered, this is the only sensible compromise. A decision has to be made and we need to get going. We agree to call every hour even if there's no news.

My husband and two children are in Bristol, my parents in Anglesey and now I'm leaving my sister in Reading. Everything is starting to feel very fragmented but this isn't the time for self-indulgent emotions; all I can think about is finding Jenny.

Sharon sits in front with Martyn and I sit in the back of the car with James and Dendy. James is very quiet, mostly looking out of the window as we travel along the motorway towards London. I need something to do and begin sending text messages to various people who won't yet know about Jenny. Dendy suggests sending a block message but I can't manage the technology so pass the mobile phone over to her. She asks me what I want to say. What do I say? 'I'm on my way to London. Jenny appears to be missing following the explosions on the underground yesterday. I thought you would want to know. Julie'.

Conversation is mostly sporadic and light. Sometimes we even laugh. Martyn finds a packet of Minstrel sweets and passes them around. Ordinary things! There are long periods when very little is said as we are lost in our own thoughts, gazing out of the window or attending to text messages on mobiles.

Traffic slows to a crawl on the approach into London. We travel alongside a small white van on the inside lane for a while before picking up speed again and moving ahead. The driver is bobbing his head around, listening to music and tapping out the beat on the steering wheel, oblivious to being watched from the neighbouring car. He's wearing green overalls; some kind of maintenance uniform, I suppose. We pass each other several times as traffic speeds up and slows down in alternate lanes.

Prelude

I ask James about the photo of Jenny taken on the steps of the Albert Hall. They were going to a Proms concert. James points out that what you can't see in the picture are Jenny's feet which had been hurting from walking around all day. She had swapped her high heels for a pair of James's trainers, several sizes too big.

Once in the thick of London traffic we debate a route to the hospital. None of us really has a clue and consider stopping to pick up a map. For a while we go with the general flow towards central London, stopping and starting and trying not to get impatient with the slow progress. There's nothing around us that suggests anything of the carnage we were fixated upon yesterday, glued to our television screens. Everything looks as normal: roads full of traffic; people meandering along and rushing about; shops open; offices functioning. For those of us in the back of the car, there's nothing to do but be patient and look out of the window. Stiff from sitting in one position I shuffle around a bit and stretch my neck, looking out through the glass roof of the car; it's a Scenic, I think. For the first time I notice tops of buildings and comment that one can't usually look up and out from the inside of a car and it's a new and interesting perspective. For a few minutes the talk is all about the buildings we pass and the architecture – architecture, for God's sake!

We pull up at some traffic lights and a police car draws alongside. Waiting for the lights to change, Martyn quickly winds down the window and asks the police officers for directions to the Royal London Hospital. The officer nearest to us asks why we want to get there, as though they can sense the urgency, and Martyn explains, indicating towards me in the back. 'My cousin's daughter is missing and we're trying to find her.' The officer turns slightly to glance at me, and then tells Martyn to follow them; they will guide us to the hospital. The lights change and the police car pulls in front of us, forging ahead through traffic and traffic signals with determined confidence and speed. At times Martyn can barely keep up, nervously pressing through a red light as the police car ignores the signal to stop. It all starts to feel bizarre and quite surreal, on the tail of a police car speeding through the streets of London – not so fast that it was dangerous, just fast enough to bring Martyn out in a cold sweat.

'This feels all wrong,' he says. 'Every instinct in my body tells me to slow down when I see a police car, not speed up and definitely not to go through red lights!'

The police car is clearly doing its best to get us through the traffic and to the hospital as swiftly as possible. Despite the tension it's impossible not to see the farcical side of this; 'Jenny would find this hilariously funny, like something out of a Bond film,' I say just as the police car indicates for us to pull over.

The police officer in the driving seat gets out and walks the few steps to our car. 'We're heading straight on now but if you turn into this road on the left it will take you down to the hospital. I hope you find your daughter.' With that he was gone and in moments the police car had sped off without giving us any opportunity to find out their names or say more than a hasty 'thank you'.

The hospital building is obscured by scaffolding and green mesh, which makes the entrance difficult to find at first. Martyn drops us off and then goes to find somewhere to park the car. Dendy goes with him. 'Don't wait,' Martyn says. 'We'll come and find you.' The remaining three of us stand and watch as he drives off down the street then we turn and enter through the double doors of the hospital.

1989

*Jenny is about eight years old. I'm rushing around, getting ready
to go out, typically late, as is my lift. It's a warm early summer's
evening; the front door is open so air can circulate through the*

house. *Greg is settling Thomas and Lizzie, reading a bedtime story. Jenny is playing in the garden, looking out for my lift.*

'She's here, she's here,' *Jenny calls out, my prompt to hastily kiss Thomas and Lizzie before running downstairs.*

'Go inside now,' *I say to Jenny,* 'Daddy will be running your bath soon.' *She's jumping on and off the wall, over the rose bushes which are in full flower.*

'I want to wave bye-bye.'

'All right, but I want to see you go inside and close the door before I leave.'

I wave a greeting to my friend sitting at the driver's wheel. Jenny is wrapping her arms around my neck and giving me kisses, lots of them, before climbing back on the wall and jumping over a rose bush again.

'Watch, Mummy.'

'Be careful, if you fall you'll hurt yourself. That rose bush is full of thorns.'

'One more jump!'

I close the front gate behind me and sit in the car, waiting, slightly impatiently, for the final assault over the rose bush. Jenny is waving at the car as she jumps; this time falling in the bush. Leaping from the car I rush back into the garden and help her up. She is shaken and fighting back tears.

'My leg hurts.'

'You're OK,' *I say, brushing her down and showing her a small graze just above her knee.*

'Look, it's just a scratch. Ask Daddy to clean it in the bath. You're lucky you didn't get a thorn.' *Taking her by the hand, we get to the door as Greg is coming downstairs.*

'Can you see to Jenny's leg, she scraped it on the rose bush? I need to go.'

Jenny gives me one more, slightly tearful, kiss before I close the door behind me and hurry back down the garden path. Apart from a few pangs of maternal guilt as we drive away from the house, I think no more about the incident.

'I'm not sure about this,' I say to my friend as we drive along. We're on our way to a religious campaign, a Billy Graham event which I have been persuaded to attend.

'You'll be fine. You might even enjoy it.'

'I suppose I ought to listen to Billy Graham once in my life, if only to say I've done it!' It's fair to say I'm curious about the impact his campaigns seem to be having. This one is called Mission England.

Stewards are enthusiastically directing people into specially erected marquees. Already I am feeling this is not where I want to be. Inside the tent, people are jostling for seats; excited anticipation seems to be the prevailing mood though there are plenty of tentative faces and baffled expressions. The sermon itself is being broadcast from London and transmitted onto large screens erected at the front of the tent. With as much of an open mind as I can muster I settle back to experience the phenomena of Billy Graham. On this occasion the good news of Jesus Christ is lost on me. It is all too much, too zealous. As people leave their seats and go forward at the speaker's invitation, first steps to a new birth, I can only look on in wonder.

'This is not for me,' I say to my friend who is looking delightedly at what is happening at the front. I want to leave but dare not leave my seat. Most of my life I have attended church, found a resonance in ritual and sacred music and enjoyed the community of fellowship. The rhythm of the church year and Christian festivals is as much part of me as the seasons of the year. I love to hear the retelling of biblical stories and engage with the mystery and exploration of faith so I'm not quite sure why I find this so alienating.

I arrive home feeling completely overwhelmed by crusading Christianity, bemused by the response of the masses and for some inexplicable reason utterly depressed by the whole experience. I turn my key in the lock, glad to be home and looking forward to a cup of tea and bed.

Greg's face is sombre and doesn't respond at all when I say I think I'm going to become an atheist. Instead he greets me with the news that he has been in casualty all evening with Jennifer, the result of a long deep gash from the fall into the rose bush. The injury required several stitches and a tetanus booster. Feelings of shock, concern and guilt all tumble out at once as I rush upstairs to check Jenny is OK. Tentatively, so as not to wake her, I lift the covers and peer at the dressing covering her entire upper thigh. Thankfully, she is sleeping soundly and peacefully. I lean over and place a kiss full of love and apology on her forehead. Propped up on the bedside table is a colourful 'Certificate of Bravery' made out to Jennifer Nicholson and issued by staff at the hospital. Downstairs Greg tells me how, after I left, Jenny pulled her skirt up to check her sore leg and noticed the full extent of the injury. Our next-door neighbour was called in to sit with the younger children while Greg took Jenny to hospital.

'Let Jenny tell you about it herself in the morning, she wants to surprise you and show off her stitches and the certificate. She was very brave.'

Ah well, I reason, as my head touches the pillow half an hour or so later, I suppose this is the stuff of childhood. It could have been worse.

The Royal London Hospital, early afternoon Friday 8 July

The reception area is crowded. Looking around there don't seem to be any notices or indications of where we might go for specific information regarding the events of yesterday. We speak to a passing uniformed nurse but she isn't able to help directly or know where we should go. She isn't aware of this hospital being a centre for concerned relatives and suggests we enquire at Reception. So we stand in the queue for the general reception desk and wait our turn. The person at the desk can't tell us anything either, but directs us to a waiting room in another part of the hospital which is being used, she believes, as a temporary incident room. Once or twice we manage to get lost en route until eventually we find a member of staff who accompanies us to the right floor, leading the way through a door where we're plunged into a sea of confused and worried faces, all turning to look at the newcomers as we enter the room. It's a montage of images and shapes, of tableaux and sounds; it's a film set with actors dressed as officers and personnel: there's a sari and several pairs of jeans in shades of blue denim; a diminutive, elderly nun dressed in traditional black habit and a young black-suited cleric, tall with a slightly stooped appearance, wearing glasses and a dog collar. He's holding a half-eaten sandwich still in its plastic container. This is not real. This does not belong to my reality, to the quiet vigil of yesterday or the gently poignant journey along the coast.

There's a round table in the corner with large flasks and trays of beakers, jugs of milk and bowls of sugar; teaspoons are scattered around the table and used sugar packets litter the surface. A seated area to the left is separated from the rest of the room by a sort of handrail barrier. Some people are sitting, talking to what I assume to be police or medical staff and others are standing around the room. Doors at the end lead out to a balcony where some people are smok-

ing, others speaking into mobile phones. Now that we're here we
don't quite know what to do. At one and the same time it is both reassuring and bewildering. Having arrived at the place we now find
ourselves hovering on the edge of someone else's drama. There's
chaos, bustle, noise, yet in the midst of it all there's purpose and quiet
calm amongst the gathered groups. There's a couple standing to our
right; the woman holds a picture of a younger woman in formal graduation robes and smiling out from the picture. I catch the woman's
eyes; they're troubled and slightly desperate. For a second or two we
connect and exchange a look born out of mutual understanding as
something between a smile and a grimace passes between us.

Martyn and Dendy arrive, talking about where they parked the
car, unsure whether it was a legal parking space. Martyn shrugs his
shoulders: 'I left a note of explanation on the windscreen and hope I
don't get clamped or towed away.' The five of us are wondering what
to do. Martyn goes off to see if he can find out anything and the rest
of us stand around, taking in our surroundings. When Martyn returns
a few minutes later, he is none the wiser. It looks as if there are
personnel moving around the room and taking details from people,
so we guess we have to wait our turn.

The nun and the cleric stand out amongst the groups of people as
they don't quite belong. I move out to the balcony, possibly to avoid
contact. Their presence symbolises that all is not well. At this moment
I need optimism and hope. The view is hardly soothing. I want green
fields and trees and flowers, not concrete and bins and pipes. I find
myself part of the other communing bodies, leaning over the balcony,
speaking into mobile phones, connecting with home, feeding the
same non-information. This is where I am, this is what I'm doing, this
is what I know, this is what I don't know. How are you? What are you
doing? Words of love and encouragement exchanged and reinforced
across the country and probably also across the world.

A Song For Jenny

A few chairs are scattered around on the balcony, but there isn't any room to sit down so we move inside and stand in a group talking and not talking and looking around, and looking lost and looking at other people looking lost. The young cleric approaches us tentatively, asking if we've had far to travel today. 'Oh, for goodness' sake, what difference does it make how far we've had to travel today?' Thankfully the words never leave my mouth. He's still clutching his sandwich pack as he comes out with one asinine phrase after another. I let the others respond while I look on barely listening; thinking, impatiently and ungraciously, that I wish he would just go away and leave us alone. We all stand there for a few minutes until the cleric runs out of things to say and we run out of responses. I know I should say something to ease his discomfort but can't be bothered. I feel irritated that we have to be subjected to his helpless ministrations. 'Is there anything I can get you?'

I want to shake him. Clearly at a loss, he shuffles awkwardly from foot to foot before suddenly thrusting out the remainder of his sandwich towards us and asking if any of us is hungry. For a moment the sandwich hovers between us like an embarrassing pause before we politely decline. I don't know whether to laugh or scream. With a rush of words none of us catch clearly he waves the sandwich in the direction of the refreshment table, inviting us to help ourselves to tea or coffee and biscuits and hopes it isn't long before we get some news. On that we're all in agreement.

Martyn pours tea and coffee into a couple of plastic beakers as a man standing close to the table informs us that the coffee is cold and the tea stewed. Nevertheless we take our beakers and move to the far side of the room where some seats have become vacant. Martyn and James stand by the window as Dendy, Sharon and I sit in a line, turning our bodies slightly in towards each other so we can talk more easily.

'You should have told him you're a vicar,' Sharon says teasingly.

Our three sets of eyes follow the cleric, still clutching his half-eaten sandwich and now talking to an older couple sitting a short distance away. We sip our tepid tea and watch his slow progress around the room, warming to him as he extends his arm and offers his sandwich again. Maybe there isn't anything else he can offer.

'I wish he'd just eat it!' I blurt out.

'Is he a chaplain?' Sharon asks.

'I don't know; he didn't introduce himself as a chaplain. I think if he was a chaplain he wouldn't be quite so ill at ease.'

'Maybe he's from a local church wanting to help in some way. He seems out of his depth.' Dendy makes a half-hearted attempt at being charitable.

We're all out of our depth, I think, but don't say.

I might have been friendlier towards the cleric but he reminds me of who I am and possibly of my own inadequacies in such a situation. With some consternation, I realise I do not wish to be reminded of my own vocational role. If I were in his shoes, I doubt I could offer people any more than a half-eaten sandwich, which is a troubling thought. I do not wish to be aligned with these two people. I am a mother, desperately searching for her child. I am Jenny's mother. I am also a priest but at the moment I am embarrassed by the fact and I am struggling to see how the church has a place in this room.

Eventually someone comes and takes a few details: my name, Jenny's name, her age, our relationship and establishes that I'm the next of kin. Between us James and I give the information asked for: any scars, distinguishing features, colour and length of hair ... We trip over each other in our eagerness to provide any detail that could help identify Jenny. It doesn't take long. All of us watch and listen intently to what the woman is saying. Apparently there are seven casualties in total in different parts of the hospital in various states and conditions and yet to be identified. It's possible that Jenny could be one of them. She'll be back as soon as she has some information. Meanwhile, we should help ourselves to tea and coffee or water. For a moment I think she's going to tell us to make ourselves at home.

The elderly nun is moving around, gliding up to people and standing alongside for a while before moving on. People are trying to avoid catching her eye. As though she spots a new set of faces in the room she moves over towards us. 'Keep her away from me,' I appeal to Sharon and turn my body pointedly in Dendy's direction, feigning a conversation. I listen to the nun talking to Sharon for what seems an age. She has a kindly, soft, prayer-like voice and Sharon is being very patient and gentle in her response. The nun has assumed Sharon is looking for her daughter. Perhaps I should engage but it's all too much effort and I remain resolutely turned away. At this moment I don't want the attention of chaplains or nuns or anything except action and people who will help me find Jennifer.

Martyn has wandered off in search of a loo and James has sat down in the vacant seat on the other side of Dendy. His head is bowed and he's staring at his rucksack on the floor between his feet. He looks far away and tired and there's something about his hunched shoulders that makes me want to stand up and shout: *Won't somebody help us please*. Of course I don't.

The room is becoming increasingly crowded; everyone is desperate for information and feeling the frustration of needing to be tolerant of a system and await developments. The room is airless. Even with the doors to the balcony wide open, there is hardly any air circulating and the heat is oppressive and uncomfortable. Some people are waving papers like fans to create streams of cooling air. Empty water bottles lie discarded, scattered around the room on tables and under chairs. Water jugs on the refreshment table are being emptied faster than volunteers can replenish them. People sporadically go over to the table and tip the jug as though expecting a stream of water to miraculously appear.

Another cleric comes into the room, bearing a tray filled with white plastic beakers. He's tall and has an air of confidence and authority as he announces: 'Iced water if anyone would like some.' He doesn't ask anyone about their journey or sympathize in pitying tones, he simply attends to a present need – thirst in a crowded hot hospital waiting room – making eye contact and smiling his care as he passes around beaker after beaker of refreshingly cold water. 'That's my kind of chaplain,' I whisper in Sharon's ear.

The nun remains by Sharon's side, watching events and commenting from time to time on something in the room or an aspect of the day. It seems that having found a sympathetic ear she is loath to relinquish her attachment and is now reminiscing, 'This reminds me of the war,' describing clearing away rubble from the streets and finding people beneath and how the spirit amongst everyone was wonderful. I dare not catch Sharon's eye.

Just as I think we can't bear any more Second World War recollections, however kindly meant and gently shared, the female staff member calls my name and comes over, we hope with some information, and the nun slips away saying something about hoping for good news and very nice to meet and talk with us.

It emerges there's a young white woman, unidentified, in IT, aged about thirty. 'Let me see her.' Either I didn't say it or the member of staff didn't hear me. There are two other women also in IT but neither match Jenny's description. One is an older woman and the other Asian. There's one woman who could be Jenny and that's the possibility I hold on to. I don't think about why she might be in IT. We describe Jenny again, going over details as requested, hair, eyes, height. She confirms what James has told us, that there is no point going to other hospitals as all casualties yet to be identified have been brought here. A police liaison service is being put in place through the hospital and so we'll be amongst the first to have someone assigned to us. We're assured that for the time being this is the best place to be.

As hard as it is – and it is hard – all we can do is wait, patiently. Restless and impotent, together with everyone else in the room, we give ourselves up to the process. The term 'waiting room' has taken on a new meaning.

Martyn goes off in search of sandwiches, supplies for the long haul, he says, even though none of us is interested in eating. It's hot. I go out on to the balcony for some space and air and attend to the now regular ritual of checking messages and rigorously calling Jenny's mobile, persistent in urging her to be safe and in contact. The latter feels like a salve to the implications of the last hour. *Hang in there, Jenny, we're on our way to you.*

Leaning over the balcony rail, for a few minutes blotting out the crowded room, I gaze down at the concrete vista, as I call home imagining the scene with Greg and Lizzie and Thomas, frustratingly dependent on us for any morsel of news. I wish I had something positive to give them other than relaying bare facts and rigorously repeating the need to stay positive. A smile escapes at Lizzie's affectionate description of Auntie Chris making them feel they weren't quite so alone any more. She tells me of friends who had called and of Sharon and Mike's older girls, Katie and Joanne, who are driving down from Manchester so they could all be together – cousins in solidarity. Lizzie's voice, sounding wobbly yet so courageous, lingers in my ear as my eyes remain fixed and staring.

Take courage, soul. This is my prayer, all I can muster.

I feel suspended between endlessly blue sky above and grey unrelenting concrete below. One contradicts the other, like my head, full of opposing forces. When I speak to people I hear my voice reasoning positively full of hope. Yet in moments of isolation this deep,

creeping fear almost overwhelms me. Ripples of it rise up threatening to break the surface and I have to take deep guttural breaths to
force it back in place. I remain calm, but it is, in truth, a fearful calm.
On my way back into the room I stop to speak to a couple who smiled
and said hello as I passed earlier. We talk for a few minutes, sharing
stories of the last twenty-four hours and sympathizing with each
other. They hope I find my daughter. I hope they find their son. This
is a very worrying time, we all agree. They seem very alone.

As the afternoon wears on more and more people arrive. All the
cultures of the world seem to be gathered here, united in purpose,
many carrying pictures of missing relatives. A Japanese couple struggle to make themselves understood. A group of young adults looking
for a lost friend bring new energy into the room as they take up seats
in the same area as us. Their chatter is a diversion and provides a new
focus for a time.

The person who spoke to us earlier and took Jenny's details
comes back. The young woman in IT is not Jenny. They checked
hair colouring and other features and distinguishing marks. I don't
know whether to be relieved or despondent. In desperation I ask
about the remaining casualties in other parts of the hospital, any
chance one of those could be Jenny? Even as I ask I know checks will
already have been made. I can't take my eyes off her face as she
shakes her head slowly. 'No, I'm sorry.' For a moment or two we
stand in awkward silence.

'What happens now?' Martyn's voice cuts into the pause.

'A police officer will be along shortly to speak to you and take
things on from here.'

For some reason I find myself saying 'thank you' before sitting
down and waiting for the next directive.

More cooled water is being circulated but we're almost too tired
and preoccupied to bother taking any. The plastic bag containing packs

of sandwiches Martyn went out for earlier lies neglected at our feet, mostly untouched. For a while after the latest information none of us speaks; we focus instead on drab peeling paintwork, metal window frames, torn or worn patches on seats and our own private thoughts. I watch as James takes his mobile from a pocket to check a text and replace it without replying.

Heads turn in the direction of the door as two police officers come in. The officers pause for a moment, scanning the room, before reading out the names of two families. The rest of the room waits expectantly for a few minutes before returning to its mix of activity and contemplation.

A young woman in a light blue shirt stands just inside the doors and looks over towards us, raising her eyebrows to enquire, 'Mrs Nicholson?' She introduces herself as Joanne, a police liaison officer. She's a similar age and colouring to Jenny. We follow her into another room, smaller with a few functional tables set against the wall and chairs pulled around. There are already two other families talking to police officers in their respective groups. Joanne apologizes for the cramped space as we settle ourselves into seats and make introductions. She's warm and friendly. Forms are systematically filled in; we respond to question after question, while Joanne writes. Descriptions and details already given are gone over again in minute detail: position and size of scar, dental work, surgical procedures, height, and vital statistics – hip measurements, chest. 'She has a wonderful bosom,' I blurt out, aghast at myself and recognizing shock in the faces of my companions at my outrageous remark. 'Well, she does!' I persist with some embarrassment.

James tries to remember what Jenny was wearing when she left for work, whether her hair was tied up or loose, what kind of bag she was carrying and what personal possessions she had with her. Between us we rack our brains for any detail that may help locate and identify her. James recites the route Jenny would normally take to work, and the timings, the unlikelihood of her being at Edgware Road travelling in the direction of Paddington. 'It doesn't make sense,' James insists over again. 'Jen would be travelling away from Paddington not towards it.' Joanne doesn't have any answers; all she can do is collate as much information as possible about Jenny and all we can do is co-operate in the task.

The interview is difficult; it's impossible not to listen to snatches of conversation from the two other interviews going on in the room at the same time, we're all in such close proximity. None of us has the luxury of privacy.

Joanne asks about Jenny's teeth, whether she had any significant dental treatment. 'She doesn't have any fillings,' I say when Joanna's pager bleeps and with a hasty 'excuse me' she leaves the room and we have no alternative but to sit and eavesdrop on what the other families in the room are saying.

On her return, Joanne explains how the police liaison service works. I feel considerable relief knowing that someone is going to be working alongside us, on our behalf, in finding Jenny.

'Where are you going now: Reading or Bristol?' she asks.

'Reading for the time being.' I give her my sister's address and phone number, then we go back into the waiting room while Jo attends to some practicalities.

After the confined atmosphere of the interview room, the open and fresh air of the balcony is a welcome change. For a few minutes we discuss the various aspects of the interview before dispersing around the balcony busy with our mobile phones.

I hear my name called and swing around quickly, my eyes sweeping past Dendy and Sharon and James in different parts of the balcony before fixing on the person coming towards me. Would I consent to having my DNA taken?

Through a haze I'm aware of a small room, a swab and plastic tube. I think I open my mouth. It is said that children only ask questions they are ready to hear answers to. I do not ask any questions of the person taking my DNA.

It's all over. Joanne tells us to go home. There's nothing else we can do here. The police liaison service will take over all the groundwork now.

'Will that be you?' I ask.

Disappointment is reflected in all our faces as Joanne explains that as she is attached to London we will be assigned liaison officers from the Reading area. We've warmed to her and built up some trust and confidence with her.

'When will we hear from someone?'

'Soon, probably in the next few hours.'

As James takes her card and puts it in his wallet, the last words we hear from Jo are: 'But if there's anything I can do, please call me.'

We're a subdued group retracing our steps down vaguely familiar stairs and corridors and leave the hospital through the same double doors that we entered several hours before, walking straight into the path of a man holding out his hand and begging for money. We're taken aback and pause, rather than stop, for a moment and look at him as we pass. All I can do is shake my head limply in response to his extended hand. None of us is in the mood to hear his tale of woe, in fact we feel he should be ashamed of himself preying on vulnerable people coming out from the hospital. He doesn't give up on us as easily as we give up on him, pushing his bike and pursuing us along the road. He continues following and calling out to us for some time before we turn the corner in our callous disregard.

Buildings have blotted out the sunshine and we walk the rest of the way to the car in shade. Double red lines follow the kerb around and I ask idly what they signify. Apparently they're worse than double yellow lines. Drivers must not stop or park on them for any reason. There isn't a vehicle in sight so the penalty must be harsh. As I follow the double red lines along the road, they seem to represent all the frustrations and 'no go' areas of the last twenty-four hours.

We don't say much during the drive out of London. Sharon calls Vanda to let her know we're on our way. Any more information can wait until we reach the house. The atmosphere in the car is pensive. The last couple of hours have been filled with words and now there's nothing left to say. We've run out not only of words but of energy and purpose too. Martyn concentrates on driving and the rest of us sit slumped in the solitude of our own thoughts. Mine are brooding and as much as I try to push troubling imaginings to the back of my mind, to keep focused on Jenny and on positive possibilities, darker thoughts niggle away at the surface of my consciousness. This day has not ended; it has been a beginning, an introduction, like the prelude to an immense piece of music.

Chapter 3

First Movement

RECOVERY OPERATION

It's a relief to be driving along a stretch of familiar road and momentum within the car is picking up as we near our destination. I lean forward, looking out for the landmarks which indicate the gap between trees and hedges where we need to turn off the main road. Martyn slows the car down; even so we overshoot the turning, spotting the obscured entrance just as we pass it. He swings the car around, swinging us with it and doubles back the short distance to turn from the main road into the approach lane leading to my sister and brother-in-law's house.

The lane gradually crumbles into a track, uneven with ridges and potholes. Bumping slowly along towards the drive, passing the two or three other properties, we're shaken out of our soporific states and begin speaking again. The tension of the journey is rapidly dissipated. When the car finally pulls to a halt, there's a fraction's pause while Martyn flexes his arms against the steering wheel, breathing a long sigh, then the doors are thrown open and our stiff bodies tumble from the car. Amidst a mêlée of greetings and embraces, we trail through the hallway, all talking at once and pour through the doorway of the kitchen in a combined state of near hysteria.

First Movement

Vanda and Stefan are looking at us with stunned expressions and have become rooted to the spot as we bombard them with overlapping words. They are standing close together as if in mutual protection against the onslaught. 'My God, you all sound so high,' Vanda finally blurts out. 'We thought you'd be tired and flat and we'd have to restore your spirits.' Finding her voice seems to galvanize my sister into action and she turns to stir a pan simmering on the stove for a moment before abandoning the wooden spoon and turning her attention to a row of glass tumblers lined up on the kitchen unit.

'Come in and have a drink.' Stefan is taking a bottle of gin from the pantry and handing it to Vanda.

'We've had a really quiet day here, apart from the phone,' she says, dropping several chunks of ice into each tumbler. 'Can you call Mum?' The ice is followed by slices of lemon and a generous slug of gin. 'I promised her you'd call as soon as you arrived.' Tonic fizzes over the top of the bottle with a whoosh as the cap is unscrewed. My sister's gin and tonic construction is legendary: clumsy but with great largesse.

Within minutes of piling through the front door all five of us hold a more than modest G&T in our hands. Dendy, a devotee of Harvey's Bristol Cream sherry who doesn't normally drink gin, magnanimously concedes, 'What the heck, I may as well start now!'

Questions and responses dart backwards and forwards. My niece Ellie comes over and gives me a hug, snuggling her head against my chest and wrapping her arms around my waist, remaining in that position while everyone talks, doubtless taking it all in. I am smoothing Ellie's hair and chipping in as Dendy and Sharon animatedly recount the dramas of the journey into London. My sister is still looking shocked at our high spirits and in her eyes I see a look which I think translates as, 'I wish I had been with you; I wish I had been part of it then I might understand why you're all behaving in this way.'

Nevertheless I believe she is glad we are all now here with her. Martyn is sitting at the table, long legs spread out in front of him. He's beginning to look sleepy. In spite of this a grin is spreading across his face at the description of the police escort. Leaning against the sink dressed in work jeans and a T-shirt Stefan's expression is intent. A high forehead combined with greying hair and spectacles gives him a prematurely wise old owl appearance. He doesn't say much but his eyes behind his glasses are narrowed in concentration, listening as though he is carefully assimilating information. He has finished his gin and has folded his arms across his chest. Every now and then he darts a concerned glance across the kitchen at James who has been talking rapidly but is now very quiet and staring at the ground.

This is the tableau, varying levels of energy gathered around a kitchen table with a pot of pasta bubbling in the background.

My nephew is standing in the doorway and looks on for a little while, hopping from one foot to the other, trying unsuccessfully to be patient, before asking James to play football with him outside. I watch them go; this is normal practice for six-year-old William. Visitors arrive, they play football with him; why should today be any different?

Everything I say to my mother is a blur, she doesn't need to tell me: 'I wish I could be there with you.'

'I know.' I can imagine how she's feeling, away from the place and one person she wants to be with.

'Let me know as soon as there's any news.'

'I will.'

I can feel my energy ebbing away but I phone home before settling down to whatever the night has in store. Lizzie answers. There's not a lot to say that hasn't already been said throughout the day. We talk about commonplace things: what's going on here; what's going on there.

'What time did you arrive?'

'About seven o'clock. Auntie Vanda had gin waiting,' I say, smiling across the kitchen at my sister.

'We're waiting for Katie and Jo to arrive and Auntie Chris is cooking.'

'William has dragged James off to play football.'

'The phone hasn't stopped ringing.'

'Nor here from what I can gather.'

'What's everyone else doing?'

'Uncle Martyn has fallen asleep on the sofa, exhausted after the long drive and a large gin, Stefan is outside with William and James and the rest of us are in the kitchen talking.' We each need to hold on to an image of the other household; it's a connection between us.

'Promise you'll call, even if it's the middle of the night.'

Thomas is very quiet on the phone but Chris assures me everyone is OK; they're all keeping each other going. By the time I speak to Greg I've run out of anything to say and resort to 'how are you?' to which, of course, there's no adequate answer. How are any of us? This big portent is hanging over us like a great louring cloud and all we can do is talk about the little things.

The gin has taken effect and I'm feeling a bit light-headed. My glass is replenished but I don't drink any more. I want to keep a clear head. Vanda and I are alone in the kitchen. 'Have many people called?' I ask.

'The phone's been ringing on and off all day. The children went to friends after school so it's been just Stefan and me here most of the day, answering the phone and trying to keep busy.'

'What have you told the children?' I ask.

'Not much; fortunately they've been out of it for most of the day. They know about the explosions and that you've come to London to look for Jenny, just the bare facts.'

She's cutting a long French stick of bread into chunks and piling it on to a platter. 'I made a big pot of bacon chilli pasta, something that would do anytime you arrived.' Between us we make space in the centre of the table for the bread.

'Dendy's a vegetarian,' I say, remembering.

'Oh!'

'That's OK,' says Dendy, coming back into the kitchen. 'I'll just pick the bits of meat out.'

Right on cue, the phone rings; although I'm nearest I don't move from the table. 'Do you want to speak to anyone?' Vanda asks as she crosses the kitchen to take the call.

'No, not at the moment,' I answer, shaking my head. 'Unless it's the police, I gave them your number.'

Ellie and William are in the bath. I offer to go and supervise and wander down to the bathroom. 'You can sit on the toilet seat,' William instructs me magnanimously.

Watching the children play is a distraction and provides some respite from the activity in the kitchen. The bath is clogged with plastic toys, an array of primary colours bobbing up and down in the bubbles.

'Auntie Julie?' William concentrates on filling a green plastic whale with water and doesn't look up.

'Yes, Wills?'

'Where do you think Jenny is?'

I wasn't expecting the question and hesitate for a moment, unsure how to answer. Truthfully, I suppose. 'I don't know.'

'Are the police going to help you find her?'

'Yes, I hope so, Wills.' I wait for the next question but it doesn't come. He seems satisfied for the time being. Ellie is engrossed in her own world of play and seems not to have heard the exchange but suddenly declares she's had enough of the bath and asks if she can get out.

First Movement

Being amongst family, and carried along by the routine of the household and needs of children and bath and bedtime rituals, offers a kind of recovery from the turbulence of the day. Despite the bustle of arrival and phones ringing, it feels like a safe harbour – a place to be normal. The children are tucked into bed by Daddy and send a message via Stefan that they want James to go and say goodnight, then Auntie Julie, then Mummy. As I lean over to kiss Ellie, she says very quietly, 'I wish Jenny was here.'

Supper is calm, or subdued, I can't tell which, though without the children we can talk more freely about the last two days. We sit around the kitchen table long after supper is cleared away; wine glasses, bottles of fizzy water and coffee remain to sustain us through the evening. Stefan says he thinks we ought to get Greg and Lizzie and Thomas here. Whatever the next days have in store, we all need to be together.

Callers are dealt with quickly; everyone is aware of the one call which could change everything. If the landline isn't ringing someone's mobile is. We soon become used to the different ring tones and incoming text jingles. Every spare socket around the kitchen now has a mobile phone charger attached and active. My sister's kitchen is turning into an incident room and those of us gathered around the table debate every nuance of Jenny's journey, as though we're inves-tigators in a strange disappearance, which in a way I suppose we are. Over and over James insists there's just no logical reason why Jenny would have been travelling from Edgware Road towards Paddington. Perhaps she's been involved in a separate incident, is lying concussed in another hospital. Who knows what knocks and bumps might have occurred in the general chaos across London? It's conceivable that she's forgotten her name and lost her belongings and bearings. The news reported people drifting into churches and halls in traumatized states. As James is talking, I imagine Jenny wandering the streets of

London, confused, not knowing where to go for help. Maybe, even now, someone is looking after her, trying to find out who she is and where she lives. It's inconceivable that Jenny has been caught up in the explosions in any significant way. We all collude with the improbability and deny well into the night the possibility that Jenny is anything other than temporarily missing.

In the allocation of beds I opt for the sofa with the logic that I'm unlikely to sleep and it's closest to the phone. Sharon is on the sofabed and Dendy on an airbed on the floor. For an hour or so after the household settles down for the night the sitting room takes on the air of a girls' dorm, with all the accompanying foolishness, before darkness and the relative silence of night permeates our senses, stilling our chatter and gradually lulling our bodies into repose.

The gentle, rhythmic breathing of my companions, now asleep, provides a reassuring backdrop to my wakeful state. I can't really decide whether I need company or solitude. The confident mask I put on during the day is laid aside under cover of night and with it all protection against fears and dark thoughts. Yet I'm glad of that. Glad of the release into whatever the darkness brings. My eyes wander over the shapes and shadows of the room, through the gap in the curtains where the midnight sky is bright with stars and gaze deeply into the endless darkness beyond, feeling the dark shadows in my own heart. I give myself up to it, wondering *where are you Jenny?* Over and over, out through the window, up into the vastness of the sky and mystery of the universe, that continuous refrain and my random prayers wing free into the timeless hold of night. *Come back to me Jenny. I will lift up mine eyes unto the hills, from whence cometh my help. Do not let this thing be true. Where are you, Jenny? I will lift up mine eyes unto the hills, I will lift up mine eyes, I will lift up mine eyes.*

I fear to sleep. Fear a missed call; fear that if I close my eyes and break the connection Jenny will be gone from me. Yet I long for the oblivion of sleep. If I sleep I can wake up and the last two days will be no more than an absurd dream; but my eyes will not close and sleep will not come and this is not a dream. My mind races out of control in waves of despair and panic and then calms again. As the night deepens I find myself muttering to the sky. *I wish I could float and the sky carry me off to wherever you are, Jenny, so I can take your hand and bring you home. Be safe; be safe; O God do not pull the shroud of darkness over her.*

Nonsense, nonsense, she's going to be all right. Tomorrow we will find her – tonight even, there could be a call. I throw the cover back and get to my feet, agitated, my mind full of negative thoughts. At a loss to know what to do I stand peering into the darkness for a minute or two, acclimatizing my eyes, then tentatively feel my way around the room into the kitchen, stepping over shoes and bags and around furniture, taking care not to disturb Sharon and Dendy. Believe, I tell myself as I turn on the cold-water tap, letting it run, believe she's alive, out there, somewhere. Don't give up on her.

I take a few sips of water, then I pour the rest into the sink and rinse the glass, setting it to drain. As I turn from the sink to go back to bed, I catch Jenny's smiling face studying me from her picture pinned to the noticeboard, caught in the glow of the night light in the hallway, her head tilted to one side, eyes questioning. I go towards it and every prayer, every longing, every thought sings in my heart as I mutely return her gaze. I trace the outline of her face with my forefinger, then place the tips of my fingers against my mouth and transfer a kiss from my lips to Jenny's.

One minute, two, three, five, I look at my daughter as I once looked at her lying against my breast, just a few hours old, on the first night of her life.

'Mrs Nicholson, Julie,' the midwife whispers, 'your baby is awake and hungry; would you like to feed her?' In the tiny side ward, with only the dim light of the maternity unit to relieve the darkness, all is still. The distant, faint and perfect cry of a newborn baby breaks the night-time silence. My first child is placed into my arms and I look down at her scrunched-up face. 'What are you calling her?' the midwife asks.

'Jennifer,' I reply, not lifting my eyes. 'Jennifer Vanda Ann.'

My baby feeds from my breast, little suckling sounds. I am in awe. I vow to love her, protect her and always keep her from harm.

As I slip back under the covers on the sofa, there's a whisper from one of the other beds: 'Are you all right?'

'Yes,' I whisper back, 'I'm fine, I just went to get a glass of water.' Which of course is a lie, I'm anything but fine.

For most of the night I watch the sky – no, more than the sky, the firmament – as if the secret depths hold all the answers. Blink and I may miss a revelation. Fragments of ancient psalms and present longings, hopes and doubts battle it out in my head. I start to count the stars; I swiftly lose track and start again. It's strangely soothing, and I drift towards sleep, only to jerk into wakefulness to begin counting again.

There's a movement beside me so I close my eyes, not wanting to give away my wakeful state and have my solitary reverie spoilt. A door opens and closes, then the flush, running water and a rustle of covers as I sense rather than see Dendy get back into bed.

I turn on to my side, facing away from the room, pull the duvet around my shoulder and nestle into the back of the sofa, blotting out the last two days and escaping into the days before.

Forcing my mind to focus on details takes all my concentration at first, and my undisciplined and tired mind keeps drifting back to the present. Eventually I settle into a random form of remembering that seems to work. With my body snuggled under covers and my mind free to wander through the stages of setting out with my parents from Bristol on Monday 4 July, journeying in the rain, arriving in the rain and spending the next two days in the rain. Happy days and endless chatter, shopping and picking vast amounts of summer fruit and vegetables, periods curled up on the sofa reading, an entire afternoon playing Scrabble and five of us squashing into my little car each time we ventured out, joking over whose turn it was to sit in the front and making sure my father and uncle had their walking sticks.

Wednesday 6 July

We drove into Bangor. I bought a new kettle and a smoothie-maker. As we drove back over the Menai Bridge on to the island the rain stopped and the sun came out. We passed a deserted pick-your-own fruit and vegetable farm and decided to stop and gather what we could while the sun shone. My father stayed in the car doing his crossword while the rest of us managed to pick for almost an hour before the next shower sent us scurrying for cover. On the way home we saw a rainbow over the bay and, driving along, watched it fade away as the sky darkened and the rain returned with a vengeance. I see again wet shoes being removed in the porch and hair towelled dry and my new kettle being unpacked, tried out and causing surprise when it automatically switched off with a piercing whistle. I see my mother putting on her glasses and reading instructions for using the smoothie-maker. With the rain falling in torrents we set to making smoothies, experimenting with weird and wonderful combinations of fruit cocktails, one tasting session after another and helping it all down with gin and tonic. The rain sloshed around outside but there was plenty of sun and laughter inside. My uncle, who rarely ate fruit, returning for one smoothie taster after another; my father demanding to know, as he topped up his whisky glass with water, how much more of 'this stuff' we intended making and what were we going to do with it all; my aunt searching cupboards for more containers and my mother washing up between batches. We made litres of 'the stuff'.

I see my uncle coming into the smoothie 'brewery' announcing that the forecast for the following day was fine and sunny. As we cleared up we planned what we might do if the forecast proved true.

Earlier Jenny had sent a text message, full of excitement and bubbling over with 'Jennyness', from the centre of celebrations in Trafalgar Square. Her office had joined the cheering crowds sharing in the euphoria following England's successful bid to host the 2012 Olympics. Her jubilant text claimed that for the first time in her twenty-four years she had watched the Red Arrows fly 'live' overhead. Jenny, full of joy and typically spreading it all around, loudly!

That evening after dinner I was doing the *Guardian* quick crossword. There was a music question about opera: which composer wrote only one opera? I thought I knew the answer but wasn't certain so I sent Jenny a text asking her if Beethoven wrote *Fidelio*. She sent a text back saying yes, it was his only opera, citing almost word for word the question as it appeared in the crossword! Remembering the exchange of text messages brings me back to the present with a jolt and all thoughts of fruit-picking and smoothie-making disappear.

Under the duvet I check my phone, scrolling through messages, looking for those last two from Jenny. Gone, I must have erased them. I close my eyes recalling her vibrant words: *'I'm in Trafalgar Square, we've all come out of the office to join the celebrations. I'm so excited and I don't even like sport! It's a fantastic atmosphere. Wow, the Red Arrows are flying overhead.'*

Then the other exchange: 'Did Beethoven write *Fidelio*? Yes, it was his only opera. Why? I'm doing the crossword. What's the clue?'

First Movement

I wish I'd kept the texts and feel cross with myself for erasing them; suddenly they seem so precious. I clutch the phone to me under the covers and close my eyes, willing a sign of life through a call, a text. No, all of that can't be gone; it's not possible, all that life and energy.

As soon as the sky begins to lighten I slip out of bed and sit at the kitchen table listening to the dawn chorus and watching night transform to day.

At 5 a.m. there's movement further along the hallway. Vanda comes into the kitchen and goes straight over to the kettle, asking the inevitable question: 'Did you sleep?'

As we sit talking over a cup of tea there's movement in other parts of the house. Vanda makes more tea and carries two mugs into the sitting room. 'Sharon's folding up bedding and Dendy is in the bathroom,' she says, coming back into the kitchen. Over the next hour, copious amounts of tea are made, the bathroom is continually in use and uppermost in my mind is wondering when the police will call and how long I can bear to sit around waiting.

By 8 a.m. the kitchen is a hive of activity and in the midst of it my sister is sorting breakfast for the children and making plans with them for the day. Vanda and Sharon make a shopping list and work out how many extra beds will need to be found. My only contribution is to claim the sofa for another night and ask Vanda if she can pick up some flowers, sunflowers if possible. Sharon suggests a tent for the youth and a call is made to close friends in Cardiff, Lizzie and Thomas's godparents. Can they bring their tent?

There are so many voices talking at once and everyone is looking strained from lack of sleep.

Martyn is making plans to collect Caroline, his wife, from Huntingdon and their daughter Michelle and her fiancé James from London. Sharon is going with him for company.

Sharon's husband Mike calls from Manchester wondering if he should drive over and bring Mum and Dad from Anglesey. Aunt Karina and Uncle Jimmie don't want to be left by themselves, understandably, but with the four of them and young Megan there isn't room in one car. Martyn is saying that he'll go and collect them when he gets back from Huntingdon.

'You can't, it's too much driving ...'

I hear all of this in fragments and feel slightly distanced from the making of arrangements. James and I seem to be the only people without an immediate purpose and the only people not yet showered and dressed. James has just come off the phone to his parents. His dad has offered to drive from their home in Gloucestershire to Bristol and collect Greg. He sits at the table looking into a cup of tea for a while and dutifully eats the toast Vanda has placed in front of him, then he takes a towel from the airing cupboard and goes off to have a shower. 'Do you think James is all right?' someone asks. We all look at each other. No one has an answer.

A bit later, on my way down to the bathroom for a shower, I overhear Stefan say quietly to Vanda, 'We need to talk to the children.'

The order of the morning is routine, it's the conversation that's different.

The shower is warm and I take my time, washing away the night, trying not to think about the implication of family gathering to be together and hopeful of hearing something soon from the police.

By the time I finish in the shower, dress and dry my hair, the household is quiet with only Dendy and James left in the house. 'Ellie and William have gone to play with friends and Vanda has gone shopping,' Dendy explains. 'Your mobile has been busy, we didn't know whether to answer it or not.' I check messages and respond to a couple, leaving the rest for later. Responding to text messages and phone calls is becoming a mammoth undertaking. Until yesterday very few people had my mobile number. How things change. On the whole, people don't expect a response. They want to tell me they're thinking of me, and ask: Is there anything we can do?

Rosey, my friend and colleague, is the only person I speak to for any length of time when she calls, taking the phone into the sitting room. I pace up and down the room for a while with the phone to my ear before settling on the sofa. We talk peacefully for quite a long while and then Rosey asks if the Bishop knows, offering to call him on my behalf. 'And what about people at your church?' She's thinking of practicalities.

'Fortunately I'm on holiday,' I say, 'so I don't have to worry about services tomorrow, they're all covered.'

Rosey's voice is gentle and concerned. It's easy to picture her on the other end of the phone, gold blond curly hair, compassionate eyes, short rounded frame and stylish, often dressed in deep pinks and purples and the colours of an English garden in full summer glory. This is how I picture Rosey now, as we speak across the country, Rosey by name and by nature. 'Rosey exudes joy,' Jenny once said but there's little joy on this occasion.

Rosey's call has opened a whole other world that I have not thought about in days, a world of church structures and faith communities, a world embraced when I took the mighty step of ordination in 2000.

My journey to ordination began many years before that. I suppose it was born out of a habit of going to church, my work developing drama and theatre projects in local communities and a sense, if not a certainty, of this thing called God. That I might have a ministry of sorts gradually emerged through life experiences and as I became more involved in the community. I grasped the challenge of faith rather than being convinced by it. I wanted to work for humanity and ordination, when it was posed to me as a possibility, seemed an appropriate path. I love people and God is a mystery that I have embraced. I find both people and God full of creative possibilities.

I look through the window and out to the green pasture of the garden. In the background I can hear a male voice describe 7/7, as it is already being referred to, as a significant event in British history. An ironic smile is passing across my face; I can see it reflected in the window pane. In 1998 I was being assessed and scrutinised over three days by a selection board. This was to discern whether I was an appropriate candidate for ordained ministry. Part of the process required me to produce an inventory of significant events in my life. On a timeline I catalogued joys, sorrows, celebrations, hurdles, successes and failures. I marked a lengthy stay in hospital as a child; the death of my grandparents; an abortive career in nursing; marriage; the birth of my children. On a double side of A4 paper I wrote about things that made me happy, things that made me sad and when I last cried.

I felt stripped bare.

All these revelations formed the basis for discussion points in the formal interviews. I was completely open and honest. I couldn't see the point of being otherwise. I enjoyed discussing literature and theology, exploring the meaning of pastoral care and delving into the mystery of the Eucharistic feast. I was a bit weak on Jesus.

My assessment, when it came, was that I was recommended for ordination training but that my training should include a rigorous immersion in scripture. I undertook this at an evangelical theological college which considered itself open. I would like to have attended a liberal catholic establishment but there wasn't one in Bristol. For two years I existed as a round plug in a square hole. By the time I left and took up my clerical collar my eyes were open to the diverse spectrum of Christianity. I had come to a new understanding of difference. At the end of my theological training I was confirmed in the knowledge that I was a woolly liberal with a catholic heart and that I did not have an evangelical mind.

My ordination, when it came, was held on the second day in July. The occasion was a significant event. Someone, I must not reveal who, gave me a set of red lacy underwear with a note which said: 'So you don't forget you're a woman under the cassock'. As it happened that was about all I did wear under my cassock that hot July day. All of us being ordained were sweltering in the heat and I was not alone in stripping down to only the bare essentials. After the ceremony I showed Jenny. She laughed herself silly and went around telling friends furtively that her mother was wearing lacy red knickers.

From the moment I took the decision to join the 'monstrous regiment' of ordained women, as it has been described, I was determined that for my children I was first and foremost their mother. They could come to church if they wanted though mostly they didn't want. Jenny came to morning worship with me once during my time at theological college. She was revising for her A-levels at the time and needed a break from study.

'Why don't you come into college with me this morning?You could come and experience college worship and then we could sneak off and go shopping.' It's a suggestion which meets with Jenny's approval. She's hoping for a new pair of jeans.The college chapel is a fairly modern building, purpose built on the site of the old swimming pool and set in sunken landscaped grounds away from the main college building. It is a tradition and expectation that college staff as well as students and tutors attend morning worship at the start of the day.Tutor groups take it in turns to lead the worship on a weekly rota.

The chapel is filling up as Jenny and I arrive.The music group is playing but nobody is singing yet.There are only a few seats left and we have to squeeze into a middle section. For reasons which will become apparent I do not like sitting in the middle.

'Good band,' Jenny whispers in my ear.

I just smile at her.

'What's the first hymn?' She asks.

It's traditional enough and we both sing with a fair amount of gusto. Then the worship songs begin; a series of choruses which are repeated in a prayerful manner. Jenny spends a lot of time looking around and taking in the atmosphere. As the worship develops pace, the chapel becomes filled with praise-filled voices and long arms are raised in the air. Jenny keeps prodding me in the ribs and when I sneak a look at her she is cowering against the volley of limbs outstretched with palms open or punching the air above in time to the music. She is taller than me by a couple of inches but we are surrounded by a throng of tall men who are head and shoulders taller than either of us. Jenny is dissolving into a fit of giggles and holding her nose.

'Stop it!' I tell her, but her expression is infectious and very soon I am cracking up as well.

She has lost all control now.

'Jenny!'

'Sorry, I can't help it.'

How we get through the rest of the service I do not know.

At last we are outside.

'Oh my god, she says as we make our way towards the car, I've never been consumed by armpits before. I wish Lizzie had been here.'

The thought of both daughters collapsing with laughter at my daily predicament is too much to contemplate.

'Now you know what it's like for me every morning. I only come up to most of the blokes' armpits. It's quite an experience, which is

why I try to sit on the end of a row. What an expression – consumed
by armpits – I think that's what I'll call my dissertation!'

Yes, there have been many significant events in my life, I think as I
turn from the window and memories of the past, but none more
significant than this unfolding event here and now.

I can't bear to sit doing nothing so I start cleaning the kitchen, filling the sink with hot soapy water and stripping the oven and grill of
any piece of metal which detaches and can be scrubbed. Dendy joins
in and sets to cleaning the cooker hob. We work in a way that is
completely uncharacteristic for both of us, scouring pans that don't
need scouring and scrubbing fiercely at oven racks. Surfaces, window
sills and everything else in sight is purged. Dendy turns from the
cooker, where she is poised with rubber gloves and clutching a scouring pad full of soapy suds, to look at me mopping the floor, and says,
'We must be the two most unlikely people to be doing this.' The irony
makes us both laugh and for a few minutes the tension in the air is
eased.

As I move around the kitchen cleaning, straightening a shelf of
cookery books, tidying a pile of school letters, pens and notepads, I
come upon my sister's diary lying open displaying end-of-term school
activities and engagements. A line of yellow Post-it stickers with
hastily scrawled food lists and reminders cover the left-hand page,
blotting out days of the week already past. The weekend section is
crammed with planned activities all now thrown into disarray. The
panic I felt yesterday is rising to the surface again and I fight to control
the sensation, closing my eyes as I did over the balcony in the hospital, drawing in a deep breath and exhaling as if to rid the fear from my
body. In a moment I've recovered.

'I'm going to have to get some more credit for my phone.' I say,
'It's running out rapidly.'

Vanda arrives back from shopping, astonished less by the transformed state of the kitchen than the fact that Dendy and I have been cleaning. We help unpack the bags of shopping. Vanda realizes she has forgotten something and will have to go out again later. 'Can you pick me up some credit for my phone?' I ask and go off in search of my purse, which is amongst the bags stored in a bedroom at the other end of the house, but don't get very far as the phone rings and I double back to the kitchen.

The phone is held out to me and a mouth forms the word 'police'. I speak to an officer with a Scottish accent who introduces himself as our assigned family liaison officer. At first I don't catch his name. There's no news but he and his colleague want to meet us at Foxhill Road, at Jenny and James's home – are we able to get there or do we need a lift? I explain my husband is on his way from Bristol so we make arrangements to meet at lunchtime. He gives me his mobile number and I ask him to repeat his name, which I jot down on a Post-it. He assures me that if there is any news in the meantime, he will be in touch immediately, asking if this is the best number to contact me on. I confirm it is, at least for the time being, and also give him my mobile number. I might have been reporting a lost cat.

The Post-it with the family liaison officer's number is pinned on to the noticeboard. James says his dad will drive us to Reading and the rest of the day begins to wrap itself around that meeting. A bunch of sunflowers now sits in a vase on the kitchen window sill alongside a picture of Jenny. Alert to all comings and goings I watch Stefan's mum get out of her car, back from feeding the horse, and cross the drive to her house. Another car pulls into the drive and one of my sister's friends gets out with a bunch of flowers. Vanda, who has been outside in the garden, goes across to greet her and her friend gives her a long hug. They move towards the house and I bolt along the hallway, reluctant to engage with anyone at the moment.

I spend a bit of time tidying my case and debate whether or not to put some make-up on, decide I can't be bothered and leave the room, then hear Jenny laughingly telling me not to forget the kick-ass lippy, which sends me back to the bedroom, rummaging in the case for my toilet bag and searching for mascara and lipstick. I even help myself to a squirt of my sister's perfume. I take advantage of the quiet and return a couple of text messages, sitting on William's bed and watching Ted, Stefan's dad, working in the garden. He straightens up, rubbing his back and catches sight of me in the window, lifting his arm in greeting before bending back to his digging, shaking his head at the ground. As I watch Ted I think of my own father and wonder what his thoughts are at the moment. They've seen so much, these old men, yet say so little.

By the time I go back to the kitchen Greg and Thomas have arrived.

I think Greg has no energy when we embrace. A light is gone from his eyes. His eyebrows, always dark and thick like his hair was once, now seem like heavy shadows above his eyes. His entire face is in sorrow. 'Don't do this,' I want to cry at him, 'Don't give up.'

A moment later I'm holding Thomas, so glad to see him and have him close. 'We'll find her,' is all I can say. 'We'll find her.' His eyes fill with tears, as do mine. There are other people in the kitchen but I'm only aware of Greg and Thomas and the blue and yellow squares on the tablecloth as the sun shines across it. I want to keep touching Thomas, ruffling his hair, stroking his back, whether to reassure him or comfort myself I don't know, I'm just so glad to have one of my children close.

Two plain-clothed police officers are already waiting at Foxhill Road when we arrive. As soon as we go through the gate they get out of a car and follow us into the house. Jenny's shoes are in the same position they were in yesterday, as though she had just stepped out of them. Introductions are made, Colin and Pauline, police family liaison officers. James asks if anyone would like a cup of tea and Pauline follows him into the kitchen asking if he'd like a hand. She has a faint Welsh accent and is chatty and friendly. Colin is more formal at first and his presence seems to fill the space in the small sitting room.

'I don't know how much was explained to you yesterday ...' he begins. 'Everything you would do yourself to find your daughter we will do on your behalf and liaise between the relevant authorities and yourselves ...' He's telling us about their role as family liaison officers, what we can expect from them, how they will be in touch regularly, a couple of times a day, either in person or on the phone; even if there's no news they will call to confirm there's no news. He talks about Jennifer (Jennifer not Jenny or Jen): can James remember what she was wearing on Thursday morning ... what time she left ... her route. I'm listening intently to everything being said yet it's the phrase 'relevant authorities' that jumps out at me and I want to ask: What do you mean by relevant authorities? But I don't question, none of us do.

Pauline is speaking now, asking for some personal items of Jenny's, her toothbrush or hairbrush, something like that, items needed for DNA testing, to help with identification. Pauline asks if she can go upstairs and it seems that she doesn't require any of us to follow. I don't know whether to read anything into that or not. When she comes down she asks to go into the bathroom and returns asking James if the items now in a plastic bag belong to Jenny, holding it out so we can see clearly Jenny's toothbrush, hairbrush, razor and a pair of earrings. Then James is asked for a photograph of Jenny. 'I'll make sure you get them back,' Pauline assures him.

Greg is asked if he would volunteer a sample of his DNA and doesn't hesitate in agreeing. 'Of course, anything that helps.'

'I'll just need to wipe a swab around the inside of your mouth,' Pauline explains, leading him into the next room. It all feels so calm and methodical, even when the police officer quietly confirms the reason for requesting DNA. Police don't usually request DNA if they believe someone to be alive. We tell him that we're still hoping Jenny will be found alive and urge the police to explore the possibility of other train or road accidents.

'She could be in hospital involved in an incident completely uncon- nected with the bombings,' James insists.

We're told this is very unlikely but any news would be given to us straight away. This is now a recovery operation. It's said so quietly, gently professional, almost businesslike and our response is dumb, barely registering what is being said as we nod our heads in dream- like submission.

Colin seems to have picked up on the variations of Jenny's name as at one point he refers to Jenny not Jennifer and then pauses and asks if it's OK to call her Jenny, looking from Greg and me to James. We're asked if we would like information on a 'need to know' basis or all details and I blurt out, 'I want to know everything.' Greg and James are more cautious.

'That's fine, not a problem,' responds Colin, making a note. Jenny's name will be released this evening as one of those formally missing. Apparently we have the rest of the day to inform anyone we wish to know ahead of it appearing in the media. 'Unfortunately we can't stop her name from getting into the media as it will be a matter of public record,' we're told.

The police officers have gone. Before we leave James collects a few things from upstairs, asks me if I'd like anything of Jenny's to take back and I pull a couple of items from the mangled heap of unwashed clothes in the laundry basket: T-shirts that smell of her and a jumper, still holding the faint odour of J'adore. When we go out through the door a few minutes later we leave her shoes where they are, in the same position they've been in for the last three days.

I struggle to remember the journey back. I remember phrases from the last hour: relevant authorities, formally missing, samples of DNA, recovery operation. The familiar world passes by beyond the car as I inhabit another world, balancing a new terrifying reality with disbelief. Four clinical phrases tip the fragile balance of the last few days and I feel as if I've moved from feeling the distant rumblings of an earthquake to standing over its epicentre, waiting with fearful calm.

I need to fight this, I need to hope and believe. I shift from one interior state to the other, from panic to determination, resolved by the time the car bears us home to state the facts, to be realistic but not dwell on the awful possibility of what is not known.

Vanda is in the kitchen when we arrive back; there's a moment of anticipation, hope, in her eyes as we come in through the open door, then one look at us tells her all she needs to know and her face crumbles. I return her look and shake my head and burst out crying.

Thomas is in the garden with Dendy, sunglasses shielding his eyes. They've been talking about a holiday our two families shared in France many years ago. I don't know what to say to him. A few hours ago I emotionally promised him I would find Jenny. Now I must prepare him for the possibility that he may not see his sister again. 'There's a chance Jenny may not be found,' is all I can bring myself to say for a few moments. He nods his head slowly, as if he's trying to swallow bad-tasting medicine.

My world is slipping away. I watch my son walk off down the garden and don't know whether to follow him or give him space. I long to hold him, to reassure him and make it all better, but this is not a cut knee we're dealing with.

'I knew you were going to say something bad,' Thomas says later, 'because when you sat down your eyes were watery.'

The heat of the garden is too intense so I move indoors and join the others in the kitchen. Vanda is standing at the work surface under the window making tea for James, his dad and Greg. We're so deep in conversation that at first not much notice is taken when Vanda goes out through the kitchen into the utility room. Moments later there's a distressed sound, someone upset, and I look up to see Martyn's car in the drive and Vanda comforting his daughter Michelle, Jenny's cousin, and everyone else looking as if they've just been given some bad news.

Suddenly the house is alive again and bustling with activity and voices. We're all gathered in the kitchen, sitting, standing, leaning against walls and cupboards. Mugs of tea proliferate around the table as we discuss the meeting at Foxhill Road. Despondent faces reflect what I feel in my heart as the details and implications of the police encounter are relayed. For the first time we articulate the possibility that Jenny may not have survived. The likelihood that by some fluke Jenny is still alive and surviving elsewhere is slowly being eroded. Martyn suggests that we need confirmation from the police that Jenny might have died. I can tell by the expression on James and Thomas's faces that they're not ready for that. Neither is Greg, neither am I. Then the subject is dropped and there's a general retreat into practicalities.

I'm unable to settle and start roaming around again. In the sitting room Martyn's wife Caroline is with Greg talking quietly on the sofa and holding hands. Greg looks shell-shocked, lost. I can't bear to look at the anguish in his face. Neither of them look up and I turn from the room without disturbing them and continue through the house into the conservatory littered with children's toys and out through the open doors into the garden. Martyn, Thomas, Michelle and her fiancé James are sitting around in the late afternoon sunshine, limbs outstretched. They all have sunglasses over their eyes and appear deep in contemplation of the sky or the grass; bodies languid and still, a sprawling tableau of spent energy.

There's such stillness everywhere. All life seems suspended in waiting. Even the guinea pigs in their run, basking in the heat, are motionless apart from sharp darting eyes. I turn the corner of the house into a wooded area of the garden. My sister is sitting on a home-made swing of wood and rope strung between two trees, gently rocking back and forth, staring into the distance. I leave her to her solitude and walk away in search of mine. I wander through the trees to the bottom of the garden and lie down in the cool grass amongst the shady patterns cast by the leaves and branches of the horse chestnut tree and pray for a miracle.

Vanda, Sharon and Dendy are preparing food and James is sitting at the table. I'm standing next to the phone so when it rings I pick it up automatically.

'Hello.'

'Can I speak to Julie Nicholson?' a female voice enquires, youngish, sounding friendly, up-beat.

'Speaking.' I hold my breath in hope.

The occupants of the kitchen stop talking and turn in my direction.

'This must be a very difficult time for you.'

'Yes.'

'I wonder if I can speak to you about your daughter Jenny.'

Something doesn't feel quite right. 'Who is this?'

The name doesn't register.

'I work for …' She names a local Bristol paper.

The voice continues to speak but I don't listen, instead I thrust the phone out and Dendy, who is nearest, takes it from me as I shriek, 'Oh my God it's a journalist.' Then my friend's outraged voice is yelling into the phone, 'How dare you intrude at such a time. Go away!'

For a brief moment, my reaction when I answered the phone made everyone think that Jenny was OK.

The call has distressed us and we're all baffled as to how a journalist located the number since it isn't listed. 'It's probably best if you and Greg and James don't answer the phone,' Sharon suggests, 'until we know who is on the other end of the line.' Lizzie has called, upset that reporters have also been calling the vicarage, which is less surprising though no less upsetting. She said they have a similar strategy in place and Auntie Chris is screening calls.

Vanda is popping out to the local supermarket and Dendy has decided to go with her so I give them a twenty-pound note to get some credit for my mobile phone.

The house phone is busy. Occasionally I speak to someone but mostly I leave it to Sharon to field and deal with callers and go and sit with Greg and James for a bit, watching *News 24*. Names and faces of missing people and victims are starting to appear on television and more survivors are talking about their experience. There's a rerun of a girl with a burns mask covering her face being led out of Edgware Road tube towards an ambulance. We've seen it several times, but watch again, each of us intent on scouring the crowds for a sign of Jenny through a backdrop of discussion on terrorists and suicide bombing.

Voices in the kitchen drag my attention away from the television. Vanda and Dendy have returned and confirm they've put credit on my phone. When I check the credit level it shows seventy-five pounds. 'Where did this come from?' I ask looking from one to the other. My sister shakes her head and Dendy admits to putting fifty pounds of credit on my phone. 'I can't do very much to help but at least I could do that,' she says.

At 5 p.m. the police liaison officer calls to confirm that Jenny's name is going to be on the evening news.

'Another person … Jennifer Nicholson … daughter of a Bristol vicar … today been named … missing …' Jenny's face is filling the television screen. She's in the room with us, laughing from outside Bristol Cathedral. Then she's gone and we're left bereft, on our knees in front of the television or hovering over it.

No one speaks or moves. Then: 'Where did that picture come from?'

'A youth production, when she was about sixteen.'

How did the media get hold of it?

While we debate the possibilities, whether the picture came from local press archives or someone involved in the same youth production, the impact of why it was on the screen in the first place, the central fact of the news, is temporarily channelled into animated speculation around the periphery. I'm not sure which is more upsetting, seeing Jenny's face blazoned across the screen or that it was released without our knowledge or that everything about the last few days is passing out of our control.

When all our debating over the picture is over, the stark fact remains that another person has been formally named as missing following the bombings on the London transport system two days ago and that person is Jenny.

11 September 2001

I'm getting ready to leave for Wells, to direct a play. My case is open and half packed. I'm running late and rushing around making sure I have everything I need for the week away. My mother is visiting and working her way through my backlog of ironing, adding item by item to the piles of pressed and folded clothes on the settee. The television is on downstairs while she irons. Suddenly she calls upstairs in an urgent voice telling me to come down quickly. Mum has stopped ironing and is intent on the television; a plane has crashed into the twin towers of the World Trade Center in New York. For almost an hour we watch the unfolding horror and devastation, Mum leaning on the ironing board while I lean over the back of the settee, watching and listening. Then, because we need to, we get on with our tasks. The shock lingers and our mood is subdued; the television remains on, but the devastation in New York does not prevent us from getting on with the day.

The next day in Wells, Jenny calls me from uni. I am due to fly to America the following week.

'You're not still going, are you?'

'If I can get my flight, yes.'

'Please don't go, Mum, I'm really worried.'

'This is probably the safest time to travel, security will be extra tight. Anyway, all flights are on hold at the moment so it may be out of my hands.'

'You have three children, what if something happens to you?' I can tell from her voice that she is upset and a bit cross with me.

'Jenny, nothing is going to happen, calm down. I would never put myself in danger.'

'Promise you won't go if there's any risk.'

'I promise.'

The trouble with danger, of course, is that you don't usually see it happening until it's upon you and by then it's too late to do anything about it. I think about those people trapped in the twin towers and how so many reached for their phones with one last message of love. I understand now what I could only imagine at the time.

After the news we don't quite know what to do so hit the gin and tonic. I drink mine too quickly so when a friend calls to see if there is anything we need I say, 'Gin!'

Lots of phone calls follow the evening news; my mother said it was a shock seeing Jenny's picture. 'You never think something like this is going to happen to you.'

A friend is telling me that my church in Bristol held a candlelit vigil last night and people have been taking flowers all day and leaving them at the church. There's going to be another vigil tonight. Everyone is doing what they can, in the best way that they can, to keep faith with Jenny. There's a kind of comfort in knowing that.

Mike and Megan have arrived. Martyn, Michelle and her fiancé have left for Anglesey; I don't remember them going. I remember discussion over needing to call my insurance company to arrange cover so Michelle and James could drive my car back. I was standing at the sink washing up some dishes and Sharon was by my side, liaising over the phone between me and the insurers. I remember Ellie and William being brought home by friends and William asking with confusion and some indignation, 'Why is everyone coming to my house?' Most of all I remember the exhaustion of pretending to be normal until bedtime.

And then the darkness and release from the day.

The heat is uncomfortable and my limbs are restless. Tiptoeing out to the kitchen without disturbing people is more difficult tonight. Where there were three of us scattered around the sitting room, there are now five with Mike occupying the sofabed with Sharon and twelve-year-old Megan sharing floor space with Dendy. Twice I catch my foot on the end of the blow-up bed and almost fall on the sleeping child.

Fed up with tossing and turning and getting in and out of bed I finally give up on trying to sleep and sit instead at the kitchen table with a mug of tea and a picture of Jenny, talking to her in my head as if she was sitting opposite me.

As soon as the first chink of light appears in the sky I replace Jenny's picture on the window ledge and creep back to bed and listen to the birds. I must have closed my eyes as the next thing I'm aware of are voices in the room and Vanda placing a cup of tea next to me and

Sharon, for the second morning running, folding up bedding and collapsing beds and looking tired and strained.

It's a quiet start to Sunday. I wonder about going to church but the thought is fleeting. Vanda offers to drive me if I want to go but here is where I want to be this morning, waiting for news with my family. The radio is on; prayers are being said in churches and places of worship up and down the country for people caught up in or affected by Thursday's bombings, for the dead, the injured, families waiting anxiously for news, the emergency services.

There's a woman on television, looking glorious in African dress, making an impassioned plea, demanding to know what has happened to her son; a mother, like me, desperate for news of her child. Her frustration and distress reflects my own, yet our response is so different. Why do I feel so calm? Should I be doing more, demanding information on the streets of London. *Will somebody please tell me where my daughter is?* I feel a sudden surge of emotion – panic – and take myself off to sit on the swing for a bit, inhaling long deep breaths, reassuring myself that I am doing all I can to find Jenny, we all are, and the police are working to help us. But I understand that other mother's desperation and the anguish in her face and rage in her voice haunts me as I swing backwards and forwards wondering what else I can do.

The Sunday papers are strewn across the table, and I pick up a copy of the *Sunday Times* and read about terrorists and suicide bombers and who they might be and pictures of missing people including Jenny. A voice calls out, 'Lizzie's here,' and suddenly my younger daughter's presence fills the kitchen.

Lizzie is the tallest of the three and the most passionate, feisty and dramatic. She doesn't walk into the room so much as bursts through the doorway. Long limbs encased in tight blue denim jeans, skimpy black vest top, long chestnut to red hair, straightened and held back from her face by large black sunglasses. In seconds, her eyes are flash-ing around the kitchen, taking in the scene and the papers on the table, on top of which she dumps her big bag before coming towards me. Our arms are wrapped around each other and we are rocking from side to side.

'Are you all right?' Lizzie is speaking into my neck, her breath warm against my skin. 'I missed you. I wish I'd been with you in London. How's James?'

'I'm fine and James is bearing up. I'm really glad you and Thomas and Dad are here now and we're all together.'

Amidst a stream of tearful greetings and hugs there's a great sense of relief at having her here with us after the distance and fragmenta-tion of the last few days. I want to sit down with her and talk, find a quiet spot, but too much is going on and the moment passes. The kitchen is filling up again, as if a central character has come into the scene and taken her place on stage. In a way she has. It is Lizzie who set the scene, Lizzie who first alerted us to the fact that something was wrong. And now she is here among us. Like a chorus we are gathered around her as she relays tales of goings-on at the house in Bristol: journalists turning up on the doorstep, Chris arriving laden with food; everyone sitting up all night talking; a never-ending stream of phone calls. And then, suddenly running out of steam for one subject, she notices empty gin bottles on the side. Her eyes open wide.

'My god, how much have you all been drinking?' And suddenly the chorus is laughing and swelling as more people arrive.

At first Ellie and William are excited to have all their cousins around but they soon become bewildered as the house and garden begin to fill with more family and friends.

Lindsay, one of my sister's closest friends arrives, bearing flowers. 'Oh Julie,' is all she says as we embrace but that is enough to commu-nicate a wealth of feeling. Watching from the kitchen window as she drives off a short while later, all I can see is a little girl with ribbons in her hair, new long white socks and black shiny shoes climbing into a car and excitedly waving out from the back window as the car pulls away. 'Do you remember when you and Lindsay took Jenny to the ballet?' I ask as Vanda comes back into the kitchen.

'Yes, we saw *Coppélia*. We had a box.' Neither of us speaks as we stand side by side looking out at the drive in contemplation of the empty space left by Lindsay's departing car.

Finally, at lunchtime, Martyn's car bearing my parents and uncle and aunt from Anglesey pulls into the drive. My mother is out of the car almost before it stops and heading towards the house before any of us have a chance to get outside.

My trusty little silver Fiesta draws up alongside and as Michelle and fiancé James climb from the car looking hot and tired they tease me about the lack of air-conditioning. 'It's called windows,' I instinctively retort. There follows a stream of light-hearted banter over the basic functions and limitations of my car before we all go inside the house to the now requisite gin and tonic.

I might have expected the arrival of my parents and aunt and uncle to be fraught with tension and emotion, but instead their relief at having arrived after a long hot journey and gladness at being amongst the rest of the family temporarily lifts the general mood. The embrace my sister and I receive from our mother transcends any need for words and I think we'll both remember that hug for the rest of our lives. I'm generally OK greeting my parents and uncle but when my aunt's eyes fill with tears as she greets me I have trouble holding my own emotion back. My mother immediately gets busy gathering up her grandchildren, declining any kind of drink. I'm beginning to think that the ritual of pouring gin as soon as visitors arrive is to give us something to do; it's a rite of passage to break the awkwardness. Anyway, it seems to work.

The kitchen has become a hive of food-preparation activity. More friends of my sister arrive laden with food and instantly depart. For me, wandering around my family, Jenny's family, is as comforting or reassuring as it gets; being in solidarity, together, caring for and supporting each other. Observing 'the youth' of the family lounging in the grass with bottles of beer; my sister, cousins and friends preparing food and pouring drinks; our close friends Steve and Ann arriving with their tent in tow; my niece changing her baby's nappy in the midst of the mêlée: all of this seems bizarre yet in a way quite wonderful despite the reason why we're all here. This is a family Mass in the fullest sense of the word.

Greg and I walk around the garden with James and his parents, a calm quintet weaving in and out of trees away from the main hub and discussing the status quo. Status quo! I mean talking about how long Jenny has been missing and the implication of meeting with the police yesterday, our current state of limbo and frustration and how unbelievable it all is. In the background the sounds of family and friends reuniting rise and fall like the crescendos and diminuendos of an orchestral movement while the gathered throng, splayed out across the lawn, looks more like a garden party than a family in crisis.

I'm reassured by everyone's presence but I don't feel part of it. The heat haze is becoming like a shimmering veil between me and my family. I'm so glad everyone is here yet I seem to be skirting the perimeter feeling more and more detached. The day is becoming a blur and I'm aware of a creeping vagueness and distance from everything going on around me. From time to time I stray into the kitchen to help but my contribution is mechanical and surplus to requirements.

William is upset, disturbed and confused by so many people and so much tension in his home. 'I want everyone to go away and leave my house!' He's very angry and shouts about bombs and blowing people up. Vanda and I sit outside with him on the swing for a long time. William is sitting on Vanda's lap cuddling in to her and when he's calm she asks him, 'Would you like Auntie Julie to tell you about Jenny and what's happening?' William nods his head and I ask him if he would like to ask me questions or for me to tell him about it.

'Tell me,' he says quietly.

So I begin trying to explain what's happening and why so many people are here, telling him simply and factually about the explosions on the underground, how lots of people have been hurt and some have been killed and how worried we all are because we don't know where Jenny is and how we're waiting for the police to find her and why it's taking so long.

'Is Jenny dead?' he asks.

'We don't know, Wills. We hope not but she might be.' I'm surprised I'm able to say that so calmly. 'That's why everyone is in your house, so we can be together while we wait to find out what has happened to Jenny. Is that OK?'

He nods his head. There's a pause and for a few minutes we all swing gently backwards and forwards without speaking. Then I ask if he wants to know anything else and he shakes his head, for the time being satisfied. After a little while he says tearfully against Vanda's shoulder, 'I think the bombers are very bad people.'

Strangely, this is the calmest and most useful I've felt all day.

My uncle is sitting at the kitchen table and seems lost in thought contemplating a glass of whisky. I sit down opposite him 'Are you OK, Uncle Jimmie?' I ask. He doesn't answer but reaches across the table to grasp my hand in one of his and as he lifts his head his 85-year-old eyes are full of tears. We sit like that for a moment or two before he gives in to the welling emotion blurting out, 'This is terrible,' to which I can only respond, 'I know.'

'I need to tell you that this is no longer a rescue operation and now officially a recovery operation.'

For a moment none of us responds. There's a pause while the relevance slowly dawns, then in an instant I grasp the significance of what is being said. The police family liaison officers are sitting at the kitchen table with us; at least one of them is: Colin. Pauline is standing close to Lizzie and Thomas. James and Greg and I are sitting at the table. Some of the family are in the kitchen but most are outside.

I listen as Colin speaks, watching his lips move. Someone asks what 'recovery operation' means. I know. I know that means everyone who could be rescued, has been. Now it's bodies and remains to be recovered. I understand the subtle shift between rescue and recovery, the difference between life and death, the difference between hope and futility. As I listen to the police officer's voice telling me what I asked to hear – everything, I told him yesterday, I want to know everything – it's as though a long slow injection of absolute despondency is being released into my system. I sit transfixed, not taking my eyes from Colin's mouth, hearing only the voice in my head, loaded with meaning. *Recovery*.

'It means that everyone who can be rescued has been and all the injured have been accounted for.' His voice is the only sound in the room.

Then a barrage of questions, lots of questions. The police are unable to confirm whether Jenny has been found.

'Where is she then?'

'If Jenny has not been found then where is she?'

'Why wasn't the Bakerloo line working?'

'What about her scar, it's very distinctive?' We tell him about the scar again in minute detail. 'You must be able to identify her from her scar.'

'This is out of character; Jenny called James several times each day. Can you track her mobile phone?'

We're being told the police are working in difficult circumstances; intense heat, poor light, asbestos; there are still bodies being recovered and the sites are littered with debris.

Jenny has not been found yet. Hold on to that thought, I tell myself, and with that thought – or hope – a new thought comes, one I can hardly bear to voice, but it niggles away until I follow Colin and Pauline out to the car and ask one more question quietly, away from anyone else's hearing: 'Is it possible Jenny may have been taken hostage?'

The question sounds ridiculous even to my own ears, and yet such things happen and I have to ask. Equally quietly but very firmly Colin says, 'No, that isn't possible,' as Pauline shakes her head in affirmation. There's a fleeting expression in the officer's face, sympathy, but something else as well, which stops me asking any more questions. As I watch the car turn in the drive before pulling slowly into the lane away from the house I'm left with a certain feeling that more is known than being revealed and for a moment I want to run after the car demanding to be told. Maybe I'm imagining it but I do believe the expression on the officer's face was knowledge. No, I'm not imagining it.

I can't settle and start wandering about the house again, feeling a terrible pressure inside me that has no outlet.

People are dispersing, preparing to leave and getting into cars. One moment I'm calm and aware of debate over car travel and driving, who is taking my parents and aunt and uncle back to Bristol, who is going and who is staying; the next moment I'm shouting, reacting over the silliest thing, whether the dog should stay here or go to Bristol. Erupting like a volcano – '*I don't care about the dog*' – screaming and yelling and bolting through the house to the farthest point until there's nowhere else to run to, throwing myself down on a bed pounding it with my fists. My father is standing in the doorway, I think having come out of the bathroom opposite, looking at me in shocked disbelief, asking what the matter is, and all I can do is pour molten lava over him and everyone else now gathering in the doorway, at the walls, the pillows and everything in my path until finally collapsing and sobbing into the pillow. *'My daughter, your granddaughter has probably been murdered by terrorists and you ask what's the matter with me.'* There, I've said it, screamed what I've been trying not to say for three days and the acknowledgment is unbearable. Sharon is sitting beside me on the bed rubbing my back until all the fire and rage and torrent of angry words have gone and all that's left is pitiful sobs.

The house is quiet and I wonder if I've been dreaming but somehow I know it was real, my outburst, the way I shouted at everyone, my father's stunned expression and my terrible frustration vented on the people who are most important to me, bearing their own pain and absorbing mine. I don't know how long we stayed like that, Sharon soothing me like a baby. I was aware of voices – *She needed to cry . . . She's been too calm . . . Better to leave her alone for a while . . . Maybe she'll sleep . . . We'll sort the dog out* – and of feeling completely empty, too empty to talk or respond or lift my head as people came to say good-bye, and then the voices faded. I suppose I must have fallen asleep.

I turn over feeling embarrassed and ashamed. William is standing in the doorway, looking at me intently with a frown on his face, unsure whether to come in. 'Can I get my cricket bat?' he asks. I want to hug him but instead I smile at him and a little while later hear him say, 'Auntie Julie is awake.' The room is darkening; it's still light outside but dimmer in the room as the evening sun sinks lower behind the trees. The house feels as if it is restored, settled, spent of turbulence and more peaceful; there's music playing, too soft and far away to tell what it is, it could be anything, but it sounds gentle and sacred, like a distant Benedictus.

CHAPTER 4

Second Movement

WAITING

Today is Monday; five days and still no news of Jenny.

Media coverage of the effects of the bombings and all things related is still fairly continuous, though television has ceased to be the focus of household attention in quite the same way as it was through the first few days. Occasionally someone will suggest we turn the television off for a while, or sometimes the sound is turned off and the picture left running. We can't bear the disconnection from news for long and invariably when one person has turned it off it isn't long before another person switches it back on. From time to time victims of the attack dominate the news, bright faces filling the television screen, full of life, relaxed and at play in informal family snapshots or smiling delightedly and proudly in formal graduation robes. There's a catch of the breath and stillness, a sacred stillness, while we listen and watch and hear the shock and sorrow and pride in the voices of those who speak of the newly dead. Then we go back to the waiting, our own waiting, and don't speak at all of the possibilities that hang over us like an ever-darkening shadow.

I slept for a couple of hours last night. One moment I was listening to the dawn chorus, one bird after another cheep-cheeping away;

I suppose they must have sung me to sleep as the next moment I woke with a start and the birds had stopped singing and the sky was light. There was a moment of blessed normality as I opened my eyes before the crushing reality flooded in and with it another feeling: that I had failed Jenny by not staying awake.

An air of solemnity has overtaken purpose. Yesterday had a momentum; today it feels as if the household has woken in a state of limbo. Languid bodies drift through the rituals of the morning. The youth have begun to emerge from their communal sleep in the conservatory last night. They move slowly and yawningly, one by one inhabiting the bathroom before congregating in the sitting room. Everything, even the tea-making and washing-up, has a sense of being slowed down this morning.

Vanda is nowhere to be seen, which probably means she's outside, on the swing. The children are in school so there's no pretence of normality. Sharon is going through the house with a vacuum cleaner and Stefan is working. Greg is sitting quietly with a book, distant and motionless, staring at the pages rather than absorbed in reading. There's a kind of disconnection separating us; we're here, inhabiting this same space, waiting for the same news, full of the same anxiety, yet we're remote from each other, each lost in our own dimension of limbo and unable to quite reach out and properly connect with the other. It's like a dream in which you can see people but can't quite reach them.

When the phone rings we're all suddenly alert. Greg and James and I are to meet the police family liaison officers at Foxhill Road early this afternoon. They want a profile of Jenny.

Vanda says she'll drive us.

Some of the questions surprise us. Is Jenny a member of any groups? Has she travelled abroad recently? Spent prolonged periods away from home? Any religious affiliations? Had we noticed any changes in her behaviour recently? This is Jenny we're talking about, for goodness' sake! Jenny sings in choirs, she goes to aquarobics, had a short holiday in Portugal last month with James, attends church sometimes – mostly when she comes back to Bristol – goes to wine bars with friends and laughs a lot. I can't begin to take the questions seriously. Colin is apologetic, explaining why such questions are necessary. I know why but it doesn't stop them sounding ludicrous.

When we're asked who Jenny's doctor is I'm not unduly concerned, it seems quite routine; after all, medical records will contain details of previous surgery which could help with identification. When we're asked if she has a dentist it's a different matter. Even though Colin chooses his words carefully, and stresses 'if there's a need … details already on file,' the implication is clear enough.

The FLOs are unable to confirm how long the wait will be for news. Is it possible Jenny is confused and wandering, traumatized, suffering from amnesia? James applies his own logic to the fact there isn't any news and the officers patiently tolerate our insistent and repeated assertions that if there isn't any news to the contrary, then Jenny may still be alive, out there, somewhere. This is the hope and belief we intend to hold on to.

Believe and it may be true.

While we rinse out the tea mugs, James points out that on the CD player in the kitchen is Elgar's *Dream of Gerontius*, a recording Jenny sang in a few weeks ago. The cover is lying open on the kitchen unit but I can't bring myself to remove the disc. Instead I pick out some of her CDs stacked against the wall, the *Greatest Hits* of Nina Simone, a Benjamin Britten arrangement of English folk songs, *Greatest Pop Divas* and one of her favourite classical pieces, Beethoven's 'Emperor' Piano Concerto.

More dashed hopes when we get back and fragments of conversations, questions and answers and non-answers. Frustration and tension rises like a tide. 'How long will we have to wait for news?' Lizzie asked the same questions I asked of the police family liaison officers a couple of hours ago.

'I don't know.'

'Maybe she won't ever be found.'

'Don't say that.'

'It all takes so much time.'

'There are a lot of body parts being recovered, the police said.'

Oh God, don't say that, don't even think it. But it's too late, I've said it and watch Lizzie's eyes open wide with horror at the image my words have conjured up. Lizzie's spirit is suddenly defused and for a few seconds neither of us speaks as she rests her head on my shoulder and I put my arms around her, stroking her hair. I'm trying not to think of Jenny blown apart and I think Lizzie is too. When we're both a bit calmer I say, 'It's a painstaking operation. I know it's hard but we have to be patient while the police do their job.'

'I'm not very good at being patient,' Lizzie says, her spirit returning as she straightens up.

'Neither am I. I've just had more years to practice.' This makes us both smile.

Lizzie and Thomas are wondering about going to Manchester later, then on to Anglesey with the Nicholson cousins tomorrow. Mike has suggested that it might be a solution to them kicking their heels here. None of us has any idea how long we will have to wait for news or what that news will be; it could be hours, days. There's lots of discussion and we're all torn over what to do for the best. In the end Lizzie and Thomas decide to go with their cousins Lucy, Andrew, Katie, Joanne and Megan, to the holiday home in Anglesey. The wait might not seem so interminable and tense if they pass the time with their cousins in a place where they've all been happy, spent childhood holidays and can chill out for a few days together. I don't know if we're making the right decision but lack the energy to resist and in a way I'm relieved. Lizzie and Thomas look as though a weight has been lifted from them.

I'm lying under the tree at the bottom of the garden.

Tears trickle along the side of my face, towards my ear and down my neck into the dry ground.

I feel an ant crawling along my arm and instinctively flick it away with my finger, hardly a movement but enough to rouse me and cause me to sit up and shift position. What looks like a four-leafed clover catches my eye and I lean forward to pluck the fine stem from a patch of grass, feeling a slight stirring of hope. Three leaves, not four. I cast the little green stem aside and begin parting blades of grass, quite idly at first and then with a growing fixation as though the most important thing in the world at this moment is to find a four-leafed clover. I search and search to no avail and finally fall back in the grass inexplicably disappointed and bereft.

There's a four leafed clover tucked inside my parents' wedding album, pressed and dried. I grew up believing that to find one was a sign of good luck, one of those childhood myths that never quite relinquish their hold on adult reasoning. On days out in the park and countryside we would pick daisies to make daisy chains and search for four-leafed clovers. My father found one for my mother around the time they became engaged, which pre-dates my existence. I made plenty of daisy chains during my childhood but never found a four-leafed clover and never experienced the regret I feel at this moment.

When I come back into the house Greg is looking for me to say that Colin called his mobile as arranged to confirm the name and contact details of Jenny's dentist in Bristol.

'Did he say anything else?' I ask.

'Not really, only that he and Pauline would call in later.'

They arrive as we're watching the news. Vanda and Sharon look out from the kitchen window predicting what colour shirt Colin will be wearing today. They've started to tease Colin over his shirt colours. There's laughter as he comes through the door and Sharon's guess of lilac proves to be correct. They share some light-hearted banter with him over what colour he'll be wearing tomorrow. As usual we sit at the kitchen table; Pauline says she was trying to get her head around who was who in the family so we attempt to fill in the blanks for her. The visit doesn't seem to be about anything in particular and is relatively informal and relaxed. 'I'm on a day off on Tuesday so you'll only see Colin tomorrow, but you'll see me again on Wednesday,' Pauline tells us as they prepare to leave. On the way out to the car there's some more teasing about Colin's shirt colour and he asks Sharon and Vanda if they have a colour preference. When one of them suggests lime green he says he'll see what he can do.

William and Eleanor are sitting at the kitchen table, fresh from their bath and dressed in pyjamas, hair still damp. William, in full competitive mode, has been talking about sports day at school tomorrow, the races he's in and how he hopes to be placed. He's high and excited and we are all putting a lot of energy into being excited with him. With a captive audience he wants to know who is going to watch and having secured a following of supporters goes off to bed willingly and in high spirits.

Ellie, conversely, doesn't want to go to school tomorrow or take part in sports day and it takes some negotiation and compromise to persuade her to follow her brother to bed. Eventually she goes, albeit in a more subdued mood than his. Vanda is looking tired and strained and tears suddenly spill from her eyes. Then almost immediately Sharon's eyes fill with tears, as do mine. It lasts moments, a welling up of emotion, overspill and release, wiping eyes, blowing noses and then we pick up from where we left off, talking about sports day and agreeing that we need to maintain as much normality as possible for the children.

'It's important for Wills that we're there,' James is saying with determination and solidarity for William.

Sharon suggests Vanda goes for part of the sports day. 'Just go for William's races, you don't have to stay for the whole thing.' That seems to determine a purpose for Wednesday afternoon at least.

Lizzie and Thomas have left with Katie and Joanne. Mike and Megan are the last to leave. After the final round of hugs and provisional farewells, promises to look after each other and keep in regular phone contact, the doors are closed on the outside world and our depleted group settle down for another night of uncertainty.

When there's any significant news we'll come and tell you in person, together. We won't relay news over the phone. We'll tell you as soon as we have any information.

Mid-day, Tuesday 12 July

Today is William's school sports day. It is due to begin at 1.30 p.m. so we will need to leave around 1 p.m.

Martyn and Caroline are leaving after breakfast, driving Michelle and her James back to London before going on to Bristol to sort a few things in the vicarage and to call in on my parents. I'm still in my pyjamas at the kitchen table, writing a list of items needed from home and explaining to Martyn and Caroline where they can be found. At the same time Sharon is on the phone to my motor insurers arranging cover for yet another person to drive my car. 'We'll gather up any post and bring it back with us,' Martyn is saying as I hand him the list. Then there's a burst of activity as everyone gathers outside, amidst hugs, assurances, choruses of 'drive carefully' and 'see you soon', to watch the four settle into the car and drive away.

The family is gathered in Anglesey, the day after Mike and Sharon's wedding, June 1977. Three generations of relatives — brothers, sisters, uncles, aunts and cousins — stand at the gates of my uncle and aunt's house shouting farewells and waving good-bye to a departing car. Four arms wave effusively back from wound-down windows until with a honk of the horn the car turns the corner at the end of the road and is gone from sight. Bodies spill back into the house and garden to resume post-wedding partying. Two uncles, life-long buddies silly with whisky and high on party spirit, fool around like court jesters while others egg them on, causing young American cousins to fall about laughing. The revelry goes on until it's time for another departure and some-one jokes, 'Rent a crowd at the ready!' which is the cue for the sequence of hugs, farewells and shouts of 'drive carefully' and' see you soon' to begin all over again.

Time is stripped away in memory and the ritual of family farewell does not change over thirty years, except this morning there is no laughter and the farewell wave is a single raised hand.

At mid-day Colin arrives. He has come to tell us that the police in London are in possession of Jenny's dental records and an identification process would now take place. We are all very composed, resigned I suppose you could say. This is the inevitable final stage that we have dreaded. Colin assures us that we will be updated on any developments as soon as possible. He isn't able to confirm how long that would take. Here we go again, an increasingly familiar response

to news, composure on the outside; blind panic on the inside. I understand what Colin is saying, what he is communicating. I don't want to
hear. Abruptly, I tell him he has to leave as we need to get to sports
day. Vanda darts a glance at me, shocked at my forthrightness, Colin
looks surprised, taken aback. But then, as equably as ever, says OK and
he will speak to us later.

'What are you going to do now?' Vanda asks after Colin has left.
The time is 1.30 p.m.

'I'm going to sports day.'

'You don't have to; I can go on my own.'

'William will be expecting us, it's important for him, we must go.'
James is equally adamant.

There is no more time to deliberate; we are already late. Greg isn't
going, neither is Sharon, so Vanda, James and I hurry out to the car and
set off, zooming out of the drive and up the lane.

It's very hot; the children are all in sun hats and sitting under specially
erected canopies on either side of the sports track. The races are
already under way and Vanda, James and I dash across the field to find
William, let him know his fan club is here to cheer him on. As soon
as he spots us we get a thumbs-up and beaming smile in response to
our wave. Ellie is nearby with a sun hat pulled right down over her
forehead, to protect her fair skin, and looking far less enthusiastic
than her brother though she does muster up a wave. Vanda is talking
to some people so James and I make our way down the playing field
in search of somewhere to sit and watch William's races.

We've settled in a shady spot under a tree. It's some distance from
the main gathering of spectators, towards the bottom of the playing
field. I suppose we're in our own world rather detached from reality,

which is maybe why we don't take much notice when a family group sitting a little way apart call over and suggest we may want to move. Apparently they had sat in the same spot earlier and were told by a member of staff to move, something to do with health and safety and children over-running the course. It seems a long way from the end of the running track and there are no visible notices or ropes cordoning off the area, so we decide to sit there anyway. If there is a problem, someone will doubtless come and ask us to move. Besides which, there doesn't seem to be anywhere else to sit which is in the shade.

The three of us are talking, speculating on how long it will take for the identification to be completed. I wish I could be there for it and not have to wait for news at a distance. We're absorbed in our own discussion and don't immediately notice trouble approaching.

A woman in shorts and a big sun hat is striding down the field shouting. She's shouting in our direction, at us in fact: '... how many times must I tell you people not to sit there ...' Her body language is fierce as she approaches, coming to a standstill in front of us, hands on hips and continuing to berate us. We're all on our feet in seconds. My response is to blurt out, rather pathetically and defensively, 'You can't speak to us like that.' James has fled into the bushes; Vanda is shouting back as though she has been stung, which in a sense she has, telling the woman in no uncertain four-letter-word terms to go away and leave us alone. The woman looks horrified and embarrassed. 'Oh, Vanda, I'm so sorry, I didn't know it was you. I wouldn't have dreamed of speaking that way ...' And as suddenly as she bore down upon us, the woman has turned on her heel and is striding back up the field.

'You shouldn't speak to anyone in that way,' I say to her retreating back, but I don't think she has heard me.

People have gathered around. The father who warned us against sitting under the tree is speaking gently, kindly, telling me how sorry he is, what a terrible time we've been having and that Jesus will be looking after Jenny now. I don't know how to respond. I wonder if he'd be feeling so confident if he was standing in my shoes at the moment. Part of me wants to cry out, how dare he, how dare he make that assumption but it's difficult to rage in the face of well intended Christian kindliness.

The scene has calmed, or deflated. We watch William win his race then leave. During the drive home there's enough outrage and hysteria in recalling events of the last hour to fuel the car and keep us from crumbling.

4.45 p.m.

Spoke to Colin, he telephoned to alert us to the fact that there is an impending press release by the police about four suicide bombers responsible for the explosions.

Early evening

Mike telephones from Manchester and speaks to Sharon. Lizzie and Thomas are both OK and in the garden with their cousins playing volleyball. Mike is going to do a BBQ for them all later.

8 p.m.

Sharon is preparing supper and talking over her shoulder to James's parents, who have driven over from Gloucestershire. Vanda is folding towels from the laundry basket and joining in with the conversation. I answer the phone when it rings, expecting it to be family or one of Vanda's friends.

'It's Colin, he and Pauline are on their way.'

James is standing next to me, 'When will they be here?'

'Soon,' I reply automatically but my mind is rushing ahead recalling earlier fragments of conversations. 'He said they – they'll be here.'

The significance is lost on no one.

This is it, I know this is it. 'You won't see me tomorrow,' Pauline said yesterday. 'We'll both come with significant news,' Colin had said. 'We'll tell you we're on our way.' There's no time to think or discuss, the car is pulling into the drive and Vanda has already gone outside to meet them. Everyone is in the kitchen, watching the doorway. Waiting.

I'm seated at one end of the kitchen table. Greg is standing behind me, his hands on my shoulders. James is seated to my right, his parents standing behind him. Colin is seated opposite me, at the other end of the table with Pauline standing slightly back.

Even as it is happening I know I will remember this moment for the rest of my life.

Jennifer Nicholson has been identified by way of dental records as being one of the victims from the Edgware Road site bombings ... body parts missing ... temporary mortuary been set up ...

I've never experienced a tsunami, but this is how I think it happens. You see it coming, a great wave approaching; you can't escape even by running. The great wave of death is intent on consuming all in its passage. Turn and run away, or stand your ground and face it.

There's no time to think now or prepare. The wave is coming closer and closer; and now I'm in the middle of it, people falling and breaking as the wave hits, forlorn animal sounds and sobbing. I reach out and touch pain beside me. I'm being forced down; someone clinging to me, dragging me under and then pulled away. The air is filled with excruciating sounds as hope and life are suffocated by an immense force.

And then the great wave of death moves on towards Manchester, to a garden where my children have tried to escape the wave and are playing volleyball on a warm and sunny evening. When the tsunami hits there, Mike will hear and see it first, and leave the BBQ he's preparing, to go to my children and his children and break up their game and they will all stand together, holding each other as the devastation takes its toll.

The wave changes course again, rising up and making ready to crash on to Bristol, to grandparents and friends, sending shock waves spiralling out, while behind and in its wake is brokenness and disbelief.

This is the only way I can describe the impact, by describing something completely outside my experience because the experience itself is beyond anything I can write.

... details of injuries Jennifer sustained ... probably twenty-eight days before Jennifer's body can be released ... arrangements will need to be made ...

'I want to see Jenny's body.'

'It's not advisable.'

'I want to see her, as soon as possible, I want to see her.'

'Where was she standing when the bomb went off?'

'Was she on the platform or inside the carriage?'

'Where was her body found?'

'How long before she died?'

'Would she have felt anything?'

The questions are endless and the explanations frustrating which leads to more questions, all met with understanding if not satisfactory answers until, for the time being, there's nothing left to say or ask or demand.

The police have gone, with an assurance that arrangements will be made for me to be taken to the temporary mortuary to see Jenny's body tomorrow.

Greg is walking away from the kitchen, passing me and going into the hallway. For a moment we cling on to each other but the pain is too great; he can't bear mine and I can't bear his. There is no comfort, only anguish, and then the length of hallway stretches between us like a desolate plain before shock numbs feeling and darkness comes down like a blind.

Twenty-eight days. What do we do for twenty-eight days? Greg and I are walking around the garden thinking about Jenny and finding some space and energy to talk. We're walking side by side but could be a million miles apart for all the words we can find. And yet there is tenderness between us as we try to be parents to Jenny in her death and give something to each other. 'I don't know how to make this better for Lizzie and Thomas,' I suddenly cry out and then all either of us can do is sob for Jenny and all the unspoken loss exposed by her death. For a while we sit on the swing, forlorn souls unable or unwilling to speak. Yet this space is calm and peaceful and shaded from the sun, protected, and provides us with a temporary sanctuary in which to be together truthfully. 'Maybe you need to go and see your mother,' I say at last, and tears begin to stream again from both our eyes as decisions are made which will for the time being leave me surrounded by the family of my childhood and restore Greg to his.

Last night we both encouraged Lizzie and Thomas to continue with plans to spend a few days in Anglesey. 'There's no need to come back,' we reassured them. 'You can't do anything; none of us can, until Jenny's body is released then we can all be together again.'

But nothing will ever be the same again, for any of us, and when Greg and I share a final embrace before going back inside it feels just that, final, as though we are saying goodbye.

Wednesday lunchtime Colin arrives; I assume with details of travelling to London to the temporary mortuary but he informs us that the
coroner is going to release Jenny's body, probably tomorrow.

'You said twenty-eight days!' The words ring out like an accusation.

'Due to exceptional circumstances … so you can make funeral
arrangements … where you would like Jenny's body taken …'

I hear what Colin is saying but all I can think is I'm not ready for
this. 'Yesterday you told me you would take me to see Jenny in the
temporary mortuary, you explained the set-up, I've imagined the
setting, I'm prepared. Now you're telling me a faceless official with
a sweep of the pen has consigned Jenny to an undertaker and I'm to
make arrangements, well I'm not ready, it's too soon.' I'm screaming
but the screams must all be inside my head as the words that leave
my mouth sound reasonable. 'This is too much to take in; I need some
time to think'.

Greg's brother David has arrived to drive Greg to Manchester to see
his mum. I'm glad they're going together. My nephew Andrew has
also arrived but he's travelling on to Anglesey to join Lizzie and
Thomas and the rest of the Nicholson cousins. I'm glad about that as
well. Mostly I suppose I'm glad that my family is being looked after
and cared for while I feel so incapable.

Jenny's body is going to be moved to an undertaker in Reading on
Friday. James has requested that Jenny comes first to Reading, where
they shared their life together, before being taken home to Bristol. It
feels appropriate; ironically, her life in reverse.

The FLO has called again, for the name and number of the undertaker we'd like to use. I wish I'd insisted on going straight to the
temporary mortuary in London. I want to see my daughter's body. In

spite of all advice to the contrary I know this is something I must do, yet the police seem reluctant now and slightly embarrassed. I'm puzzled by the change in attitude and sense that pressure has been put on the FLOs to dissuade me from going to the mortuary. Yesterday the FLOs were making arrangements for me to be taken to London, now I'm being put off – or that's what it feels like, persuaded it would be better not to see her or at least to wait until her body is moved to Reading. It's so difficult to take a stand and argue in the face of reasoned concern. There's a compromise: I won't go to London to the mortuary; I'll wait until Jenny is brought to Reading, but I'm not happy about it.

I don't have the energy to fight. I want to demand I'm taken direct to London, to wherever Jenny is. I can't bear to think of her alone and uncared for. 'Who is looking after her body?' I ask. Who is honouring her, taking care of her? Nobody has answers, only advice: 'Better to let her body be brought to Reading and see her there … less distressing.' Better for whom? Why am I not fighting this more? Fear, I'm afraid. I acquiesce, see sense, behave sensibly even if that means I live with the realization that I am abandoning my child to bureaucracy because I didn't insist hard enough or long enough for an alternative.

Eventually I do what has to be done and telephone Derek, an undertaker in Bristol whom I've known and worked with over the past three years. Predictably Derek is gentle and professional, offering to go to London in person, bring Jenny's body to Reading, to an undertaker he recommends, and ensure that Jenny is treated with all dignity and respect. Later, when we are ready, he will bring her from Reading to Bristol.

I've heard people say that it's the not knowing which is the worst time, the waiting. I don't feel that to be true. In the not knowing there is hope and in the waiting there is possibility. This – reality, facts,

confirmation – is worse; all the hope and possibility we've nurtured
and cherished through the last week is gone, smothered by the fact of
death. Numbness is creeping through my body again; curled up on the
sofa my eyes fix on the doorway and over and over I see Jenny walk
through, kick off her shoes and smile. This is not comforting, it's a
longing.

'Julie, my dear,' the voice of our one-time parish priest, now
retired, is thick with emotion. I'm in William's room, standing at the
window overlooking the garden, my mobile phone pressed against
my ear. I am glad of the emotion in his voice. He is asking me about
Jenny, asking if I feel able to talk about all that has been happening.
Talking to him with his gentle easing out of information is proving
therapeutic.

'Would it have been instant?'

'We think so, from her injuries.' I can't bring myself to tell him
what these are though and he changes the subject.

'Have you heard from the bishop?'

'Yes, he's called most days. I couldn't ask for more care and
support. He's put his press officer in touch, to advise us and to deal
with media interest on our behalf.'

'Good, good.'

'Everything feels so difficult. The police family liaison officers are
great. I don't know where we would be without them but there is so
much officialdom between us and Jenny.' I tell him about the recent
conversation over seeing Jenny's body and my need to pursue it. For
a moment he is horrified, 'Do you think that's wise?'

'The police are trying to dissuade me but it is something I must do.
I want to know and see everything.'

'Yes, I can understand that.'

Then he seems unable to speak and his voice is breaking, so much
so all he says is 'Dear Jenny, dear Jenny.'

There's a pause for recovery and then, 'How is Greg?'

'I don't know. He's become very quiet, withdrawn. Shock is affecting us all in different ways.' It's on the tip of my tongue to say *I think this will destroy us* but something prevents me. This is not a time for discussion or analysis of my troubled relationship and marriage. This is about Jenny. Instead I blurt out in one breath, 'I want a requiem mass for her will you take it?'

His voice is full of emotion again and after agreeing to my request, which I haven't yet spoken to anyone else about, he surprises me by bringing up my ministry.

'This is probably not what you want to hear at the moment but one day your ministry will be richer because of this terrible experience.'

It's true I don't want to hear it but I don't mind because I know he really believes in what he is saying.

'What did FJ say?' Vanda asks afterwards.

'He said "Dear Jenny,"' and I start to cry again.

Thursday 14 July

There is to be a national two-minute silence at noon today, followed by a vigil in Trafalgar Square later. Martyn is driving James and me to London so we can meet up with some of Jenny's friends at St Paul's Cathedral. We were a bit late leaving and there's lots of traffic and now a growing anxiety that we may not make it in time. On the outskirts of the city Martyn suggests James and I transfer to a taxi and a driver who will probably know side streets and the quickest possible route. 'I'll catch up with you later,' Martyn calls after us as we get out of his car into a passing taxi which has slowed down for traffic lights.

Once we explain where we want to get to and why, the taxi driver is pulling out all the stops, taking a crazy wriggle route, driving as fast as he safely can, even cutting down a couple of one-way streets. 'Close your eyes,' he tells us. The driver is doing the best he can to get us to St Paul's in time for the two-minute silence but as we approach the area police are already stopping traffic. We can see the dome of St Paul's in the distance. The driver has taken a U-turn, swinging the cab around and pulling up alongside a uniformed policeman, winding the window down and rattling off a quick plea to let us through – which he does – adding, 'Your best bet is to get out and do the rest of the journey on foot as everything is about to come to a standstill.' The taxi driver gets us as close as he can and then advises us to run, refusing to take a fare but asking for a picture of Jenny. As I close the door of the taxi I see him place the picture of Jenny on the dashboard and rest his head in his arms on the steering wheel. Then we run. I tell James to go on so at least one of us has a chance of making it to the cathedral in time.

The great bell of St Paul's begins to toll, marking the start of the two-minute silence. James has disappeared from view and I know I'm not going to make it to the steps in time. Everything has come to a standstill: traffic, people on foot and people who have poured out of offices to stand in huddles. Breathless and just short of the cathedral I stop and lean on a water hydrant, clutching a folder of pictures, snapshots of Jenny in Greece. A girl rushes by seeming oblivious to anything around her until a man halts her, saying, 'Can't you stop for two minutes?' But she speeds on. Maybe like me she's trying to get somewhere. And now the bell has stopped and there's only silence, in the shadow of this immense cathedral yet not quite in sight of its great swathe of steps; where only a few weeks ago I watched Jenny running towards me, her long sun-tanned legs striding out from beneath a blue denim mini-skirt and sky-blue top, clutching her mobile phone to her ear, talking as she ran and waving with her free arm.

Where shall we go for lunch?

We're walking through Paternoster Square, deciding where to eat. Earlier I had travelled up to London by coach with colleagues for an event in St Paul's: the consecration of our new bishop. The coach was held up on the motorway and was late arriving so we had to slip into the back of the cathedral after the service had begun. I couldn't see much of the proceedings and felt a bit detached from it all. I didn't have an order of service so was only able to mumble my way through the hymns. Towards the end of the service, as the new bishops were being presented to the congregation, my phone began to buzz in my pocket — on silent thank goodness — with a text from Jenny saying she was leaving work and would be with me in about twenty minutes.

'Is the service for the Bish over?'

'Nearly,' I texted back. 'See you on the steps.'

There was such a jam getting out of the cathedral, so many people wanting to greet the Archbishop and newly consecrated bishops that I decided to slip out of a side door. The sunshine was momentarily blinding after the darkened interior of the cathedral; the bells were ringing out in celebration and people were standing in groups laughing and chatting, friends and colleagues reunited. I sat on the steps, slightly apart from the main buzz. There was a group of tourists on my left; one of them asked me what was happening. I explained the Archbishop of Canterbury had consecrated two new bishops. This was a mistake, I soon came to realize, as I tied myself and the tourists up in knots trying to explain consecration and the role of bishops in the structure of the Church of England.

'Can we meet him?' one of the tourists asked, referring to the Archbishop.

'You can try,' I replied, 'He's the one with the biggest hat,' which made them laugh. And then I spotted Jenny running and waving and the next minute we were hugging and walking off together towards Paternoster Square.

We decide we're not in a hurry for lunch and that we would just walk and see where we end up. We end up at Smithfields — way off course, so we head for the Barbican Centre and have a late lunch in the terrace bar.

'Inside or out?' the waiter asks.

'Oh, out,' says Jenny, 'let's make the most of the sun'. I sit in the shade and Jenny soaks up the sun. We drink pink fizzy wine and talk about such a lot, her hopes and aspirations, her love for James and their plans for the future. I talk about something she has already guessed at. I hadn't intended to tell her, it just emerges, about Greg and me; that we have spoken about separation. Some of the lightness seems to go out of the day after that. It becomes more sombre, gentle but less innocent, yet very precious as a result. We walk part of the way back to St Paul's hand in hand, as we did when she was four and had ceased to do by the time she was twenty-four. When we say goodbye, Jenny says she can't bear to let me go. We are both tearful and laugh at what we refer to as our mutual silliness.

'Everything will be all right,' I tell her, with a note of sobriety. 'Dad and I will sort things out. Whatever happens between us, you, Lizzie and Thomas are still our children and we are still your parents. She is nodding and looks sad as she waves me off on the coach.

A myriad of images fill the silence and the silence is filled with longing, for beauty gone from the world. Dark eyes intrude, a newspaper image, unwelcome, and I drive it away, fixing my gaze on Jenny and clinging to the water hydrant as if it were her.

And then it's over. The bell tolls to mark the end of the silence as it marked the beginning. I don't move immediately but watch as people move off or turn away and disappear back inside buildings. Traffic begins to move, slowly at first until within moments normal activity along streets and pavements is resumed. Strangely it doesn't matter, I might have expected to want the moment to last but even the bustle and commotion seems to me to have a quality of music about it, reassuring almost and which gives the interval of silence and stillness meaning. People stopped, paused in what they were doing and it felt like a common bond of humanity hung unspoken between us all.

'Fermata: A pause in music indicated by a sign.'

One last look at Jenny captured in a photo standing against a rock in a blue bikini, sarong tied around her waist, eyes squinting against the sun laughing, before tucking the picture safely away in my bag and hurrying to join James. He's surrounded by an unexpectedly large group of Jenny's university friends and work colleagues on the steps of St Paul's. It's a wonderful sight.

Jenny's work colleagues have invited us to a lunchtime concert in the church of St Mary-le-Bow. It feels like a good and gentle thing to do. First, James and I go into the cathedral to light a candle. Spontaneously, I don't know why, I say I would like to see a priest. We're taken by a verger to the vestry door and sit and wait on a narrow bench. A few minutes later the door is opened and an elderly priest steps towards us, smiling. 'How can I help you?'

'I don't know. I'm a priest in Bristol, my daughter has been killed in the bombings; this is her partner, James.'

I'm gabbling and don't really know why I'm here, why I've dragged James through the cathedral to find a priest and now I feel nervous and ridiculous. The priest won't know what to say because there is nothing he can say that will help and I dread words of comfort and reassurance. However, he doesn't utter any words other than, 'What is your daughter's name?' Instead, he has taken our hands and is holding them very firmly in his and that is how we remain for quite some time.

'I'm a very old man now,' the priest is saying as he lets go of our hands. 'But I will pray for Jenny and for you every day for the remainder of my life.'

When we arrived at St Mary-le-Bow someone else took hold of my hand, Jenny's boss, who was very kind and spoke of Jenny warmly, and then told me how his son was the same age as Jenny when he died of cancer a few years ago and that prior to his death he was doing the same work as Jenny in the same office. It was a poignant exchange and I felt less isolated in my grief as we spoke and he shared some personal experiences of his own grief. 'It doesn't go away,' he said simply.

Each piece of music seems picked or chosen just for Jenny … I know that is not the case, yet even so, piece by piece there is a resonance, a connection. Every now and then I take a tissue out, ready to wipe away a tear before it escapes down my face or builds into a torrent while all the time the music is washing over me, holding me. *It doesn't go away* the phrase repeats itself, picking up the rhythm of the music *it doesn't go away* as I fix my eyes on the deep blue of the painted ceiling *it doesn't go away* and in the repetition I know there is a quiet truth communicated, heartfelt from one parent to another *it doesn't go away* and finally I have to close my eyes against the threatening tears, forcing them back, and further back as I've done so many times this week and I think of Jenny, seeing her behind closed lids alive and laughing and singing and I want her here sitting next to me and loving the music and nudging me in the ribs and opening her eyes wide in unspoken communication, delighting in a motet by Orlando Gibbons. Someone from the choir is speaking, introducing an arrangement of Leonard Cohen's 'Hallelujah', 'which we would like to dedicate to the victims of the London bombings.' Scrapping around in my bag for a dry tissue proves fruitless and so I resort to the soggy mess of a ball in my hand. I think I'm going to fall apart, it's all too much to bear, the memory, the pain and the longing. Behind me someone begins gently massaging my shoulders; I don't look around, not yet, in a moment maybe. Now there is only music, beautiful, haunting music … 'a blaze of light in every word, it doesn't matter which you heard, the holy or the broken hallelujah …' and the pathos and tenderness of the moment that needs neither explanation nor defining but is in its own way a perfect expression of things felt. At the end of the concert, it's no surprise to see Charlie sitting behind me, smiling.

Afterwards a group of us sit in Paternoster Square for an hour or so, extravagantly drinking champagne and remembering. Charlie is talking about the day he and Jenny met at university, running across the campus from the music department, both late and sneaking into the back of an English lecture, trying to be quiet but giggling so much they disrupted the lecture and were told off. Tender, talented, fun-loving Charlie has made us laugh; sad, regretful laughter but laughter nevertheless. A group of the friends are going on to the vigil in Trafalgar Square later; James has decided to join them but I think I'll make my way home. Enough is enough. The effects of the day, combined with lack of sleep and a couple of glasses of bubbly is taking its toll and my energy is starting to flag. Besides which I think it will be good for James to spend some time with friends. 'It's OK,' I say when he and Charlie offer to accompany me to the station 'I'll jump in a taxi.'

Famous last words! I'm beginning to despair of ever flagging down a taxi. Rush-hour traffic is whizzing by in every direction – I couldn't have chosen a worse time to make my way home. Black cab after black cab hurtles by and not a yellow 'For Hire' sign to be seen. Every taxi is occupied and any vacant cabs are all travelling in the opposite direction. Perhaps I'll have more luck on the other side of the road so, pushing against the jostling, heaving stream of pedestrians all intent on their own journeys, I walk back up to St Paul's and over to the other side of the road, feeling all the time as if I'm swimming against the tide.

I don't know whether to stop someone and ask for help. I've been here for twenty minutes now and still no taxi for hire. My head is throbbing with concentration, scanning the distance for taxis, rushing towards one pulling around the corner, waving my arm as it comes into view but to no avail as someone has got to it before me by running into the road, dodging the traffic and leaping into the cab while it's still moving. In growing frustration I decide to give up and get the tube and determinedly start walking in the direction of the nearest underground. With each step I become more and more hesitant and finally come to a complete stop, filled with fear at the prospect of getting on to a tube. Even going into the tube station is not something I can contemplate. Stationary and dithering, people bump into me, which causes mutual apologizing, much tutting and an occasional smile.

I resume rushing up and down the pavement, turning my head this way and that, frantically searching for a taxi, panicking more and more as the streets get busier and the whole world seems to be crashing into me. I can't breathe and feel as if I'm going to faint. Shall I go into a shop, tell them I'm having a panic attack? No, they'll think I'm mad. Breathe deeply, slowly, imagine a brown paper bag. Tears are welling up; I want to be home, out of this place. Calm down, I tell myself again, walk back to St Paul's, sit in the cool and quiet and wait for the rush to die down a bit, or walk to somewhere less busy. Suddenly a taxi has pulled up in front of me, dropping off a passenger. It's a silver taxi, maybe that's why I didn't notice it approaching, intent on scanning the road for the more distinctive black.

'Sorry, love, it's not for hire, I'm going off duty.' I've opened the door to climb into the back of the cab and my heart sinks at the driver's words.

'Please, I need to get to Paddington.'

'You must be joking, that's right across town.'

At first the driver seems impervious to my plea, shaking his head dismissively and preparing to move off. 'Please,' I plead with him again as I continue to hold the door open, remaining rooted to the spot with one foot on the pavement and the other inside the cab. For the first time the driver has turned in his seat to look at me properly. His eyes are piercing as they scrutinise my face. I meet his eyes with my own and hold on to the gaze, not flinching. After a slight hesitation during which neither of us moves he rather reluctantly agrees to take me. My 'thank you' is heartfelt and unqualified. I scramble into the cab and slam the door shut (before he has a chance to change his mind), wearily sinking into the seat.

'Are you OK?' the driver asks.

'I am now, thank you.'

'What brings you up to town?'

'The two-minute silence; I wanted to be at St Paul's.'

'Did you know someone in the bombings?'

'My daughter, she was killed at Edgware Road.'

'I'm so sorry.' There's a pause before the driver continues, 'Do you mind me asking, what was your daughter's name?'

'Jenny. She was on her way to work in Shaftesbury Avenue.'

'Terrible.' He's shaking his head again, this time in disbelief. 'Well you just sit back and relax and we'll soon have you at Paddington.'

The driver glances back at me regularly during the journey to the station but does not speak again until pulling up at the taxi drop-off point. 'Are you sure you're ready for this?' he asks, turning around to speak to me and indicating the crowds of commuters filling the concourse.

'Not really but I'll be OK once I'm on the train.' I assure him that there will be someone to meet me at the other end. 'How much do I owe you?' The driver doesn't answer immediately and appears to ignore the money in my hand.

'Where are you heading?'

'Reading.'

'Why don't you stay where you are and I'll drive you there?'

Exhausted, dreading fighting my way through another crowd of people, queuing for a ticket and without any thought to how much the taxi journey to Reading will cost, my response, all I can manage to say, is another but equally heartfelt 'thank you', and then I add, as much as to myself as to the driver, 'So much.'

When I call Vanda from the back of the taxi to explain what is happening, she suggests meeting at a service station to avoid driving into Reading. It all feels much calmer now and once or twice when the driver looks into his mirror, our eyes meet and we exchange a smile. Concern is reflected in his eyes, what he sees in mine I don't know, but I hope he recognises gratitude.

Sharon and Dendy are waiting. The driver is out of the taxi and opening the door for me. We both begin speaking at once:

'Looks like your family are here ahead of you.'

'I can't tell you how grateful I am ... How much do I owe you?'

'You don't owe me anything.'

Despite my protests he will not accept any payment. Instead he has taken my hand in his. 'You must have a very bleak view of the world right now and I want you to know that there are still good people left in it.'

Before I can reply, ask his name, say anything at all, the taxi driver is back in his cab and driving away.

Friday 15 July

I had more sleep last night, exhaustion probably, from the efforts of the day. Before bed I couldn't stop thinking about the taxi driver and his generosity. I talked about him all evening, felt compelled to tell the world about him, his generosity and act of kindness. I wrote the story down and asked a friend to write a press release which can go through the police press office. Then when I woke this morning and was making a cup of tea, it dawned on me, perhaps that's the whole point – the fact that the driver is anonymous, a stranger whose kindness and humanity made a difference. Nevertheless, I'm still going to try and find him.

A newspaper is on the kitchen table, displaying pictures of the four suicide bombers' impenetrable eyes, or maybe it just seems that way to me. I study the picture of Mohammed Sidique Khan more closely than I do the other three. Did Jenny look into those eyes, I wonder, in the instant of her death or seconds before? The mere thought of it is intolerable and I thrust the paper to one side, turning it over so the faces of the bombers are hidden from view.

A squirrel is stealing the birds' food. I've been watching from the kitchen window. First the squirrel frightened away the little birds and now it is systematically dismantling the feeding tube. The squirrel is hanging upside down by its tail from the guttering on the side of the house and is feeding on the nuts and tearing at the metal cage until it manages to pull apart the tube from the base and the remaining peanuts fall to the ground. The squirrel is unconcerned when I tap on the window, stopping only to jerk its cheeky head from side to side before gobbling up the nuts and scurrying away. I am filled with rage, so angry that it makes me cry.

Saturday 16 July

I've been asked if I'd like a priest with me when I go to see Jenny's body, encouraged at least to have some therapeutic support. The police are concerned about the impact her injuries will have on me. I know I will be OK and that this is something I want to do on my own for my daughter, and for myself. In this one thing I feel strong, empowered, as if Jenny were drawing me to her, compelling me to attend to certain things. I know this is born out of my own need and maternal longing but I feel I must see for myself and touch for myself; I must care for her in death. In the simplest mother-and-child ritual, I want to tuck Jenny into bed and prepare her for sleep. I believe with all my heart that this is what Jenny would want from me.

I am going to anoint Jenny's body. In religious terms anointing is a symbol of the indwelling of the Holy Spirit but more importantly for me it is a ritual which transcends words. It reflects the intimacy of mother and child, the intimacy of loving human touch.

I have rejected the challenge of faith over recent days. I know this. I have had no room for what at some point in the future I must encounter. I have barely prayed and yet the image I have carried in my heart is the Pieta. The image of a suffering mother who has had her heart pierced. It is an image of a mother having her child's body restored to her when everyone else is done with it: broken, damaged and with all the life gone from it. It is a compelling image, full of love, suffering and grief. At the moment, I feel it is all that faith has to offer me.

The little phial of oil, loaned by a local priest, is in a large Georgian silver container. There is some mirth amongst my family that this costly item is delivered to the house in a Tesco carrier bag.

When we arrive at the undertaker's in Reading Pauline is waiting. Apparently we're early and they're not quite ready for us. We're shown into a small reception room, James and his parents, Vanda and

Sharon and me. There's a little park opposite the undertaker's building and I spend a little bit of time in there before going in to see Jenny. I've been with dead bodies before and anointed people who are close to death. This is different. Pauline has come across to fetch me and to explain one or two things. Vanda and Sharon are waiting in the hallway; both have offered to come in with me but they understand when I say this is something I want to do on my own. Pauline isn't giving me a choice and leads the way down a dimly lit corridor.

Nothing has prepared me for entering the room and seeing the coffin. No imagining or past experience. It is stark and shocking and real. For a while all I can do is stand and stare, too full of fear to move forward.

Pauline has taken my hand and guided me over to where I am now standing looking down at my daughter's body shrouded mostly in muslin. 'You can hold her hand,' Pauline is saying gently. My hand is warm and shaking and Jenny's is cold and still. It isn't enough. I want to lift her body out, hold her in my arms and breathe life into her. I make do with leaning over and kissing every finger, examining them as I did when she was born. Her nails are flush with the end of her fingers. 'She kept her nails short, because of playing the piano.' I realize I've spoken in the past tense.

I've balanced the small phial of oil on the corner of the coffin and handed the larger silver container, along with the carrier bag, to Pauline, saying, 'Don't drop the silver, it's probably worth thousands!'

I can only anoint Jenny's hand and place my hand under hers, resting my gaze for a moment at both our hands resting together on the cover. Then I dip the middle finger of my other hand into the oil and prepare to anoint her with the sign of the cross. 'I can't remember the words!' I cry out in panic.

Pauline is standing back in the corner of the room. 'I'm sure whatever you say will be perfect.'

Second Movement

And so I proceed with anointing my daughter's body. 'In your beginning I anointed you with water, blood and milk, blessed you with tears … and now I anoint you with oil in the name of this mystery we call God …' The words continue, not liturgically correct but from the very depths of my being and tears flow and merge with the oil on Jenny's lifeless lovely hand until there are no more words, only tears and sobs, from a mother standing over her daughter's coffin and a police officer in the far corner of the room.

I believe it was for this moment that I was ordained a priest.

'It's Jenny,' I confirm to the others. 'I could tell by her hands.'

When we arrive home I know I must phone Greg and Lizzie and Thomas and my parents but I think I must be a little bit in shock, I'm finding it difficult to talk and can't stop shaking. Vanda is steering me into the sitting room. 'Sharon and I can phone the family and you can speak later. Why don't you have some time on your own? I'll make some drinks and bring one in for you.'

A few minutes later she is back with a gin and tonic and places it on a small table next to the sofa. 'Would you like some music on, one of Jenny's CDs?'

It's very quiet; the trees outside give a natural shade to the room and a gentle breeze is moving the curtains. Ignoring the gin and tonic, I curl up on the sofa in a foetus position with Jenny's T-shirts rolled up in a tight little bundle. I feel so full of Jenny and so empty of anything else.

The music is heart-wrenching and soothing all at the same time, a Benjamin Britten arrangement of folksongs:

Down by the salley gardens my love and I did meet
She passed the salley gardens with little snow-white feet …

Jenny and I are lying curled up together on the sofa, having an
afternoon nap; she's two and a half.
　'Am I squashing the baby in your tummy, Mummy?'
　'No, the baby's very cosy and warm.'
　'Shall I sing a song for you and the baby?'
　'That would be lovely.'
　She made up a song and we drifted off to sleep together.

She bid me take life easy …
But I was young and foolish, and now am full of tears.

WAKING

The gin has been removed and a mug of tea is in its place. The CD has stopped playing. I can smell the scent of freesias. I'm awake, but I feel asleep. My eyes seem separate from my body; my seeing self is roving around the room, drifting over furniture while my body remains moulded into the sofa, unfeeling and immobile.

A large brick fireplace extends along the opposite wall, red brick after coarse red brick. I see it now as I might look on an icon. What last week was a large rustic feature fireplace has now become a shrine. A family hearth with large green plants in pots and a few candles in holders has become a different stage, crammed with flowers and pictures of Jenny. Massive yellow and orange sunflowers with heads the size of small plates are propped against the rough backdrop and stand out against the mass of summer flowers of all kinds and colour in vases and improvised vases. Jenny in a white T-shirt, Jenny with a glass of wine, Jenny, Jenny and more Jenny in the pictures, in the flowers and in the candles and still the verdant green and trailing leaves of pot plants dressing the set at either end. More candles and cards on the mantelshelf, 'thinking of you' cards. I see them now, from a short distance. Not sympathy cards — those are in the kitchen, a growing pile of expressed loss and grief. In here are cards and messages which have been our companions during the days of waiting. These belong in the room, on the hearth; the others have no place here, not yet. These still speak of hope. But even as my eyes remain fixed my mind is contemplating the shift between what is hoped for and what is. Very soon there will be no place for the card displaying a field of sunflowers with one standing out tall above all the rest, inside expressing the hope and belief that Jenny will soon be restored to us, safe and unharmed.

There's a cobweb or two in the corner of the fireplace long since abandoned by their maker. Little fronds trail and move with the warm air. My eyes linger with the cobwebs for a while before moving on around the room. If my mother and aunt were here the cobwebs would be gone, dusted away. In any other circumstances there would be amusement, laughter, teasing. Now the cobwebs are just something else to observe, note and pass by.

Dried candle wax has dropped on to the carpet and formed a hard crust. A few stray petals lie fallen and scattered on the red bricks. There's a line of dust between the carpet and the edge of the fireplace where the vacuum cleaner hasn't reached, an even line running the length of the fireplace, dulling the green carpet with grey.

This has been a room in waiting, an inherited carpet and colour scheme waiting to be decorated. Despite my sister's frustrations it is a place for children to fall laughing into squidgy sofas. A waiting room for a waiting family! Everything about the room is warm and comforting, and throughout the week it has provided a sanctuary, a safe haven in the centre of the house, with only a sprawling beautiful garden to look out on. There is no ugliness in this room. Feeling the warmth and knowing the view is behind me – I need only turn to look – the sofa is like a sanctuary within a sanctuary from which my body still cannot or will not move.

My eyes roam clockwise, the only way I can see the room without moving my head. The television is switched off. A child's rocking chair is pulled close to the screen, abandoned at an angle as though someone had been summonsed away or grown tired of a programme and vacated the seat in a hurry to run outside with a ball. There's an empty red plastic plate and beaker on the floor next to the chair – evidence of William stopping for a snack and rushing on with life.

Up two steps on to a split level where a tall cabinet is stacked with CDs and a sound system and a picture of Vanda and Stefan on their wedding day, smiling out from the deck of the SS *Great Britain*. Vanda in cream lace, a band of gold and white flowers in her hair and Stefan in morning dress, arms around each other and toasting the camera with flutes of bubbly. There are baby and toddler pictures of Ellie and William. Another trailing green plant draws my eyes away from the cabinet and on to the glass-panelled door closed against the kitchen. I can't hear voices so guess Vanda and Sharon must be elsewhere in the house.

There's another larger cabinet on the back wall full of crystal behind leaded glass doors, which are mostly obscured by yet more abundance of greenery. House plants thrive in this room. I've never noticed before. The dining table and chairs usually dominate this raised level of the room. Now the table is against the side wall with chairs pushed underneath and to the side, moved at the weekend to make space for an airbed. The table is piled with newspapers of recent days on one side and children's colouring paper and pens and craft stuff on the other side. I don't linger at the table except to fleetingly consider that the paper on one side of the table reflects destruction and devastation and the paper on the other side reflects creativity and play.

Back down two steps. Long windows fill almost the entire length of the room opposite the fireplace and behind the sofa where I'm lying. The curtains are pulled back carelessly, bunched up behind the sofa, heavy drapes with panels of cream, green and beige with birds on them and some worn and torn patches in the cream lining. My sister hates these curtains, 'I can't wait to change them,' she said yesterday.

The door to the kitchen opens, drawing my eyes away from the curtains in a blink.

Vanda is standing next to me picking up the untouched mug of tea. 'Your tea has gone cold; I'll get you another one.'

'What happened to my gin?'

'We came in and said we didn't think it was such a good idea for you to drink alcohol in case you were in shock so Sharon made tea instead.'

I don't remember any of this.

'I remember Jenny wearing that when she was here the weekend before last.'

I realize Vanda is referring to a lilac T-shirt, the outer layer of the bundle of other T-shirts I've been cradling in my arms, holding it like a baby between my face and neck. 'It still smells of her.'

I offer the bundle to Vanda and she breathes in the scent deeply as I did before her. Then we both weep for a while and after that I am properly awake.

CHAPTER 5

Third Movement

We all need each other and each one of us makes a difference

I had intended to wash my face and hands and change my top, but Vanda is directing me into the bath in much the same way she directed me on to the sofa earlier, closeting me away from the business of the house and giving me space. After our weep over Jenny's bundle of T-shirts she suggested I might like a soak in the tub with a gin and tonic. I declined the gin but welcomed the bath. 'There's plenty of bubble stuff. Just give the hot water twenty minutes,' she says, opening the airing cupboard and feeling the hot water tank. 'I'm popping out to pick up the children.'

Sharon has made a fresh cup of tea and the two of us discuss the visit to the undertaker. 'I don't think Jenny's funeral will be for a couple of weeks. We have to take her home to Bristol first and I'm not going to rush things. I can't get my head around her death yet, let alone a funeral … and there's the matter of … well, you know, the other things we need more information about … items she would want to be buried with that haven't been identified yet.' There's a pause while neither of us speaks and drink tea.

I break the silence. 'How long did you wait before Matthew's funeral?'

'About a week. The undertakers dealt with everything.'

Conversation drifts backwards and forwards between Jenny and Sharon's baby son Matthew.

How easily we sit here, sipping our tea and talking about the death of our children. At the mention of Matthew's name a multitude of stored memories are opened up and refreshed. Sharon's eyes are a testament to the fact that grief can bubble to the surface at the mere whisper of a name and that a span of sixteen years is no guard against sorrow. Recalling Matthew's quirky little ways is almost to reach out and touch him. Remembering how he would hook his finger under the feeding tube attached to the side of his face and pull it from his nose, which sometimes seemed like an act of defiance, causes us both to smile. 'Do you remember how he would bounce his leg up and down when he was happy?' Silly question, of course she remembers; he was her son.

'It was his left leg,' Sharon adds without having to think about it. 'He liked being in his bouncy chair and would bang his leg against the fabric to make the chair spring up and down even more.' Maybe that was his way of laughing. I remember the mass of toys adorning his room, more than our other babies, and bright primary colours strung across his pram. His cot was so full of toys that you hardly noticed the large oxygen cylinder on the stand behind the cot or the booty of medicines and drugs. The night Matthew's frail heart finally stopped beating is etched on my memory, even though I wasn't there. Mike was doing Matthew's late feed as he always did. Sharon would do the early morning feed so had just gone to bed. Shortly after getting into bed she was woken by Mike calling out to her that there was something wrong and that they were losing Matthew. Sharon jumped out of bed as Mike came into their bedroom holding Matthew in his arms and, as the three of them stood together, Matthew drew his last breath.

We talk about some of our memories of Matthew, but not all. Sharon doesn't talk about the night that Matthew was born and the days and weeks that followed the diagnosis of Down's Syndrome and severe heart abnormalities. Nor does she talk about the choices and decisions that came with a prognosis. I suppose there is a time to speak of some things and not of others.

'I can remember the day of Matthew's funeral,' I say to Sharon. 'Mike had asked the family not to wear black. We were at the house waiting for the funeral cars to arrive. Arrangements and simple bunches of flowers were spread on the ground, outside the kitchen door. There were lots of flowers, but mostly I remember blue irises. All the family was downstairs and someone asked where you and Mike were. I went upstairs to check and saw you both standing together on the landing, your arms around each other looking out from the window on to the street below. You both looked so sad as you waited. I didn't disturb you and thought how close you were and that you didn't need anyone else in that moment, just each other.'

'I don't remember that.' Sharon is wiping her eyes.

'All the children from Katie and Joanne's school lined the path to the church.'

'The whole school came. It was next door to the church.'

'Mike carried Matthew's coffin. He carried it so tenderly in his arms from the car, along the path and into church while you walked by their side. I'll never forget it. The coffin was covered in blue gingham and it was so tiny.'

Matthew was loved and I hope he felt it. Jenny was and I hope with all my heart that she knew and felt it too.

I've found some Crabtree and Evelyn lavender bath gel in Vanda's stock and squirt a generous helping into the water gushing from the taps. I sit on the side of the bath watching the bubbles form until it is satisfyingly deep and foamy. My towel isn't very big so I decide to fetch a larger one from the airing cupboard, one that I can wrap around me. 'I forgot my bath towel,' I say to Sharon, going back into the kitchen and opening the airing cupboard door.

'I suppose I ought to think about going home.' There is reluctance in Sharon's voice. She's standing at the sink, looking out beyond the kitchen window, deep in thought, washing some dishes. Every adult in the household has had periods standing at the sink in this way, alone and musing into the distance. Our thoughts are our thoughts and I suppose we only share a fragment of them.

'It'll seem strange without you here. I wish you could stay.' I know it's selfish of me to say it but it's true.

'I don't want to leave either but I have to go back and sort things out, work and Megan's school.'

'You can't put your life on hold indefinitely. Megan must be missing you.'

'Yes, she is.'

I knew this moment would come but it doesn't make it any easier, another separation.

'We need to decide what to do about the holiday …' Sharon and Mike are due to go on holiday with Martyn and Caroline the week after next, to France and Italy. '… I don't feel like going.'

I can understand her predicament. Any thought of holidaying would be the last thing on my mind at the present time.

'If the funeral isn't going to be for a few weeks it might be better if I go home now and come back later if you need me.'

We continue to talk about funeral considerations and holiday logistics while Sharon dries the dishes. It isn't until she has finished wiping down the sink and is hanging the tea towel to dry over the cooker handle that she picks up the earlier conversation about leaving.

'Vanda and Stefan will need to start getting the house back to normal.' She adds: 'Well, you know what I mean, for the children's sake.' And of course I do know what Sharon means, despite normal being a relative state.

The visit to the undertaker's has brought us to a new stage. It is a transition, I suppose; we're emerging from a waiting period to a point of arrival. Even after the pronouncement of death we were still in waiting, waiting for Jenny's body to be restored to us. While we waited, everything was put on hold. Now we all, in our different ways, must think about what comes next. What has to be done? Where do our responsibilities now lie? It is not easy. James has gone home with his parents for the remainder of the weekend and now Sharon is making plans to go back to her life in Manchester. We have been cloistered together for more than a week. People have come and gone while Vanda and Sharon and I have remained constant companions. I ponder these thoughts while soaking up to my neck in bubbles and now wishing I had a gin and tonic to hand.

I place my hands over my stomach, wishing it was a bit flatter. As I rub the sponge over the now less than firm mound I can't help thinking about babies and bathtimes and laughter. I liked soaking in the bath when I was pregnant, stroking my hands across the firm baby bump and watching it grow as the baby developed. 'Immensity cloistered in thy dear womb …'

Jenny loved being in the bath with me when she was a toddler and would chat incessantly about her unborn baby sister. She would sit opposite me trying to make her tummy protrude like mine. 'It's my baby Sophie,' she would say. Why Sophie, we never could work out, nor why she was so convinced it was a baby girl. As it happens, she was right. When Lizzie was born, we gave Jenny a baby doll which she promptly named baby Sophie! Hardly without realizing what I'm doing, I'm frothing my hands with soap and forming a circle with forefinger and thumb to blow soap bubbles into the air. Froth, bubble … froth, bubble. Greg would spend hours on his knees by the side of the bath, making bubbles for the children. When I made bubbles there was always disappointment. 'You can't do it very well, can you, Mummy? Daddy's bubbles are best.' I would get fed up but Greg was much more patient and enjoyed the bubble-making sessions.

When the girls were in their older teens they used to laugh and tease me, about times they were in the bath and I would come in, pull the lid of the toilet seat down and sit on it. 'Whenever you did that, we knew you wanted to talk to us about boys and sex or drugs or periods and stuff.' Then they would tease Thomas and warn him to beware of Mum sitting down in the bathroom. 'It means she's going to talk to you about the birds and the bees!'

I'm tired of thinking and lie back in the bath, studying the dolphins on the shower curtain, nothing more than that. No thinking, no more remembering, just watching the dolphins, bright blue dancing shapes on plastic folds.

I've freshened up and remade my case, sorting clothes which need washing and generally creating a bit of order. Out of necessity we've all had to live out of bags over recent days. None of us 'visitors' has had more than the minimum amount of clothes so it's been relatively uncluttered. My case started off in Vanda and Stefan's room and has progressed to William's room through the week. 'Why don't you move into William's room?' Vanda suggested earlier. 'He's quite happy sharing with Ellie and you can have your own space.' Now the household has thinned out a bit there's more bed space and less reason to use blow-up beds and floor space. The need to be in close proximity to the phone has been negated with confirmation of Jenny's death so there doesn't seem to be any good reason to continue sleeping on the sofa, at least during the night hours.

The bundle of Jenny's clothes has been lying on the spare bed while I've been tidying my case. I make a space for the bundle and after holding it close for a moment and kissing it, I place it in the case and tuck a few items of my own clothes around it. I attend to this as lovingly and carefully as if it were a baby being settled down in a crib for a sleep. I even talk to the bundle: 'How mad is your mother becoming, Jenny?' There is no answer, of course. Though I think her reply might be to say it was OK and to be as mad as I liked. After nestling the bundle into the case I zip the lid closed but then change my mind and open it up again. Closed, the case is too much like a coffin. These are strange thoughts and fancies and I am very glad of William's appearance in the doorway.

'Auntie Julie?' There is a question in his voice.

'Yes, Wills?'

'How big was the bomb?'

'I don't know. It's a good question.'

'It must have been quite big to kill Jenny and the other people.'

'I expect we can find out from the police.'

'Do you think the bomb was this big?' William is forming his hands to the size and shape of a football.

'Maybe.'

'Or was it this big?' He is now stretching his arms around and in front of him as though he was holding a large beach ball.

'Probably not that big because the bomber carried it in his backpack.'

'What was the bomb made of?'

'Chemicals mostly, I think. Daddy and James might be better to ask about that.'

'I expect the police might know.'

'I'm sure they will.'

'Can you ask them?'

'Yes, I will.'

'When?'

'Next time we see Colin, probably Monday, I'll ask if he can find out.'

'Mummy said would you like a drink?'

'Tell her yes, please. I'll be there in a minute.'

As soon as William has gone, I write down all his questions in my notebook. These are the questions I need to be asking the police, with the simplicity and directness of a six-year-old boy.

Vanda and Sharon are preparing supper; a gin and tonic in large bulbous glasses stands within easy reach of both. Another has been freshly poured for me, crammed with ice and a thick chunk of lemon. Tonic bubbles are still sparkling on the inside of the glass. It looks inviting and refreshing. 'I'm ready for this,' I say gratefully. There is nothing quite like a long cold gin and tonic at the end of a hot day. This is the first one I have really appreciated all week. 'Can I do anything to help?'

'You can make a salad if you like.'

Vanda has passed me a chopping board and is pulling salad ingredients from the fridge and I'm relaying William's questions.

'Oh no, do you mind?'

'No. I'm quite glad of the questions. William is only asking questions of me that I want to ask the police.'

'You should write them down.' Sharon is measuring out rice.

Stefan has come into the kitchen for a refill. 'William has been asking what the bomb is made from.'

Vanda, Sharon and I all laugh and he looks at us, a bit nonplussed.

'That's my fault. He asked me and I'm afraid I chickened out and told him to ask you or James. You're the scientists, after all.'

'I suppose so. Anyone for a top-up?'

Stefan is presented with three empty glasses.

'I thought you'd never ask,' Sharon teases him.

Ellie has come into the kitchen, probably in response to our laughter. She settles herself next to me, leaning her head on my shoulder and preparing to absorb whatever conversation is going on around her. 'Can I have some of your drink, please?' she says sitting up. I give her a sip of my gin and tonic. 'Can I have the lemon?'

It feels odd to be in a bed again, after nights on the sofa. We had a late-night session after dinner and probably drank too much wine. Whatever the reason for my current state of insomnia, the fact is my mind feels very busy and I'm wide awake. Being in a bedroom on my own at least means I can switch on a light without worrying about disturbing other people. Vanda has put a couple of magazines on my bed, so I pick one up to browse through. Endless pages of celebrities showing off new country homes, displaying babies in designer clothes and indulging in lavish weddings do nothing to improve my mood or help me sleep, in fact quite the reverse; they unsettle me and now I feel cross. After huffing and puffing my way through a few more pages of people beaming out from charity lunches and award ceremonies I finally toss the magazine aside and get out of bed to find my book. But I can't settle to reading that either. The book has been lodged in the lid of my case since I arrived last week. The corner of a page is turned down, marking the place I stopped reading and which, as it happens, was the morning of 7 July. I doubt I'll ever go back to the book to finish it and toss that aside as well.

Third Movement

Futile attempts to get to sleep have ended in frustration and I'm writing instead. Not writing exactly, more jotting down words and thoughts – whatever is on my mind finds itself on the page …

Motionless, violated, broken
Your body
My heart
A perfect coupling
Sorrowing.

You lived in beauty
glorious
you died in darkness / darkly
lonely / alone
tunnel
not of love.

You died not in my arms
or his held
by love
but in a tunnel
darkly
blasted by hate.

My child,
My beloved child
killed
murdered
slaughtered.

A Song For Jenny

I must try not to hate
I must
Try
I must
For Lizzie and Thomas's sake.

Cloistered – cloistered together – shut up – sheltered
Immensity cloistered in thy dear womb – John Donne
Cloistered in a family womb
Sheltered – by family.

The notebook and pencil is open on my lap. I've been staring at the page for a long time, maybe ten minutes.

'We all need each other and each one of us makes a difference.'

I don't know why I wrote the line, it just flowed from my head to the page like the rest of the words. As soon as I wrote the line I had a flashback – I suppose that's what it's called – to when Jenny was home studying for her master's degree at Bristol University.

I'd come home from work to find Jenny browsing through bookshelves in my bedroom looking for something to read. She pulled out *The Seeing Stone*, the first book of a trilogy written for children and based on the young Arthur of Arthurian legend by Kevin Crossley-Holland. I'd been given a set by the author while I was working on a community theatre project a couple of years previously. 'I'll give this one a go,' she said. Over the next few weeks Jenny read her way through all three books and would frequently read a passage out.

I'm lying in bed, reading with the bedside light on. Greg is down-stairs watching television. The sound is carrying upstairs. I'm just thinking I might go down and ask him to turn it down when Jenny bursts into my bedroom. She is dressed in red tartan pyjamas and a pair of James's football socks. Her hair is flying all over the place, long blond out-of-control wispy curls down after her bath. She is waving a book at me. Her voice is excited, as if she'd made a sudden discovery. She's jabbing her finger against the cover of the book proclaiming, 'This book is wasted on children. Listen to this ... "I want everyone to know we all need each other and each one of us makes a difference." Wow! That is so true. Would you like a cup of tea, I'm going to make one?'

'Yes please, and can you ask Dad to turn the TV down?'

Jenny has left the book open on my bed. 'King of The Middle March', 'Astonishingly brilliant' is quoted on the front cover. I think Jenny and I would both agree with that. The line she read out comes at the end of the book. While she's downstairs I pick out the line and re-read it. It is a simple phrase of profound philosophy; words of truth and hope. Jenny comes back bearing two cups, placing one on my bedside table.

'Dad's taken Misty around the block so I've turned the TV off.'

'Thanks.'

While we drink our tea she sits on the end of my bed talking about her dissertation, which she has been working on.

'I've got a title, "The Eden Myth Revisited: Nature, Supernatural Power and Female Power in Twentieth-Century British Opera".'

'Impressive.'

'Now all I have to do is write it. I want to begin with Eve the temptress and discuss whether she is the tempter and cause of man's fall or liberator of female awareness.'

'Who else are you going to use?'

'The governess in Turn of the Screw and Morgan in Gawain.'

Ten minutes later, she is gathering up the mugs and putting them on the bookcase.

> *'Thanks for letting me ramble on about my dissertation. I'm*
> *really excited about it.'*
> *'I know you are and it's a pleasure.'*
> *'I'm going back to bed to finish Arthur now, nite nite.' Leaning*
> *over to retrieve the book she plants a kiss on my cheek then patters*
> *back to her own room, leaving me smiling at the empty space.*

Well, now I'm looking at another empty space but I'm not smiling.

'We all need each other and each one of us makes a difference.'

As I contemplate the line on the page, it's like an epiphany, a sudden realization of what has been going on in the household over the last nine days. The house and the people in it have provided a place of safety, care and protection. While I was talking to a friend a few days ago I said I didn't understand why I couldn't bear the thought of going home; why I needed to be here. The friend, who had been widowed, said he thought that when we're hurt we need to retreat to a place of safety. I'm certain he was speaking from experience. Since the moment Jenny was missing I have needed my sister and my cousins and they have been with me all the way. These three people from my childhood represent a time of safety and security. I know that now. I also know that I have not only retreated to a place of safety, but I have retreated to a people of safety.

We all need each other and each one of us makes a difference.

The difference people have made to me this week, and not only me, is extraordinary. Even through the bleakness and horror – or maybe in spite of it – there has been the best of humanity. Encounters with taxi drivers, and strangers in churches and on trains, is a testament to this. We all need each other. We need each other's understanding and compassion and care. All these acts of kindness equate with love and benevolence. It is what makes us human, I suppose. The safety I have felt by being here with my family, feeling sheltered, protected, knowing that my children are being cared for, is all part of needing and being needed.

I can't stop writing, scribbling wildly to get words on the page before they disappear from my mind. I must not forget one phone call, one platter of food left on the doorstep, one offer of a lift, one act of generosity or one empathetic tear. I must not forget the people who, when they could do nothing else, have offered their prayers. If I forget these things I may forget my own humanity. The page is a messy montage of ideas and crossings out and repetitions, intelligible to no one but the writer. And then I'm done. I must find the name of the taxi driver. This is my last thought before closing the book and getting up to make a cup of tea.

On the kitchen table is a newspaper. For the first time I look properly and deeply at the picture of the suicide bomber responsible for the death of my daughter ... *and the difference you have made, Mohammed Sidique Khan, is not for good. It is dark and wicked and wrong and I am full of loathing for what you have done* ... His name repeats itself over and over as I make my way back down the hallway to the bedroom carrying a cup of tea. I feel no compassion for him.

Sharon is going home today, Sunday 17 July, ten days after the bombings and nine days spent here together. Her impending departure is a wrench. She has been such a significant part of this week and shared so much that it is hard to see her go.

The weekend is marked by arrivals and departures. With James gone and Martyn and Caroline also gone we are quite a depleted household compared to last weekend's mass of family and friends. Lizzie and Thomas are back from Anglesey with Joanne and Katie plus boyfriends. They travelled in two cars and arrived with a flourish, as if they were returning from holiday. As soon as they came into the house their mood changed. It was as if the weight of grief, the reality of Jenny's death had been temporarily held in abeyance and was again closing in around them. Away from the house, they could laugh and play and recapture a time and a place in which Jenny was alive. Anglesey gave them that. Now they are back, Thomas is becoming more withdrawn and Lizzie more agitated. I encouraged them to go and then to stay away. Perhaps we have all colluded to keep Lizzie and Thomas at a distance as a form of protection. Even in this house they have been remote from me, from my narrative. They have been outside when I have been inside, at play with cousins when I have been occupied with callers. And some of the time, worst of all, I have retreated into a silent and invisible world where they have not been able to locate me.

Soon they will be 'en route' again, either home to Bristol or onwards to Dorset. The fragmentation is not easing. Lizzie is due to start work on a play for the Edinburgh Fringe Festival next month and is agonizing over whether to continue or pull out. She's torn between wanting to be home with everyone and having the distraction of something life-giving and fun. After speaking to the play's director she has decided to throw herself into rehearsals and see how it pans out. Thomas is going to spend some time with his cousin Andrew but wants to collect a few things from Bristol first. Vanda said she will drive them back, collect post from the vicarage and call in to see Mum and Dad.

This process has become our daily morning ritual, talking through what everyone is doing, establishing who needs to be where and organizing lifts, travel and shopping lists.

Thomas is watching television when I take a cup of coffee in to him. I've hardly spent any time with him throughout this whole period. When he has been here there has been such a lot going on and he has stayed in the background. When he was in Bristol it was mostly Lizzie or Greg I spoke to on the phone and the rest of the time he has been in Anglesey or Manchester with his cousins. I have not given him much time.

'How are you doing Thomas?'

His response is to shrug his shoulders in a hopeless gesture.

'I miss Jenny.' His face is crumbling.

'You can always talk to me.'

'I know. Auntie Vanda said I can talk to her as well.'

'As long as you know you don't have to bottle things up.'

'I don't get it. I don't get why the bombers did it.'

'What do you mean?'

'Why they wanted to kill people in their own country. Why couldn't they go somewhere else to do it? Jenny was so good. Why did they have to kill her? I hate them for what they did.'

I don't understand it myself so how can I help Thomas? I don't want him to hate yet I can't deny him what he feels towards the people who killed his sister.

'Whatever you feel is all right Thomas, as long as you keep talking about it. Don't bottle it up. Will you promise me?'

'Yes. I promise.'

He smiles. 'Mum?'

'Yes?'

'How are you?'

'About the same as you.'

'You can always talk to me you know.'

'I know.'

Then he grins at me and I think that somewhere in all this mess we are OK. There is a calmness between us; an understanding.

Lizzie has been looking at some of the newspaper reports and has become very upset over a particular set of pictures of the four bombers. 'How dare they put a picture of these murdering bastards next to a picture of my sister?' She has picked up a pen and is scribbling over the page, wielding the instrument with ferocity until the four faces are covered in blue ink and the paper torn. Then she flings the pen down. This is happening in the midst of coffee being made and handed round and various other conversational exchanges, all of which is interrupted for a beat and resumed. There is concern for Lizzie's upset, though not for the act itself, which has proved to be something of a welcome release and is probably the first 'household' expression of rage directed towards the bombers all week.

'We all need each other and each one of us makes a difference.'

I'm standing in a small boat watching the shore. People are fading further and further away from me. I don't know if I'm on the boat and everyone else is on the shore or if I'm on the shore and everyone else is in the boat, moving away. Perhaps there's a part of me in both places. What I feel most strongly is an increasing remoteness from people, except the people who have been here in this house. It's as if I'm the one who has died, not Jenny. Jenny feels so alive, so present and so real. I feel detached.

I'm not really standing in a boat or on the shore. I'm standing in the drive next to Stefan as we watch Vanda drive off with Lizzie and Thomas to Bristol. Vanda's is the last car to depart. 'Will you be OK if I get on with some work?' Stefan asks as we turn to go back inside the house.

'Yes. I'm going to make some coffee then sort a few things out.'

While I'm making coffee the post van arrives. Stefan has gone out to collect the bundle of post. He spends a couple of minutes talking to the postman before coming back into the kitchen and sorting through the post. 'I'll leave these for the boss to open,' he says, putting a pile of cards on the table. 'The boss' refers to Vanda. 'You know where everything is. Shout if you need me. I'll be in the garage.'

He's taken the mug of coffee I handed him and gone out through the connecting door between the kitchen and utility room. In a few minutes, Stefan will be working alongside his father, sawing wood, making bird feeders and listening to Radio 4.

It's an odd feeling, being alone. Liberating, to some extent, but a bit lost as well.

After tidying the kitchen, I call and have a chat with my mum.

She's telling me about friends and people who have visited and how relieved she'll be to see Lizzie and Thomas later.

As I talk to my mum on the phone, Stefan's dad is walking across the drive. He raises his arm in greeting as he passes the kitchen window. He keeps walking and is shaking his head, mouthing, 'Terrible, terrible,' the same two words he repeats every time he catches sight of me.

Mum is asking when Greg will be coming back from Manchester.

I tell her tomorrow or the day after.

Then she asks whether Greg will be coming back to Hampshire or going straight home to Bristol.

'Bristol.'

Then the inevitable question. 'When do you think you'll come home?'

'I don't know. I'll stay here until Jenny's body is taken back to Bristol. I'm not going home without her.'

'When do you think that will be?'

'It depends on James. We'll probably decide tomorrow. I'll stay for Vanda's birthday on Wednesday at least.'

The conversation changes direction to the subject of Vanda's birthday and the awkward business of cards and presents. Mum is debating what kind of card to send and what to write in it. 'I still want to wish her a happy birthday, even though I know it won't be.'

'Sharon said the same thing. She left a card with me to give to her.'

'What will you do?' Mum asks.

'I don't know. I thought about buying her a rose tree, from Jenny, sort of.'

'They can't grow roses there. The deer eat the flower heads.'

'Oh yes. I'd forgotten.'

'What are you going to do today?'

'While it's quiet I might start thinking about the funeral.'

'People are asking me when it will be. What shall I tell them?'

'Tell them we haven't decided yet.'

After putting the phone down I wander along the hallway to collect my notebook from the bedside table in my bedroom. I told Mum I might sit in the garden and gather some thoughts about the funeral so that's what I'll do. My case is open and the card left by Sharon for Vanda's birthday is lying on top of a muddle of clothes and toiletries. The handwriting is neat and recognizably Sharon's. I can't help smiling to myself as I consider the writing. It's an echo of Sharon and seems to reflect the transition I felt earlier. *I was here. I may no longer be here but something of me remains ...*

The notebook is resting on my lap with nothing to show for the hour or so I've spent trying to focus my thoughts on a funeral. It just won't work. I'm not ready to plan a funeral. I will never be ready to plan my daughter's funeral. I think about anointing her body, about whether her hair was loose or tied back when she left for work on 7 July. I think about where she is now and if there really is a heaven. I do not think about her funeral.

Third Movement

I'm walking around the back of the house thinking about Vanda's birthday and wondering what to give her. It's a pity about the rose tree and the issue of the deer. Apparently they get in from the adjoining woodland and eat the flowers. There are masses of large rhododendron shrubs so the deer must not like eating those, or maybe the shrubs are too tall for the deer to reach.

There is no sign now, outside this house freshly emptied of people, of the trauma and enormity of the past ten days. The only evidence is inside the house and inside my head. Out here, it might be any other summer Sunday. White plastic chairs are strewn around the garden where yesterday people moved them into the sun or out of the sun. Automatically I pick them up and replace them around the table on the patio. The table is a bit messy with red wine stains. I fetch a cloth and cleaning fluid from the kitchen, rubbing at the table and cleaning it as best I can. Even so, pink rings remain. Various toys are scattered around the garden, played with and abandoned. There's a child's red and yellow plastic car, which once belonged to Thomas, a red wheelbarrow, a red plastic table with play cups and saucers, and copious bats and balls. A large combination climbing frame and slide stands at the bottom end of the play area. The end of the slide is inside the paddling pool so the children can come down the slide and splash into the pool. I've pushed the larger toys to one side and am now collecting up the smaller items to replace in the conservatory, which doubles as a play room.

The day is getting hot. Vanda put towels out to dry before she left. Already they're bone dry. 'Don't do anything, just relax,' were Vanda's instructions before she went, which is all well and good except now I need to be occupied. Each towel is taken down, folded and placed in the laundry basket, which has been left on a patch of grass next to the rotary line. As I move around the line removing towels, I catch my leg on a side of the laundry basket and immediately feel the sting of heat against my flesh. The plastic is very hot and is burning my hands as I carry the laundry inside. In the utility room the washing machine is whirring frantically, heralding another load of laundry ready for the washing line. By the time the towels are stored away in the airing cupboard the machine has rattled and juddered to a stop. The locking mechanism prevents the machine door opening straight away so I fetch a pair of sunglasses and drink a glass of water before pulling the bedding out and hanging it on the line to dry.

I can't resist sitting by the side of the paddling pool cooling my feet in the water. The heat is causing my ankles to swell and the water is a refreshing relief. There are a few dead flies or mosquitoes on the surface of the water but they're easily flicked out by a toy spade. The only sounds are birds, buzzing insects and the distant industry of Stefan and his dad working in the garage. I have my eyes closed. Despite sunglasses the glare of the afternoon sun is intense. It is also sleep-inducing. There are no interruptions or disturbances and if it were any other circumstance, I might be thinking: Peace, perfect peace. Before long I'm drifting on the edge of consciousness with only the discomfort of the chair and the drone of a nearby bee to keep me from falling into complete oblivion.

Normally I might move rapidly away from a bee if it came too close; I certainly would from a wasp. Here in this soporific state, I have neither the energy nor inclination to move away or to mind. Every now and then I think the bee must be so close that it has landed in my hair. It doesn't matter. It could sting me and call all its bee friends to sting me and it wouldn't matter. I think I would just sit here unfeeling and let it happen. The bee's drone is not unpleasant. It is not musical either, to my ears. It is more elemental, part of the pulse of a summer's day and best heard at a distance.

Third Movement

Greg and I and Jenny, Lizzie and Thomas were holidaying in Anglesey. We were staying with Karina and Jimmie. Our friends Dendy and Phil were staying in the house next door with their children Tim, Nick and Charlotte. It was a glorious day so Auntie Karina suggested going to Newborough Beach on the other side of the island. It's a lovely beach surrounded by pine trees and sand dunes. We decided to take a picnic and make a day of it. The children were excited and impatient to get going, though that didn't stop them arguing over who was travelling in which car. To get to the beach it was necessary to drive into the pine forest, park the car and walk the rest of the way through long grass and sand dunes.

The sea was beautifully clear and safe for children to splash about in without getting out of their depth. The beach was littered with holidaymakers, mostly families, but it wasn't too crowded and there was plenty of room to spread towels around. The children had all been for a swim and we had just finished our picnic. Jenny, Lizzie, Tim and Nick were with other children playing on the sand dunes. We could hear the mass of children screeching with laughter as they scrambled up the dunes to the top, jumping into the soft sand below to shouts of 'Geronimo'. Thomas and Charlotte were playing down at the water's edge where the sand was wet enough to dig. The rest of us were lounging and chatting in the sun, keeping half an eye on the younger children.

I'm not sure who first became aware of the big black cloud in an otherwise clear blue sky. Suddenly there were shouts and people running and pointing in the general direction of the sand dunes. The black cloud was a swarm of bees. The beach lost its calm, relaxed atmosphere in an instant as parents rushed around gathering up children. Lots of people headed down to the sea as men shouted out instructions to get in the water. Most people just sat on the beach in wonderment. Fortunately our friend Phil knew a bit about bees. He was watching the cloud. 'They're not aggressive,' he said. He thought they were probably separating from a colony which had become too big and were swarming to find a new home. 'The best thing to do is sit calmly and quietly and wait for the swarm to pass.' I'm not sure I shared his confidence but other than panic and flee, there wasn't really an alternative. Phil and Greg went down to the water to collect Thomas and Charlotte, who crawled slowly along the sand to join us as bees began to fill the air.

We covered the younger children with towels and told them to lie very still and not worry about the loud buzzing. With one arm over one of the children, I slowly reached across with the other arm to retrieve my sun hat — at least my head could be protected! All the earlier panic of the beach evaporated into complete stillness and quiet as people became engulfed by the swarm.

Being in the midst of a mass of circling bees might have been frightening. Strangely it was not. The thought of the swarm was worse than the fact of it. I kept my eyes generally closed, squinting now and then to see the air black with bees. The sound was unforgettable, purposeful rather than frightening, and the whole passage of the bees was quite mesmerizing. When the swarm passed, the beach was instantly alive again. People began engaging with each other and talking about the experience. The older children came back from playing in the sand dunes, completely oblivious to the drama on the beach. 'Oh yeah,' Nick said, 'we saw the bees.'

Phil and Greg took the children to see the swarm settling in one of the pine trees. The four of us remaining, Karina, Jimmie, Dendy and I, settled back to our lazy afternoon on the beach. There was still some buzzing. It sounded very close. 'I can still hear a bee,' I said to Dendy and Karina. We all looked around

*and decided the sound was probably in my head, an echo of the
swarm.*

'You must be imagining it,' Dendy said.

*'Oh look!' cried my aunt as I took my sun hat off. There was
a bee in the crown. We watched it fly off in the direction of the
swarm, amazed that it had been in the sun hat all the time the
hat was on my head and that it hadn't stung me.*

As my present bee persists with its drone, I think about the swarm and
the day on the beach and how perfect the past can seem. The day was
idyllic, and memorable because of the swarm. We were in the eye of
the storm, albeit a storm of bees. I'm surprised by the thought that I
feel exactly the same now as I did that day, in the midst of the swarm.
There is something wild and unpredictable raging all around and I
am engulfed by a dark cloud, yet here in this moment in this garden
there is quietude. The swirling confusion has abated. I know the chaos
will return, but for now there is calm and I am in harmony with a bee
as it drones gently in and out with my consciousness.

Something has changed today. I'm not sure what. But something
has.

Vanda has returned with many cards, every one full of love and disbelief. Behind the handwriting people are struggling to find appropriate words. There are simple messages of condolence, outpourings of
grief and attempts at comfort. 'We have no words, only our love …
our thoughts and prayers are with you all at this time … I can't believe
Jen has gone, she was one of the sunniest people ever … If there's
anything we can do …' Each card is opened, read and added to the
stack received on previous days. Some are so beautifully expressed

and evocative, we can only weep more tears – 'My heart is breaking for you all, for your pain and for your loss' – and the tears are best when we laugh through them at particular joyous recollections of Jenny.

My last and best memory of Jenny is at Reading Group. She lay back on the sofa and with great glee related how one day she managed to find a very good reason for not studying and then spent nine solid hours reading *The DaVinci Code* from start to end.

She was sparkling, funny, happy and living life to the full.

This memory of Jenny will live in my heart for ever.

One card bears an image of hands raised and open. The message inside reads 'God is holding Jenny in his hands.' It provokes an angry response from me. 'If God is holding Jenny in his hands now, why wasn't he holding her in his hands when she died? Why didn't he keep her safe?'

There are a few cards like that. The impact is greater with some than others. I'm trying to see beyond the rhetoric to the people writing. Every card is kindly meant, I know that. Even so: 'How can people write things like that?' Vanda asks.

'I don't know, maybe because they believe it. Perhaps in reassuring others, they reassure themselves in the process.'

'Do you believe it?'

'No, I don't believe anything is that simple.'

'How does anyone know?'

I don't have any answers, for Vanda or for myself.

Opening that particular card has done nothing for my earlier sense of equilibrium. I feel a bit churned up by it so rather than dwelling on that which disturbs, I decide to apply my energies to something more productive and go outside to get the washing in from the line. The notion of God holding Jenny in his hands when only yesterday I looked upon her lifeless and mutilated body is anathema and I will not entertain the thought. I pull the bedding roughly from the line, scattering pegs all over the place not knowing whom or what to rail against.

Vanda has poured three glasses of red wine. She and Stefan are sipping theirs and talking at the kitchen table. I leave them to it and take my drink outside with the remaining unopened cards. The first card opened has the picture of a cross, a candle and a bunch of grapes on the cover, saying 'Now that Life's Work is done Peace'. The words don't do anything except fuel my irritation but inside a person I don't know is rather wonderfully offering a Holy Mass for the repose of Jenny's soul. At this latest gesture of kindness from another stranger, my irritation quickly dissolves.

Another card begins: 'In sure and certain hope ...' words used at the end of a funeral service. 'In sure and certain hope of the resurrection to eternal life ...' I do not want to think of those words. I haven't been sure or certain about the resurrection at any stage in my adult life – least of all now. Like Shakespeare, 'so have I heard and do in part believe.'

One of Jenny's work colleagues has written a letter: 'How I miss those morning chats and your cheerful daughter who brought me a laugh and a smile each morning ... I am so sorry for your grief but I am so pleased to have known Jenny ...'

'What are you doing out here? It's getting dark. You'll be bitten by mosquitoes.'

'I'm coming in now.'

'Stefan and I are going to bed. Will you be OK on your own? There's more wine in the bottle if you want another glass.'

I don't have any more wine but I do open one last envelope before going to bed. The card is a close-up photograph of tiny pink cyclamens in a garden. Fine stems emerge from a patch of green leaf. One pink flower in the foreground is bright and vibrant, the others are slightly out of focus, ethereal-looking, more like the gossamer wings of butterflies than flowers. Inside the card the sender has written out a poem.

I read the poem over and over in bed. The stars are compelling and I talk to Jenny through the stars. *You are pure music to me and you will live for ever in my heart. Your tune will incessantly remain.*

CHAPTER 6

Fourth Movement

At the end of every great opera the heroine always dies

William is standing by my bed. I'm aware of him as I struggle out of sleep into consciousness. He's watching me and doesn't speak until he is satisfied that I'm fully awake. 'Morning, Wills.'

'Auntie Julie, what book was Jenny reading when the bomb went off?' Clearly William has picked up fragments of conversations.

'*The Magician's Nephew.*'

Under his thick, as yet unbrushed mop of brown hair, William's eyes are big, round and deeply brown as he considers his next question. 'How do you know?'

'Well, I don't for sure, but I think that's the book she was reading because she told me she had bought a copy and was going to read it on her way to work during the week.'

William is looking at me as if he's not quite sure whether or not to believe me. 'Is that what James thinks as well?'

'Yes.'

'What page do you think she was on when the bomb went off?'

'I don't know, Wills, but I expect she was about halfway through.'

There's a pause and I sense he's deciding whether to ask another question. 'Mummy said would you like a cup of tea?'

'Yes please.'

A few minutes later William is back. 'What was the story about that Jenny was reading?'

'It's an adventure about a boy called Digory. I'm going into town later with James. I'll buy you a copy.'

He doesn't seem overly impressed by that and it's clear that already his mind is racing on to something else. 'When the bomb went off was Jenny standing like this?' William is standing as though he has a book open in his hands, looking down at the page.

'I hope so, Wills.' (Because if she was she wouldn't have been looking at her killer. I don't say this to him.)

'When the bomb exploded did Jenny fall like this' – he mimes falling backwards – 'or like this? – falling sideways.'

William is getting into his stride now and there is no hint of the tentative in his voice. I find I am as curious to know the answer to these questions as my nephew.

'Probably backwards, because of where her body was found.'

William does not ask me where Jenny's body was found. Instead he entertains me with another mime. 'I expect Jenny fell like this.' He makes a 'boom' sound and falls dramatically back and down to the floor. He lies there for a second or two, eyes closed, arms outstretched, until Vanda's voice pursues him along the hallway.

'William, are you dressed yet?'

'Quick, go and get dressed before Mummy gets here.' Either my urgent conspiratorial whisper, or his Mummy's voice, or maybe a combination of both, succeeds in raising William from the ground. In a scramble of red and blue, William is on his feet pulling his pyjama top off and heading for the doorway, narrowly avoiding a collision with Vanda coming into the bedroom carrying a mug of tea.

Vanda's hair smells of shampoo. I can smell the herbal essence as she leans over to put the tea on the bedside table. There's a whiff of something fruity as well. Straightening up, my sister crosses the short distance to the window. Her white sandals make little snapping sounds flip-flopping against the heels of her feet. As she moves through the room the combination of shampoo herbs and fruity shower gel hangs in the air.

The curtains are already partially open. Last night I went to sleep as I have done every night since I've been here, watching the night sky and sending thoughts and pleas into the stars through a gap in the curtains. Now the gap shows a patch of clear blue sky and clump of green shrubs. In one swishing movement Vanda has thrown the curtains fully open, filling the room with light and revealing more blue sky and a greater expanse of garden. For a moment, before turning back into the room Vanda is framed against the window. Her hair is still wet and combed back away from her face, ending in a straight line at the base of her neck. When her hair is dry, fair coppery highlights will stand out against an otherwise brown bob. Vanda's hair is as thick as mine is fine, the same brown hair inherited by William along with her eyes and smile. She's wearing cropped blue and white checked cotton trousers and a plain white T-shirt so that everything about her looks and smells fresh and clean. There is nothing about her garb or demeanour which suggests the awfulness of what we have been living through. To an onlooker, this is such normal behaviour, with one sister forging her way into the day, full of energy and purpose, and the other ruminating her way into wakefulness and activity. It was ever thus. Now one sister reclines in bed, drinking tea while the other sits on the side of the bed, resting for a moment and talking. If you look at us both closely, you can see drawn faces, and eyes which are more than merely tired from lack of sleep. Our faces and our eyes are speaking of things beyond words, revealing fragments of sorrow and loss already burrowing deeply and permanently into our being. I know this, because I can see my sister's face and look into her eyes as if they are a reflection of my own.

At first the talk is mainly about Vanda's birthday and the need to make a bit of an effort at teatime, if only for the sake of the children. We decide that while the children are in school, we'll go into Reading on the train and have lunch and a bottle of wine at one of Jenny's favourite restaurants. Conversation progresses to me going home.

'You can stay as long as you like,' Vanda assures me.

'I know but I have to go home sometime and the longer I leave it the harder it will be. Maybe I should go on Thursday, after your birthday, if I can arrange for Jenny to come back on the same day.' Our voices are flat as we talk about Jenny's body and making arrangements for her to be taken home to Bristol. 'I don't want to go home and leave Jenny in Reading. I want us to go home together. I'll talk to James about it later,' I say finally, which seems to motivate us both into action, Vanda to scoop up the empty tea mug and head for the kitchen and me to throw the bed covers back and go into the bathroom.

Vanda's natural instinct for list-making has provided some order to the day. She's scribbling away on a pad of yellow Post-its. Some of these will end up stuck to the dashboard of her car, some will overlap on her diary page and some will be fixed to the kitchen noticeboard. One is slapped on to the kitchen table: a reminder for Stefan.

'So you're going to call Colin then I'll drop you off in Reading at Jenny and James's house, then you're going to walk to the undertaker's and come back with James and his mum later?'

'Yes.'

While Vanda is sorting breakfast out for the children I phone and speak to Colin, requesting a second visit to the undertaker's to see Jenny's body again.

'No problem, Julie.' His distinctive Scots accent has become familiar now. 'I'll make a phone call to the undertaker's to pre-warn them so they're ready for you.' We each collude with the pleasantries of language when we both know the underlying truth is that his call will ensure Jenny's body is taken from a cold functional place and made presentable. Her injuries will be concealed beneath white muslin before the coffin is once again wheeled into a cool, dimly lit room with soft music and flowers. Thus the experience of viewing death is made as gentle as possible. *Humankind cannot bear very much reality.*

I need the reality. I need to encounter the brutality of my daughter's death and feel its harshness. How else am I to believe it?

Foxhill Road, Monday 18 July
James is making a cup of tea. I'm watching as he sets the kettle to boil, takes two mugs from the cupboard and drops a tea bag into each mug. His actions are slow and robotic. Even though his height and physical presence dominate the small kitchen space it's as if some part of him is far away.

Grief has come too early to James. It shows its bleakness in his hunched shoulders. Jenny's death is the death of their future together. It is the death of possibility … of their children, grandchildren, their hopes and dreams. *How well you have loved my daughter, James, and how well she loved you, and how cruelly she has been wrenched away from you.* Again I feel stirrings of rage against the destructive force which has annihilated such beauty and potential. I feel the rage rising, perfectly in tune with the steam forcing its way from the kettle.

'When do you think you'll come back here to sleep?'

James turns around in response to my question. 'I don't know. My parents are keen for me to stay with them at the moment.'

'I expect they want to look after you and make sure you're OK.'

'I might come back after the weekend and see how I get on. How are things at Vanda and Stef''s?'

'Quiet. It's a bit strange now that everyone's gone home.'

'Have you decided when you'll go back to Bristol?'

'The end of the week, probably. Will you be OK if I arrange with the undertaker for Jenny's body to be taken back to Bristol at the same time?'

'Yes. I just wanted her here for a little while first, where we shared our life.'

'I know. It's been a good thing to do.'

While we've been talking, James has changed his position and is leaning now against the kitchen unit with hands tucked behind his back and legs outstretched and crossed at the ankles. A crumpled T-shirt and swathe of washed-out blue denim ending in well-worn trainers might not have been the first clothes that came to hand this morning, but they might have been and as he becomes aware that the kettle has switched off and turns to flick the switch to bring it back to the boil, the word which leaps into the forefront of my mind is dejected. That's how James looks to me in this moment: dejected and crumpled – inside and out.

From where I'm standing with my back to the sink I can see beyond a small alcove at the end of the kitchen and along a passage-way to the bathroom. The bathroom door is ajar and Jenny's toilet bag is propped on a shelf above the cistern.

'I wonder how long it will take for Jenny's personal effects to be returned.' This is more of a shared thought than a question, possibly prompted by the sight of the sponge bag. Of course James doesn't have any illumination to offer, only more questions.

'Have you asked Colin and Pauline about her bag and phone?' he asks, without turning around this time.

'They're going to make inquiries. I'm not sure whether they go direct to the coroner for that kind of information or through the Met. I suppose her bag could have ended up anywhere.'

'Yes, but there must be photographs of everything found at the scene.'

There's a pause in conversation while the kettle comes to the boil again and James pours hot water into the mugs.

While he goes over to the fridge for milk he resumes speculating on where Jenny's phone might have been. 'If she was texting Michaela at work, she would probably have had it in her hand or pushed it into the back pocket of her jeans. She always sent me a text on her way to work, usually telling me what a rubbish journey she was having.' The irony of this doesn't escape either of us. James is on a roll now. 'If it was in her pocket the police would have listed it with the rest of the items she was wearing, unless they're withholding all the phones to check them out.'

This possibility hadn't occurred to me and as James throws the soggy tea bags into the rubbish container and replaces the milk in the fridge I absorb the implication of what he has just said before responding. 'If she was rushing to get from the Bakerloo line to the Circle line, she might have dropped the phone in her bag, out of the way.'

James reminds me of what Colin said earlier in the week, of the fact that there were hundreds of items to be identified. Our conjecture as we drink our tea is that inevitably some items may never be linked to a particular owner or be too badly damaged to identify, even destroyed with the force of the explosion. The item we keep returning to is the silver cross and chain we believe she was wearing around her neck. It was her most consistently worn piece of jewellery. We are both becoming quite fixated over these things. I do not believe the items hold any intrinsic importance in themselves. Their value is in their connection to Jenny and the story they can tell us about her last hour. They are missing links in a confusing set of circumstances. Most of all they are the treasured last things she wore and touched.

A few moments ago we were animated in our conversation, driven by a need for information. The cloud has descended again and inertia has settled upon us. For the time being our stock of energy and words is exhausted. 'Go and look through Jen's things if you'd like to. I'll clear up in here.' James has taken the empty mug from my hands.

Unsure, feeling slightly as though I'm intruding, I climb the short flight of stairs from the entrance room to the small landing at the top. To the left is Jenny and James's bedroom and to the right a spare room which doubles as a study and storage room. For a few minutes I do nothing more than sit on the edge of the bed in the spare room, looking around. The computer station in the corner of the room has been deserted. The machine is switched off. Papers are spread all over the desk. I don't suppose James has touched it since the day Jenny went missing. The linen basket is still full to overflowing. I'm tempted to rifle through for more of Jenny's used clothing to take away and add to my bundle. Instead I stand at the window gazing out at the houses opposite, wondering if the neighbours have any clue as to the misery unleashed within these walls. As they leave their houses in the morning, closing doors behind them, getting into cars or striding off down the street, there is probably no realization whatsoever. You'd never know, standing out there in the quiet and empty street, that the face at the window is the mother of a dead child; or that the man downstairs washing mugs in the sink is the distraught lover of a young woman recently blown up by a terrorist bomb. You may not even notice that you hadn't seen the buoyant young couple from number 77 for several days. Or that the only people entering and leaving the house are plain-clothed police officers and family with bowed heads and heavy hearts.

From the outside this dear home looks the same as any other in the terrace of two-up-two-down Victorian houses. It is a façade. The heartache is politely hidden. No one need know. I have to turn away before I start screaming at the wheelie bins looking ridiculously large and out of place in the tiny strips of front gardens.

Their room is full of her. Inside the door is the free-standing mirror transported here from Jenny's bedroom at home. A couple of scarves are draped casually over the corner of the frame. Tentatively I touch a blue turquoise scarf. Why tentatively, I don't know. Or perhaps I do. Death has made it sacred. The scarf was bought to match a pair of earrings Lizzie gave her for Christmas. Even before I lift it to my face I know it will smell of Jenny's perfume. The fabric is soft against my skin and I inhale into its folds deeply as if the scarf was an oxygen mask, breathing in Jenny and the scent of J'adore and breathing out memories …

Jenny is coming downstairs with a pile of books in her arms and thrusting a scrap of paper at me. 'Here's my Christmas list you asked for.'

J'adore
J'adore
J'adore

'Does that mean three bottles of J'adore or the only present you'd like for Christmas is a bottle of J'adore?'

'Surprise me!'

… And later, after Christmas, hair bundled back in a hurry, turquoise earrings dangling from her ears and the turquoise scarf wound loosely around her neck, she is shrugging into her denim jacket. 'I'm going to the pictures with Jess. Don't know what time I'll be back. Don't wait up.' She kisses me on the cheek and is gone, slamming the front door shut behind her. All that's left is a gust of air and a waft of J'adore trailing in her wake.

The memory is so strong that Jenny herself might have taken the scarf from my hands and draped it back over the frame, leaving me staring at my own sad reflection in the mirror.

On a chest of drawers there is a large bottle of J'adore. Almost furtively I pick it up, removing the cap to squirt a small amount on to the inside of each wrist, just enough to keep the scent with me for a couple of hours. I expect one of the last things Jenny did before leaving this room on her last morning was to squirt a jet of perfume on to each side of her neck. She would have replaced the top, as I am doing now, before going over to the bed to kiss James goodbye and setting off for work.

If only she had decided to stay home for the day. If only she had overslept, if only something had delayed her, if only I had chosen that moment to call her and slow her journey down, if only she had missed her train, if only she had got to the end of the road and realized she'd left her purse behind. All these things are possible and happen to hundreds of people every day. Why not Jenny that day? If only I could have kept her safe and if only a certain dark stranger whose name I will not utter in this room had never been born.

Even as my futile and hopeless longings rage on from one 'if only' to another I know that I must soon wake up and bring my senses to an acceptance of things as they are, not as I long for them to be.

Staring at the bed, at the pillow where Jenny slept next to James, I realize I do not fully believe in her death. I know the fact in my head but as yet the fact has not reached the rest of me.

James has come into the room. 'Have you looked for Jen's cross?'

'Not yet. I didn't like to disturb too much.'

'I think this is where it would be.' He's taken a small square trinket box from the bedside table and opened the lid. 'This is the stuff she mostly wore.' The box is full of necklaces and rings and bangles. James and I sit on the edge of the bed, side by side, with the box between us. Item by item the contents of the box are sifted through, untangled and laid out on the bed cover. Together we try to work out which necklace she would have been wearing. All week James has been pretty sure of it being the silver cross and chain, quite a distinctive contemporary design. We've drawn a blank. No sign of it here.

'There are some more boxes in the cupboard.' James has gone over to a long, built-in, narrow wall cupboard and pulled out a small green holdall. I recognize it from home and move over to join James, now kneeling on the floor, as he begins taking out boxes of various shapes and sizes. There are several small ring boxes, some empty. One ring box has a couple of crosses and chains wedged inside. Another flatter box has a few more, loose crosses and delicate chains which had become tangled.

'I didn't know she had so many crosses,' I say, partly to James, but it's more an observation, really.

'I don't think she wore any of them.'

They are all dulled now, the sort of crosses and chains that little girls might wear. I look at each one in turn trying to place them as gifts or recall the point in time when each was given. 'This was a christening present.' I hold one of them up, allowing the chain to hang over my fingers.

There is no sign of the particular cross and chain and we are now certain she must have been wearing it. There are loads of earrings but there are so many and such a lot of similar studs that it becomes an impossible task that we soon give up on. One box is dark red velvet with a strong clasp. Inside is Jenny's silver baby bracelet. Engraved on the inside is *Jennifer 14.12.1980*. As it lies inanimate on its satin bed in the box, I see it not in its box but on her chubby baby arm at her christening. She was eight weeks old. Before leaving the house for the church we had taken photos of her arrayed for the ceremony in the family christening robe and adorned with her first piece of jewellery.

I had thought this might pass down to her babies, but now it is nothing more than an icon, a precious symbol that can do no more than evoke a cold wet day in December when family and friends had gathered together in celebration and Jenny was named and commended to God in a Christian rite of passage. 'Surround this child with Your love; protect her from evil …'

The last box I open contains a silver charm bracelet. James has started packing the boxes back into the holdall and asks if I want to take anything back with me. 'No, keep everything together for now.'

There are several miniature charms attached to the bracelet, a new one given for each birthday through Jenny's early childhood by one of her godparents. I spread the bracelet in the palm of my hand and work my way around the charms, fingering each one. There's a pair of silver baby bootees, a clown with legs and arms that move, a peacock, a ballet dancer, a filigree heart, a cat playing with a ball, a windmill with a tiny handle to turn the sails, a rocking horse, and a boot which unclips at the sole to reveal minuscule characters from the nursery rhyme 'There was an old woman who lived in a shoe'.

While I've been meandering around a little girl's charm bracelet, James has replaced all the necklaces and bangles laid out on the bed back into their box and restored it to the bedside table.

Everything in the room is left as left by Jenny.

On the way to the undertaker's we walk part of the route that Jenny took to the station. It's quite companionable, even though conversation is focused on details of the bombings which continue to trouble us.

'How can the police be sure the bombings were carried out by suicide bombers?' James is picking apart information we have either been given directly through the police liaison officers or that we've picked up in the media. 'The bombers might have been duped into transporting a package, unaware it was a bomb.'

'You mean it might have been detonated by remote control or something?'

'Yes.'

Our pace began quite briskly, and has now slowed down as we ponder these things 'The police seem pretty sure it was four suicide bombers; they must be to have named them, surely?'

James is not prepared to accept what has been communicated to us without question and as we talk I realize that neither am I.

'If the police are certain, there must be evidence.' James adds.

'I'm going to write all this down,' I say to him and stop in the middle of the pavement to rummage in my bag for the little black notebook I now carry with me everywhere. James waits while I write, offering more questions. 'Do the police know whether the bombers were working alone or part of a wider network?'

As we set off again we continue to consider all sorts of possibilities, including how unlikely it seems that the bombers would have been working alone. 'If the bombs had been detonated externally, the perpetrators could be anywhere by now.' We're passing the hospital and can see the undertaker's in the distance. James has speeded up his pace again. My short legs and flip-flop sandals are no match for his long strides and trainers and I'm getting slightly out of breath trying to keep up and talk at the same time. Much of our journey has been along leafy green side roads with plenty of shade from overhanging trees but now we're alongside a busy main road in the full glare of the sun.

'We still don't know what happened to cause Jenny to switch from her regular Bakerloo line route,' James says as we approach the junction opposite the undertaker's building. He presses the button on the traffic control and stands with his hands in his pockets while we wait for the traffic to stop.

Despite the fact of Jenny's death we still need to know what happened to interfere with the route and why Jenny was apparently travelling west through Edgware Road when she was meant to have been travelling east. The certain knowledge of Jenny's death has done nothing to diminish this. If anything, it has caused us to want every last detail of her journey. We've asked the FLOs but they seem to be having difficulty getting information from the Met. 'Surely the underground authority must have a record.' James is insistent that the information exists somewhere. The traffic is whizzing by and we have to raise our voices to be heard above the noise.

'We need to sit down together and write all these questions out systematically and not cross them out until we have a satisfactory response.' When we see Colin and Pauline our minds are so full of everything it's easy to forget what we want to ask.

'Do you get the impression that Colin and Pauline are getting frustrated by the lack of information available to them?'

I do but as we make our way across the road to the undertaker's there isn't time to delve any further into the effectiveness of communication between the Metropolitan Police and the Family Liaison Officers, except to acknowledge that we need to be careful that questions are not lost in transit and that the police must be inundated with questions from families.

How can everything still appear so normal and unchanged when our whole world has changed? 'Doesn't it make you want to shout at people and tell them what's happened?' James's mother Elizabeth has echoed my thoughts. It's true, I want to scream at the crowds in the street and groups hurrying in and out of Waterstone's: *Don't you know what's happened? How can you go about your lives so normally when our world has collapsed?* The irony is that we are looking every bit as normal as all the other shoppers populating the town. This might be any day and any routine shopping trip. The fact that we've all just come from the undertaker's and are going into a bookstore to buy copies of the book Jenny was reading – researching for me – as she was blown up by a terrorist bomb is neither here nor there.

The irony is highlighted when I spend quite some time selecting a card for Vanda's birthday from the rotating card stands in the book store. Finding a card with a suitable image is proving difficult as I take cards off the stand, glance at them and then put them back in their little wire basket holders. Nothing is quite hitting the mark. I'm wondering about a card which is covered with a mass of sweet peas, delicate and colourful – maybe too colourful for our present mood. As it appears to be the last one on the stand I decide to keep hold of the card until I make my mind up. I continue rotating the stand until it sticks; I give it a little tug to set it moving again and, when it still refuses to move, a stronger jerk, which brings forth an 'oh!' from the other side. To my embarrassment there's an elderly lady also attempting to look at cards. 'I'm so sorry,' I say, adding hastily, 'I was so absorbed I didn't realize you were there; I thought the stand had jammed.'

'That's all right, it's easily done. Perhaps it would be better if we rotated around the stand.' She's smiling and doesn't seem too perturbed. 'There's so much choice, isn't there?'

I don't really want to engage in conversation but neither do I want to add insult to injury by appearing rude, so I make do with a simple, 'Yes, there is,' and a smile. We continue rotating around the stand, both of us picking out cards, looking at them and replacing them in their wire baskets.

'That's very pretty.' The lady is looking at the sweet pea card I'm still holding. 'I love sweet peas; they're one of my favourite flowers.'

'Mine too.'

'I'm looking for a bereavement card but it's so difficult knowing what kind to send. It's for a young person. She was killed in an accident at the weekend. Her poor parents must be devastated.'

I can't believe I'm hearing this.

'Where did you find your card?' She hasn't noticed the effect her words are having on me.

'I'm afraid it was the last one but you're very welcome to it.'

'Are you sure?'

'Yes, I was about to put it back anyway. It's not quite what I want.' I give it to her.

'Do you think it's suitable?' She's asking me that!

'I think it's perfect.'

'Yes, so gentle and lovely. If you're really sure I'm not depriving you?'

'Not at all. I'm looking for a birthday card and there are plenty to choose from.'

'That's very kind. Thank you. I'd better put this one back. It came from another stand but I don't suppose that matters.'

I hadn't noticed that she was also holding a card. I know instantly it's the right card for me: a cluster of dried honesty, semi-transparent mother of pearl petals, with a faint black outline around each petal and sketched on a cream background.

After paying for the card and three copies of *The Magician's Nephew*, agreeing with the sales assistant that yes, it was a lovely day and going back to join James and his mother who are waiting patiently just inside the doorway, browsing at books to pass the time, I'm beginning to wonder if this is all real. I half believe that Jenny will suddenly emerge from behind a book stand and we'll set off for ha ha bar as we have done a dozen times before.

As we leave the store, I think there is no such thing as normality. It's just a mask behind which people conceal their sorrow.

The table in my sister's kitchen is currently an island of calm. There's activity all around with Ellie and William in and out of the kitchen and Vanda making cold drinks for everyone and preparing school lunch boxes for the following day. So often this week the kitchen has represented a two-dimensional space. The ordinary and everyday routine of a family kitchen is functioning alongside an extraordinary and surreal parallel existence. The two worlds meet at the table, which is at times busy and chaotic and at times, as now, a place of reflection, gathering and sharing. Two home-made ice-pop containers lie discarded next to large partly drawn-on and coloured pieces of paper. Various coloured pens are scattered across the paper and across the table.

'I don't know whether to tell you … I asked James what he thought …' Elizabeth is sitting with me at the kitchen table. Vanda has just handed us both a glass of water and swept the evidence of children's colouring activity to one side to clear a space on the table. She's picked up the empty ice-pop containers and thrown them into the sink. '… but it's such a wonderful story of Jenny – how I'd like to remember her …'

After saying goodbye to James and his parents I'm at a bit of a loose end. It's been a long day and I'm left with an overwhelming sense of things ending again, as I did when Sharon left.

'Are you going to come and sit outside?' Vanda asks as she pours out three large gin and tonics. 'When all else fails have a very large gin and tonic.' Someone gave me a mug once with that caption written around the outside. There's an element of truth in the saying.

'I need to phone Greg and Colin first,' I say as Vanda hands me a glass.

Stefan has come into the kitchen, fresh from having a bath, and all three of us now have a very large drink in our hands. There's a habitual rather than heartfelt 'cheers' and we each take a simultaneous mouthful. Vanda and Stef take their drinks outside to where the children are playing on the slide and I set my glass temporarily to one side and pick up the phone.

First of all I speak to Colin and explain the decision to head back to Bristol on Thursday — that's the twenty-first — and ask if it's possible for Jenny to be taken home the same day. His Scots burr has become so familiar I almost hear 'aye, Julie, that shouldn't be a problem' before he speaks the words. He's asking about everyone, how James is, if Greg was still in Manchester with his mother and whether Sharon arrived home safely. When I tell him Sharon wants a daily update on the colour of his shirt he laughs. 'I'll have to choose very carefully.' During the conversation I ask about Jenny's personal effects, the items James and I talked about earlier at Foxhill Road and how long it might be before the items were returned. He's going to get back to me tomorrow.

As Greg and I speak I can picture him standing in the dining room at his mother's house in Manchester, looking out from the window to the distinctive red gold sumac tree dominating the front garden. When I say, 'I'm arranging for Jenny's body to be brought back to Bristol,' Greg appears unable to speak. Even over the distance, from opposite ends of a telephone connection, I can see him screwing his face up, every muscle working and constricting to control his emotion. In my mind's eye I imagine his free hand clenched into a tight fist. He's trying not to break down. With a huge effort and deep intake of breath he manages to speak. 'Yes, yes.' It's hardly audible but I think affirmative.

'Do you think you might want to see her?'

'No, I can't but I'd like to know she's close to us.'

'She will be.'

Now neither of us can speak, both fighting back tears and keeping the floodgates firmly sealed. I cannot bear my husband's pain. In a matter of days we have almost become strangers. In Greg's grief he cannot bear to look at pictures of Jenny; in my grief I want to be surrounded by them. I wonder how we will reconcile the two aspects when we return home.

We can talk about the dog normally, at least, and how kind people are being and how we think Lizzie and Thomas are coping.

Greg hasn't raised any issues relating to the bombings or police dealings and I haven't volunteered any information – scant as it currently is. Now, I think, is not the time.

Now is not the time for many things. Greg and I need to sort out our relationship. Our marriage is over. In our hearts we both know it. But there is no time, no emotional space to deal with more than our daughter's death and to attend to the wellbeing of our other children. The issues that are before us, marriage, relationship, separation, are for the future. They must wait. Now is for Jenny.

I need to go outside, not where Vanda and Stef and the children are but somewhere on my own. I let myself out through the front door and walk up and down the drive in front of the house for a few minutes. I want to run and run and run but there's nowhere to go. I want someone to put their arms around me and tell me everything is gong to be all right. I want my beautiful daughter not to be dead. I want to tear my hair from my head and dig my nails into my flesh. I don't know where to put the energy, so much energy I can't contain. I keep pacing backwards and forwards, covering the same patch of ground between the porch and the garage door until the panic has subsided. Then when I feel steady enough and calm enough I go back inside and take up my gin and tonic, walk out through the kitchen, along the utility passageway, into the conservatory and out on to the patio to join my sister and brother-in-law.

Equilibrium is restored as we sip gin and talk about the day. To speak of anxiety and panic attack seems somehow out of place in this restful setting. The moment has passed. I content myself with watching my niece and nephew letting off steam by racing up and down the slide and swinging backwards and forwards along the climbing frame.

The next day, Ellie has summonsed me into her bedroom. 'I'm making a card for Mummy's birthday.' She wants to show me. Unlike William, Ellie does not have a stream of questions about the bomb. We spend a bit of time with the card, Ellie sitting at a small desk, colouring and cutting out and I'm sitting on the edge of her bed, watching.

'When will Lizzie and Thomas be here again?'

'I don't know. Soon. I expect you might see them in Bristol next.'

'Mummy said we can go when school finishes.'

There's a gap in conversation while Ellie gives all her concentration to the card and continues colouring in when I ask the next question.

'Do you mind having lots of people in your house?'

'No.' Ellie shakes her head and after another short gap. 'I wish Joanne could come back again.'

Jo spent a lot of time with Ellie when she was here last weekend and she's quite similar to Jenny in nature.

'I think Joanne is going to come and stay in Bristol for a couple of weeks so you'll see her again soon.'

'How much longer will you be staying?'

'Just a couple more days – until Mummy's birthday, then William can have his bedroom back.'

'I wish you didn't have to go.'

'I need to get back to see Uncle Greg and Lizzie and Thomas and Grandma and Grandpa.'

'Will James be coming again?'

'I'm sure he'll visit lots and he's coming for Mummy's birthday so you'll see him the day after tomorrow.' At this she brightens up.

Even so, I wonder what is going through Ellie's mind in these questions. Maybe she's feeling, like me, the loss of people going away.

Tuesday evening and the garden is full of shadows cast by trees in the dusk light. The sound of birdsong is thinning out now and slowing down. How different it sounds to the morning chorus where every bird seems to compete for supremacy of sound. Their evening song does not diminish the silence of the garden; rather I feel the birds are drawing me into the silence. Their lingering notes seem to me to be like the final chords of a piece of music, music which has been listened to and transported the listener to another dimension, suspended from the reality of immediate surroundings. The music has transported the listener for a while and now it is bearing him back gently before retreating into silence.

There is a single phrase which echoes in my head as the last strains of birdsong linger in the air. It bears Jenny's voice across whichever dimension or time that separates us. It bears her voice, releases her physical, vibrant personality.

Elizabeth's voice from when she spoke at the table yesterday mingles with Jenny's ... *I don't know whether to tell you ... but it's such a wonderful story ... how I want to remember her* ... Elizabeth's voice fades into the picture she's given me of Jenny. It has come to life now as I walk on in silence around the darkening exterior of the·house, past the double doors of the garage and the mound of logs, piled high and ready for the winter fires. Worn grass and dry cracked earth mixed with wood dust and shavings suggest recent labour and self-sufficiency. A wooded, working area of the garden is adjacent to the drive, a clearing which leads into the trees where I disappear from view, around the corner of the house, to sit on the swing of many melancholic hours.

I know Jenny was excited at the prospect of *La Bohème*, her second trip to the Royal Opera House in a year but her first First Night. I know she wore a knee-length skirt in dusky blue and deep grey with a blue grey top and black high-heeled shoes. I know this because she told me herself. I know that she saw Dame Judi Dench in the audience and how delighted she was to be sitting just a couple of rows behind her favourite actor. 'She was sitting just in front of us, Mum, she's stunning.'

'What about the opera?' I laughed 'Did you enjoy it or was the main attraction JD?'

'It was wonderful, the whole night, I didn't want it to end.'

Now Elizabeth has filled in the gaps so I can see Jenny rising from her seat after the final notes had been played and the tumultuous applause had died down and the audience was preparing to leave the auditorium. Thanks to Elizabeth I can see my joyous daughter with bright, alive eyes turning to her and proclaiming in a loud voice: 'At the end of every great opera the heroine always dies,' then laughingly adding as an afterthought: 'Well, perhaps not every but certainly the most romantic and dramatic.'

And I wonder if Dame Judi was amongst those in the audience who turned to glance at the vivacious young woman. If the actress had glanced around, she could not have had any idea that the young woman who had derived such joy at seeing her in the flesh would die at the hands of a terrorist in one day short of two weeks from that moment.

Mimi, the heroine in *La Bohème* sings:

> 'My story is brief …
> I love those things
> which possess such sweet enchantment,
> which speak of love and springtime,
> of dreams and visions,
> those things that people call poetic.
> Do you understand?'

At the end of every great opera the heroine always dies. And all the mother can do is be carried by the swing and weep into eternity.

When I go inside I head straight for the bedroom and take out my notebook from the case. On the otherwise blank page where yesterday I wrote 'Funeral' I now add with a firm hand: 'Jenny's quote for order of service: At the end of every great opera the heroine always dies.'

There will be no sleep tonight. I do not need to lay my head on the pillow and toss and turn for an hour to come to that realization. It's been a long day, and busy, and my head is full, too full for sleep. Even so, when I finally climb into bed after spraying my ankles and arms with mosquito repellent, it's almost too much effort to lean across and turn the bedside light off.

I must have slept because I've been dreaming. The pillow is damp. I've woken myself up crying. The room is dark so it must still be night-time. I can remember fragments of the dream. There was music, the Humming Chorus from *Madama Butterfly*. I can only vaguely remember the tune now. It was so clear in the dream. In the darkness I sit up and turn the pillow over, and then lie down again and try to remember the rest of the dream. The more I try the more elusive it becomes. Jenny was walking away from me, I was calling after her but she wouldn't stop. That's all I can remember. Why did I know the music so well?

I need to focus on something to go back to sleep or put the light on and forget all about sleep. I try to recall the soothing sound of the Humming Chorus again but it's well and truly gone. Even though it's hot in the room I pull the duvet up around my shoulders for bodily comfort and fix my mind on the night of the Humming Chorus.

> *Lizzie is in the back of the car and it's her first trip to the opera. 'Can you tell me the story before we get there please?' I booked last-minute tickets earlier in the day. Jenny is sitting next to me in the front passenger seat and provides a potted version of* Madama Butterfly, *which Lizzie sums up as: 'So basically she falls in love, gets dumped, has his baby and then kills herself?'*
>
> *'Pretty much, but it's more beautiful than that.'*
>
> *'Are there any well-known songs?'*

'There's the Humming Chorus ... um, can't remember any more but you'll probably recognize them when you hear them.'

'One Fine Day' I chip in.

There's barely time to order drinks for the interval and the girls decide to have one now as well. No sooner have we got drinks in our hand than the bell sounds for the audience to take their seats. It's no problem for me as I only have tonic water on account of driving but the girls have a glass of wine, which they're forced to drink rapidly.

Our seats are not the best, the last but one row at the back of the circle.

'When I booked the tickets I was told there was a restricted view of the surtitles but I said it didn't matter as we knew the story.'

'Well I don't!' says Lizzie.

'Yes you do, I've just told you.' Jenny is reading the programme and thrusts it at Lizzie. 'Here, have a quick read of the synopsis.'

Lizzie turns to me to say under her breath but loud enough for her sister to hear, 'I hope she isn't going to be my mother all night!'

As the opera begins, it soon becomes evident that 'restricted view' means bottom half of each line of surtitle.

'Stop it, Lizzie,' I say in a loud whisper as she is sliding ever further down her seat to see the surtitle and being predictably dramatic about it.

'But I can't read it!'

By the interval Jenny and I had followed Lizzie's lead and so had the entire row, which is quite comical and we can't help but see the funny side on the way to the bar.

'I've got neckache.'

'It's better to have no surtitles than half a surtitle.'

'Well, we were warned.'

The row of semi-prostrate bodies produces even more giggles in the second half – helped along, no doubt, by wine.

After the show I watch them make their way back to the car, arms around each other, emulating the Humming Chorus, and just a little bit tipsy.

Far from sending me to sleep, focussing on such a strong memory has had the opposite effect and I am now fully awake and standing at the window looking out at the stars. All I can see is Jenny and Lizzie together, walking towards the car, slightly ahead of me on the narrow pavement. It will never happen again. These wonderful sisters who could be fighting one minute and best of friends the next will never walk arm in arm along the street again. The terrible sense of ending that has pursued me all day has finally caught up with me, in the night when I can't escape the darkness. With a gasp I know that Jenny is gone, wrenched away. I knew it yesterday and the day before but now I know it in a different way. I know it as an ending, a terrible, murderous ending. Jenny's life, which was lived in beauty, has ended in cruel disregard and violation and I am awakened to death with more bleakness and more anger than I believed I could ever feel.

As I continue to look out at the night all the other endings of the past days seem to feed this bigger, final ending and with the realization I sense that something is changing. There's a bend in the road around which I do not wish to go. My focus must change from being in this place to leaving it. In two days I'll be going home to face whatever is there to be faced. Jenny's funeral and then whatever unknown place waits beyond that. It's a prospect that disturbs me.

CHAPTER 7

Fifth Movement

SYMPHONIC POEM

I read somewhere that an order of medieval monks believed insomnia was a call to creativity. Maybe that's true. Maybe it's born out of necessity, a compulsion to release mental energy. Ideas and worries that will not be stilled by sleep play on the mind and on the heart until they are attended to. Anguish is better out than in but in the night there are limited channels of release. I am discovering this fact profoundly. Once the 3 a.m. cup of tea is downed and the night sky no longer holds my attention, there is only pacing the room or putting it all down in writing. So that's what I do, pour out my anguish and unholy thoughts into my notebook. I suppose those medieval monks might say that was creative, it's better than pounding the pillows anyway.

The day is gone
I'm standing in the same place
Not fully awake
Unable to sleep
Half dreaming as
One day slips by into the next.

Thirteen todays have become yesterdays. The multitude of hours have passed in slow time through the changing lights of each day, from dusk, into the darkening night, the black hole of deepest night and onward to redeeming first light.

I want to hold on to these days, to the preciousness of existing in the unreality of believing that I can stretch out my hand and pull back what has gone. Even as I indulge in this hopeless present longing I know the future is beckoning onward and will not be ignored.

'The night has passed and the day lies open before us.' The new day should be full of possibilities, not impossibilities. *The night has passed and the day lies open before us*. Words from the morning office, which I always thought to be beautiful and full of hope and promise, scribbled across my mind and across the page. Except the night has not passed and the day when it dawns will be full of shadows and I am angry with the words. I come away from the window and pour my melancholy into the pillow, part longing for suffocation, ease from this awful inward pain.

Bear it
Or be borne by it.
Remain with pain
Or leave.
Leaving others with more pain.
Untenable
Jenny would have chosen to stay.
I must stay
Despite
Grief
Rising in the distance in every direction.

Fifth Movement

I am not going to run from it
Silly to imagine I can beat it, overcome it like some enemy.
I will stand and wait for its inevitable force
Face on
Embrace it
Be absorbed by it
Go where it takes me
Hope I'll survive it.

Is this the beginning of grief?
I am not sure where or when grief begins.
Not in the trauma or shock of impact.
It comes later,
Creeping, rushing, seeping through crack and crevice of body, mind
and spirit.
Insatiable.
When shock wears off, grief takes its place.

Will I fight it?
No.
Will I run from it and hide?
No.
I will embrace grief,
Sorrow, heartache, anguish, pain, misery, unhappiness, angst, woe.

The night has passed and the day lies open before us.

I did sleep, eventually, last night. I can't remember dropping off, only
waking with my glasses still on and my pencil and notebook alongside

me in bed. Surprisingly even a minimum three or four hours' sleep has given me a determination and new energy to start the day. Instead of lying in bed ruminating under a dark cloud I've stirred and showered and dressed within half an hour of waking.

Vanda is in the kitchen. 'I'm not going to forget this birthday, am I?' she says as I hand her my card.

'No,' I reply, watching as she opens the envelope.

After reading what is written in the card Vanda places it on the kitchen window sill alongside Jenny's picture and the vase of sunflowers. 'I can't believe we're not going to see her again,' she says, reaching for a tissue.

'Don't start or you'll set me off and my mascara will run!'

Through the kitchen window we watch the post van pull into the drive from the lane. Stefan has gone out to greet him. They exchange a few words then Stefan waves him off and joins us in the kitchen, sorting through the pile of post and passing most of the envelopes over to Vanda. A few birthday cards are already propped up on the table alongside discarded envelopes and home-made cards from Ellie and William. While Vanda is opening her post, Stefan has switched the computer on in the office to look up train times.

'What time do you want to leave?' Stefan is calling out from the next room.

Vanda glances up from reading a card to look questioningly in my direction.

'Up to you, I'm more or less ready.'

'Eleven or eleven-thirty,' she calls back to Stefan while passing me some cards to read.

Each card contains beautiful, heartfelt variations of 'I know you won't have a really happy birthday this year but I want to wish you happy birthday anyway.'

Fifth Movement

Stefan has jotted train times down on a Post-it pad. 'Give me a shout when you're ready to leave,' he says, retreating back into his workshop.

James and his parents arrive, followed by a couple of Vanda's friends who have called in with flowers. In the general mêlée there are many phone calls, including a rather wistful call from our mother. A delivery of flowers I had ordered from a local florist arrives: sunflowers on behalf of Jenny, who would undoubtedly approve of the gesture. 'From me-ee in absentia,' she might laughingly have written in any other circumstance. There's a minor upset when Vanda searches out the vase Jenny gave her the previous year on her birthday only to remember it had been broken by William during a game of indoor football. The vase came from Pier. 'I'll buy you another one, we'll call in on our way to lunch,' is the only comfort I can offer.

We're expecting a visit from the Family Liaison Officers so it's no surprise when the scrunch of tyres on gravel alerts us to the fact that they've arrived. There's a light-hearted exchange between Vanda and Colin over the colour of his shirt which is a vibrant lime green. 'In honour of your birthday,' Colin jokes.

'I needed my sunglasses this morning,' Pauline quips. The banter continues for a few minutes, until we sit down at the kitchen table. Then, as though an invisible line is drawn, the mood changes into one of professional formality. Colin takes his notebook out and places it on the table in front of him. This means business.

An interim death certificate will be posted to the FLOs within the next two days and delivered to me by hand. Apparently an inquest will be opened to determine 'cause of death' and then immediately adjourned until a later date. Colin explains this is routine procedure where there is an ongoing criminal investigation. At a later date there will be an inquest proper. The FLOs are not able to confirm when this might be. While Colin glances down at his notes I think there is nothing 'routine' about any of this.

Colin has made a note of our desire to have all Jenny's personal effects returned and in particular, information about the silver cross and chain. Although he is able to confirm all items were going to be cleaned by a specialist team of property restorers prior to being returned to the family, he isn't able to confirm which specific items this relates to but will do his best to find out.

He goes on to explain that the Metropolitan Police are arranging to meet victims' families in London on Sunday, for a current appraisal and briefing. This will take place at a prearranged venue, the Royal Horticultural Halls in SW1. Families are to be updated on the investigation into the bombings and to hear from guest speakers involved. Would any members of the family like to attend? There will be time during the week to prepare any questions we need to ask. Details of the venue will be kept secret to ensure no unwanted publicity.

This is more information to absorb. Colin is waiting for my reply. 'I expect so but we need to think about it and speak with other members of the family. Is there a limit on numbers?' He thinks two or three from each family. My mind is racing ahead. I'm due to go home tomorrow. This will mean travelling back to London from Bristol early Sunday morning or coming back here on Saturday. 'There's no hurry,' Colin is saying. 'Shall I give you a call in the next day or two when you've had a chance to decide what to do?'

I hear but fail to engage as Colin explains about the police victim support service. The service offers counselling to family members. My mind is still focused on more immediate questions, which is possibly why my response to this last piece of information is somewhat dismissive.

'Can we look at Jenny's clothes that she was wearing?'

Colin hesitates for a moment before saying he would clarify whether or not these were sent off for forensic examination and will get back to us. I wonder if I should read anything into the hesitation.

'Where exactly was she on the train? Was she sitting or standing? How many other people were in the carriage?' James is asking the questions.

Colin says he will try and get an answer to these questions straight away.

When one of us asks if death would have been instant, which is something we've all anguished over, Colin tells us that in his opinion, bearing in mind her injuries, death would have been instant. He can't assure us of that for certain though. We've raised this before but until there is some evidence, either from the police or the coroner, we will have to keep on raising it.

We're on to discussing the difficulties I've had in seeing Jenny's body fully. It's true that I eventually saw her at the undertaker's but that was not as I would have wished and followed quite a tense struggle over what was deemed advisable for me to see. 'Whose decision was it that prevented me from seeing Jenny's body when I first requested it?' This issue has been playing on my mind and I needed to ask the question. Colin explains that the ID Commission had viewed the photographs of the body and was of the opinion that it would be better if Jenny's body were not viewed fully. With every fibre of my being I want to cry out that I am her mother, how dare anyone tell me what I can and can't see of my daughter. Instead, when Pauline intervenes to say that of course it is my right and no one is preventing me from seeing Jenny's body, all I can manage to say is, 'Well, it isn't being made very easy.' It shouldn't feel like a battle.

Then the moment has passed and Colin is asking about funeral arrangements. I tell him we are thinking of 16 or 17 August but need to clarify a few details before confirming. Both FLOs are being professional. If they are wondering why there's such a time lapse before the funeral they have not commented. I'm relieved as I'm not sure I could really explain.

After they've gone, it's back to birthday mode. This is like being on a pendulum, from birthday to briefing and back to birthday with more decisions to be made after that.

The birthday lunch is a subdued interlude, gentle and with much talk of Jenny. Despite the bottle of bubbly and being in one of Jenny's favourite haunts, or maybe because of it, we never quite capture the spirit of birthday joy that was our intention in setting out today. There is so much to mourn and the mourning has barely begun. Continuing to talk about her in a public place becomes almost unbearable. Not talking about her is impossible. The bubbly at least is a temporary salve to tears. We ching-ching our glasses and exchange the customary 'cheers' and, from me, a toast to Vanda for a 'happy birthday lunch'.

I am pleased when we are able to sit in the same place as I did with Jenny when she and I last came here, on a squidgy brown leather sofa at a low table. Vanda and I both order the same dish of griddled salmon. 'I can't remember if Jenny had duck or salmon,' I say unnecessarily as we settle back into the comfort of the sofa and await our food.

'One brûlée with two spoons please,' Jenny asked the waiter, smiling. He tried to persuade us to have one each but we weren't being seduced into more fat and calories than was absolutely necessary. We had been to Pier for some candles and then John Lewis to buy an electric mixer so James could make meatballs (this was Jenny's reasoning anyway!). I bought it as their housewarming present as I'm sure she hoped I might. As we walked to ha ha bar for lunch Jenny linked her arm in mine and told me how happy she was to be back in Reading with James and with a master's under her belt. She didn't need to tell me, it was evident in her eyes and

voice and the way she swung the carrier bag of candles to and fro
as we walked along. She oozed ebullient life. Like 'Jupiter', in
Holst's Planet *suite, Jenny the bringer of joy.*

Remembering is both a comfort and a pain but not at the moment in equal measure. As Vanda and I methodically flake our way through mutual fillets of salmon, I feel little comfort, only the deprivation and loss of joy. This is all the more emphasized by the rising crescendo of voices and laughter ringing out from tables of other diners, and from clusters of friends standing around in groups enjoying a lunchtime drink. It must have been equally busy and noisy when I was here last with Jenny. The difference is that she and I were part of the buzz and contributing to the din. Today Vanda and I are outside the noise, or so it seems, lunching in our own embryonic space. Our voices speak softly of birthdays past and present, of cakes and Pimm's parties, while the language of death and funeral arrangements tremor close by, suspended from speech for the time being.

'Is everything all right?' a waitress asks as she passes by, referring to the food, not our emotional state.

'Yes, delicious, thank you.'

After lunch, feeling slightly tipsy, Vanda and I wander around Pier and buy a vase to replace the broken casualty of indoor football. There is pleasure in finding an identical vase. Something of Jenny restored.

The remainder of the birthday passes in a montage of images: the world speeding by outside the windows of the train on the way home; sunflowers being transferred to the replacement vase; tea with birthday cake which Stefan has organized; a chorus of 'happy birthday' around the table; Vanda blowing out the candles on the cake. The children are happy and satisfied their mummy has had a birthday party of sorts. When it's all over Vanda looks strained by the effort. Nevertheless, it was a good thing to have done.

By evening, plans have changed. I am no longer returning to Bristol tomorrow. In the light of the police briefing it makes sense to stay on here until the weekend. There are many conversations about the briefing and logistics of attending, and about Jenny's body being accompanied back to Bristol. In the end a decision is made that James and I will attend the briefing and Greg will return home from Manchester to be in Bristol and close to Jenny. Greg's words echo in my head: I'd like to know she's close to us.

I understand that completely. I also understand I could go home and be near Greg and Lizzie and Thomas. I know that. I could go home to be with my family and come back on Saturday but for some reason which I am presently too numb to analyse, it is easier to justify staying put.

Colin is wearing a blue shirt this morning: police blue. There is an air of formality around today's briefing. I have discarded my usual summery trousers and T-shirt in favour of a black skirt and top and James has donned a shirt. 'Shall I put those in the boot?' Colin is referring to bunches of flowers we're both holding.

'Yes, thanks. They're for Edgware Road.'

'They're lovely.' The boot slams shut.

When Colin called to confirm plans for today, he asked if James and I would like to visit Edgware Road following the briefing. We said we would.

'Did you write down the questions you wanted to ask?' Colin asks as we get into the car.

'We certainly did!' I omit to add that it was over a bottle of wine and late at night, and we are still feeling the effects of both. The early start isn't helping, which is probably why James has opted for the back seat, to switch off more easily during the journey.

Colin explains we'll be driving via a police station in Slough to pick up another FLO who is deputizing for the day in Pauline's absence.

Conversation on the first stretch of the journey is largely about circumnavigating Slough and its appeal as a tourist attraction as we get caught up in traffic jams, wrong turnings and eventually poring over the road map in a supermarket car park.

The motorway stretch is a bridge between two worlds. The closer we get to London the more specific the conversation becomes, particularly over the question of the bombers and likelihood of accomplices. The face of the Edgware Road bomber is intruding on my thoughts more and more. I say his name every day now, Jenny's name first and then his name, the name of Mohammed Sidique Khan. His image, the one in the media, the only image, seems to be reflected in the window of every car we pass. I wonder, out loud as it happens, how many others might have been in on the planning and orchestration of the bombings. Speculation doesn't really get me anywhere. Did Khan have a wife? Wouldn't she have had knowledge or at least some idea of what was being planned?

'You'd be surprised at what couples don't know about each other's activities.' Wendy, the deputizing FLO's response is matter of fact, devoid of cynicism. She gives us an example of a case where the wife had no idea of crimes her husband was involved in over a period of two years. I feel I'm gently being put in my place and go back to looking out the window to think my own thoughts on the subject.

'Aye, it's hard to believe, I know.' Whether Colin is referring to couples generally or the bomber and his wife specifically is unclear.

We're soon driving through the familiar sights of Victoria, busy with traffic and tourists, then along the Embankment of the Thames and past Vauxhall Bridge.

I used to know all the London bridges. Their names and order were recited in primary school along with times tables and kings and queens of England. I mention this irrelevant piece of information as we pass by the bridge. Wendy is busy scanning a sheet of directions but Colin quips about being let off such subjects at school north of the border. Once we turn off from the main road it's another world: unfamiliar streets empty of people; office buildings shut up for the weekend. Colin has slowed his driving down so we can spot street names. 'We're looking for Greycoat Street and Vincent Square,' Wendy says, reading out directions from the back.

We pull up outside the venue just after 11.30 a.m., half an hour before the briefing is due to start. Uniformed police officers are either side of the entrance to the building and one of them steps forward as Colin winds down his window. He's directed to park at the end of the road. 'I'll drop you here and come back when I've parked up.' Within a couple of minutes he's back announcing he found a shady spot to park the car. The four of us together walk up the few steps into the building.

There are police everywhere. Watchful eyes follow us through the entrance into the lobby. There's a turnstile type of security to pass through. We were told to bring ID but it doesn't appear to be required. Our names are ticked off on a list. Colin and Wendy show their warrant cards. On the other side of the turnstile James and I are welcomed, handed a briefing pack each and invited to help ourselves to coffee and take our places at a table in the main hall. Colin and Wendy suggest we find somewhere to sit while they fetch the coffee.

'This feels like a clergy conference,' I whisper to James as we cross the vestibule, glancing at officials lining the route through to the hall. 'Welcome, conference pack and coffee; all that's missing is the name badge.'

The hall is overwhelming: a vast space packed with people sitting at large round tables. I'm struck by a series of images: pristine white tablecloths, flowers, cups of partially drunk coffee, plates of biscuits, and faces: a montage of serious and sombre faces. The room is loud with murmurings, though it's not noisy. If nervous anticipation has a sound, this is it. Moving further into the hall it's unclear if there is a specific seating plan or if we sit anywhere we can find a space. Tables in every direction are occupied. 'There must be more than one family to each table,' James is saying as we both scan the room searching for an empty table or name cards signifying where to sit.

The uncertainty is making us both agitated. I'm becoming tetchy. 'This isn't a wedding reception; we shouldn't have to trawl around tables searching out where to sit.' The atmosphere in the room is tense and anxious and immediately transferrable to anyone walking into the space. Yards away I could attempt a light-hearted comparison to a clergy conference. In here there is no place for jocularity. Many heads are strained across tables deep in conversation. In contrast there are people in twos and threes sitting silent and remote. James and I are swallowed up by the atmosphere. We are in the body of the whale. I feel like an outsider and yet part of it. I belong here; we both do. That realization comes as quite a shock.

'Do we sit anywhere?' I ask a woman with long dark hair sitting at the nearest table. Just as she is replying 'yes' and nodding her head in affirmation, a woman in a dark blue skirt and white blouse comes towards me. She's wearing a badge which I'm unable to read as I don't have my glasses on. She is gently touching my elbow and pointing forward. 'There are a couple of empty tables at the back of the hall.' We follow the direction in which she's pointing and start to weave our way through the network of tables and strangers. I feel exposed as most other people are already seated and instinctively watching the new arrivals. With relief we locate a table and sit down, looking out for Colin and Wendy. This is not the first time I recognize how essential the FLOs have become. At this moment they are something between a safety net and a security blanket!

The starched white of the tablecloth is even more pristine close up; there's not a ruffle or crease in sight. The flowers at the centre of the table are a mix of soft summer colours. In fact the room is arrayed like a wedding reception, with only the pained looks and body language of the occupants to say that it isn't. There are many suited men who I assume to be police or officials. On the other side of the room is a girl in a head and neck brace. The metalwork stands out from the crowd of people around. Instinctively, I look over the room to see if I recognize anybody. Of course not, why would I? Faces from television and newspapers, brief interviews with grieving relatives over the past week have slipped now from recall. The room is too full to single anyone out. I look again at the girl in the brace. Was she injured in the explosions, I wonder?

I'm surprised that survivors might be here as well as families of those killed, and equally surprised at how disturbed I am by the prospect.

James is studying the briefing pack and has drawn my attention to a separate piece of paper expressly stating that general questions will be taken but today's briefing is not an opportunity for specific questions to be addressed.

'What does that mean?'

James shrugs his shoulders. 'I think it means we won't get answers to any of the questions we've written down.' He pushes the folder away dismissively, commenting, 'It's just a PR pack,' and we ponder the point of the briefing if not to address families' questions. We come to the conclusion that it is, literally, a briefing and appraisal but I can't help questioning why Colin suggested we came armed with a list of questions and say as much to James.

'Perhaps he didn't know either.'

While James is checking his phone, I've opened the folder of papers and taken out the itinerary of the day. There are some top people here including HM Coroner and senior investigating officers from the Metropolitan Police and Anti-Terrorist Branch. Under each emboldened and underlined name and rank is a bullet-pointed list of each officer's responsibilities and, presumably, the areas they will cover this morning. There is even a Senior Identification Manager (SIM). I say 'even' as until this moment it would not have occurred to me that such a role existed. His role, amongst other things, is to ensure that: 'The victims of this terrorist incident on the 7th July 2005 were recovered in a dignified manner and to ensure correct identification so that forensic evidence was secured.'

'Have you read this?' I say to James, indicating the relevant point. 'He should be able to answer some of the questions we have.'

'Yes, but we can't ask specific questions.'

Colin and Wendy arrive with coffee and a plate of biscuits. 'Did you know we can't ask specific questions?' I ask, passing the loose sheet of paper towards Colin. His response is much the same as James's, only stronger and less pragmatic.

I glance across to the table next to ours on the left – there are no tables to the right, only the partition separating the refreshment area from the main hall. A woman about my age catches my eye and smiles. There's also a younger woman at the table about Jenny's age, with long fair hair, and a man who is sitting looking straight ahead. His arms are folded across his chest and there is something about his still-ness which is far from relaxed. He seems uncompromisingly deter-mined. *I'm not going anywhere until I get some answers.* I find that reassuring. There are two others at the table. From their demeanour I guess they are police officers not family members. They look differ-ent to the others at the table, less stunned. They appear watchful and detached and the man is wearing a blue shirt, like Colin, police blue. He leans across the table slightly, to say something to the man with folded arms. Still this man doesn't move, other than to slowly, almost distractedly, nod his head up and down a couple of times while keeping his head fixed firmly forward.

Activity at the front of the hall attracts the attention of the room. I can't see very well. Other than a single podium the room is on one level. A female officer is standing on the podium and introducing herself as the superintendent responsible for facilitating today's event. By straining my neck I can just about manage to see the top of a line of heads sitting on a row of chairs alongside the podium, but I can't properly see the senior investigating officers and guest speakers when they are introduced. They are on the same level as the rest of the room. There is also something wrong with the sound system. A man with headphones behind us is sending messages, waving his arms and trying to communicate lack of sound back here. People are indicating that they can't hear and there are mumblings that the sight lines are really poor. 'Did you get any of the names?' I ask James. He didn't. 'Why didn't someone think to install an adequate platform?' Without waiting for a reply I look around at frustrated faces attempting to get the technician's attention and after a bit of a kerfuffle the sound is adjusted. The struggle to see is too much of an effort so I give up and put my energy into hearing what is being said. At least the briefing papers set out who everyone is so we can put names to faces later.

Who's who and what their particular responsibilities are become clearer as we're taken through the events of the day from the police and emergency services' perspective. Being given an overview of the investigation and a detailed account of the process of rescue and recovery is helpful. It's useful having more context and some blanks filled in. Now and then I jot down a note but on the whole I just listen to a narrative of events with words and phrases that belong in detective fiction or police drama. I find I can listen and take notes quite impassively, as I might at a business meeting. In a way this is business. Detached, I note details of how many calls the Casualty Bureau took on the day of the bombings – 43,000 – and how calls were prime time and cost 40p per minute. I scribble details of the criteria of identification of the victims: primary being dental, DNA and fingerprints; secondary being jewellery and visual (I may have misheard the second word but I suppose it relates to scars and markings). Facilities at the mortuary are described and assurance given that the victims were treated with dignity and respect throughout. Throughout what, I wonder.

Significant timings are given: emergency services' response times; times between initial reports of power surges to confirmation of explosions; and so on. The time of each explosion is given. I add this information to the page even though the time has been etched on my mind for seventeen days. It is the demarcation time between life and death, a qualifying moment for those who survived and those who didn't. The speaker is talking about commuters being directed away from the underground system towards overground transport. His voice is fading. My thoughts are fixed on 08.50. Would Jenny have glanced at her watch a moment before impact? I place a question mark next to the time, knowing there will never be an answer. With the speaker's voice fading in and out of my consciousness I see Jenny looking up from her book, taking in the people around her and checking the time on her watch, a slight look of anxiety on her face as she realizes she'll be late for work. Then I see again an explosion which has no sound, only an image of a startled face with terrified eyes as Jenny is blown backwards out of the carriage still clutching the book in her hands. I've no idea if this is how it happened; it's only what I see in my imaginings. In the absence of detail I add my own. I hope as I hope every hour of every day that there was no time for her to be terrified.

The speaker's voice has changed and I am jerked out of my reverie back into the present, which in truth I never left, only slipped away from for a moment or two. And while I've been in that other place, daydreaming, I've been doodling. Questions marks, treble clefs and the letter J appear as repeated symbols along the foot of the page.

Before open questions begin we're told that a microphone will be moving around the room and that if we want to ask a question, please can we raise a hand and wait for the microphone to be brought to us. We're reminded to keep our questions general. We should not ask questions relating to our particular situation. Hackles are already starting to rise, mine included, especially when question after question has very little to do with Jenny's circumstance.

Many questions being asked are of a general nature but specific to one site and therefore not relevant to everyone else. A number of questions are from survivors of the bombings – that soon becomes apparent. A lot of issues seem to arise from the emergency services' response times and the handling and evacuation of commuters from the underground sites in particular. A woman is complaining that there was no one taking down names or details as people emerged from the underground. All these issues can be raised and yet I am unable to ask when Jenny's body was brought out from the tunnel in Edgware Road. There is too much going on here, too many perspectives. It's not helpful, bundling us all together in this way. I'm beginning to wish I hadn't come today and I can't bear this feeling of wanting to stand and scream at some of the complainants that they should just be glad to be alive. This is a mess and I don't want to be part of it.

A man near the front is on his feet; I'm not sure he's even waiting for a microphone. My view of him is restricted. He's not quite shouting but his frustration is evident: *'Please stop referring to this as an event or incident or MTI … it is murder! Please call it that!'* The enraged outcry is passionate and accusatory and sparks collective applause and foot stomping. I find the mass reaction alienating and disturbing. There is too much pain. It can't be contained. Somebody needs to calm the room down.

The response when it comes is apologetic and calming. There is wisdom in it, an acknowledgment of error and an understanding of sensitivities.

Despite the now more settled room, people continue not to get satisfactory answers to their questions. Many receive 'I'll investigate and get back to you' type of responses. This is not going down well and there are heated reactions to the lack of information available. Basic requirements for speakers to be seen and heard are not being met for at least a third of the room; someone is saying, 'It's clear we have got this wrong today … we'll get it right from now on,' but part of the sentence is lost in the hubbub. One of the speakers, I can't see who, is now giving a personal assurance that all the issues raised this morning will be addressed fully. I guess we can't ask for much more.

The questions James and I came with are not lifted from our paper and remain largely unresolved, but there are a few I am able to frame in general terms. One is a request for clarification as to what the problem was on the Bakerloo line that caused passengers to be diverted. After some conferring along the panel, the speaker's response is that he wasn't aware there was a problem. However, he has promised to investigate for us. Nor is the panel able to confirm whether the Edgware Road train was moving or static when the bomb exploded but they say they will sift through witness statements to find out. I am advised to liaise with FLOs on that question. It seems pointless to retort we already have and that this is one of the reasons we have come here today.

There are so many people asking so many questions and inevitably there are crossovers. I want to know if we will see copies of the identification report and gain some clarity on the process of identification. Someone else is asking a similar question. Some of these issues are in the realm of the coroners, of which there are four, one for each site. Apparently we will get this information if desired.

A considerable number of questions relate directly to the transport system. Again and again queries relating to the underground, busses, directions given to commuters at the time of the explosions, availability of CCTV footage, are being raised until someone reasonably asks why there isn't a representative of Transport for London here at the meeting – someone who *would* be able to provide much-sought-after information. 'Unfortunately' – and very frustratingly – 'there are no representatives from that body here today …' My head is aching with concentration. James is scribbling a question down on the page open in front of me, between my jottings and doodles: 'How powerful were the blasts i.e. whole carriage fatalities?'

Time for questions is running out. The superintendent is drawing the session to a close and taking a final question. There are voices, but I'm not aware of what is being said. I have something on my mind, something that has been troubling me all morning. I'm on my feet, my black-sleeved arm in the air. 'I'm sorry we've taken our last question.' The superintendent is saying from the front. I hear the voice but resolutely remain, arm upstretched, eyes fixed forward and holding my ground. One of the panel is pointing towards me, indicating he will take the question.

As it happens, it is not so much a question, more an outpouring of feeling. 'I have no doubt the intention of today was pure, and I can only speak for myself, but it feels like a PR exercise … You say this is not a day for specific questions; well I only have specific questions. I am a mother whose daughter was killed in this "incident" as you call it … You need to listen and engage and take me seriously, take all of us seriously. This is real; we in this room are real people whose lives have been irredeemably wrecked by what has happened. Real living people have been brutally slaughtered in an act of mass murder. Please do not speak in jargon and treat us like anything less than mature, adult human beings. Understand that we have lost beloved children, parents and partners but not the power of thought or intellect.'

Did I say all of that? Maybe I did, maybe I didn't. I might have said more, I might have said less. The room is quiet and I am on my feet so I must have said some of it. My retreat into my seat again is nothing if not abrupt, a defendant who has made a heartfelt final plea. In my embarrassment I hardly register a response, if indeed there is one.

Lunch is announced. The panel is dispersing and one of its members is skirting the edge of the room. I realize he is making his way towards our table. Now he is sitting down, introducing himself; thanking me for what I said and imploring me to believe in the sincerity of today's event. I do. The emotion in his face is like a gift. For the first time since stepping inside this building I feel a connection. He begins to explain, assuring me he would do his best to respond to specific questions. Then there's a girl in front of us. She's falling against the table and words are spilling out in a rush; she's saying over and over, 'I'm sorry, I'm sorry, I'm so sorry I'm here and your daughter is not'. I don't know who she is. I want to talk to the police officer; instead I'm standing up and moving around the table to the girl, holding her. She has put her head on my shoulder and I try to comfort her: an instinctive gesture.

Even as I offer comfort I want to cry out, 'I'm sorry too. I want you to be Jenny. Why must I hold someone else's child when the only child I want to hold is my own?' I don't know what to do with this embrace. Even as I say 'It's all right; it's all right,' I know it is not. Nothing here is all right, not the tall angular limbs or the bony shoulder blades beneath my hands or the antiseptic smell of shampoo. I want to be freed from the head resting on my shoulder, from the smell of it and from hair which is dark where it should be fair and short where it should be long. There is none of the soft warmth and ebullience so familiar in Jenny's embrace, no daughter curves moulding into mine, no familiar smell that I have known for twenty-four years and clung on to in a rolled-up bundle of clothes for the last two weeks. Repulsion is rising in my gut, 'Why can't someone come and take this girl away?' Black trousers and white shirt; Jenny would not be wearing these clothes. I have been given the wrong daughter to comfort, someone else's daughter. Yet I can't abandon her. So as she leans against me her whole body trembling, I do not push her away or reject her, even though she is not who I want her to be. While I stroke this stranger's back and feel the warmth of her body through the light fabric of her shirt I think of my own daughter lying in a coffin without warmth and without her mother. I believe this thought causes me to hold the girl closer even though my mind is far away from her. I have gone to Jenny, raised her from the coffin and drawn her to me. I have enfolded her in my arms, crooning as we rock backwards and forwards, 'It's all right, it's all right, it's all right.'

It seems the girl was on the Edgware Road tube, in the same carriage as Jenny. Other people are gathering around, all firing questions at once, eager to find out what happened, what did she see? The police officer has also stood up and is saying something to Colin, handing him his card and moving away from the table. I want to shout after him, 'Don't go. I need to talk to you,' but there are now too many people and too much confusion. I see all of this across the short divide of the table which is rapidly turning into a gulf. Through the growing throng I can only watch him go. The girl on the next table has come over and is asking about her brother and is joined by her mother, followed by her father who puts his arms around his daughter's shoulders urging her back. 'Come away,' he says, leading her to their table as the mêlée around the survivor risks becoming out of control.

My heart goes out to the survivor as I watch her walk slowly back across the room, shaking and head bowed, supported now by a friend or relative. I didn't even ask her name. For a moment I want to follow her, tell her again that it's all right but the truth is it isn't and from this moment never will be again. Someone lived while Jenny died and I don't quite know what to do with that stomach-churning fact.

Afterwards, when the commotion has settled down and we are restored to our tables, I think this is the most authentic occurrence of the day. The whole room is volatile, too volatile to mix survivors and newly bereaved together. It could have been catastrophic and for one young woman it very nearly was. We are all drawn into this ghastly tragedy but our experiences are very different. It is too soon to have such raw experiences with all the accompanying shock and trauma in one equal space. It was a mistake to bring us all together today, to be subjected to each other's distress.

I never want to feel again as I have felt in these last few minutes, sorry that someone else is alive when Jenny is not.

The family on the table next to us have left. I realize I know nothing about them except that a brother and therefore a son was killed with Jenny in the Edgware Road bombing.

In a way, lunch is a relief. Getting up and moving around provides a release from the tension of the morning. The light and elegant buffet is more a refreshment than a feast. I'm weighing up whether to take a bite or a complete mouthful of a portion of cucumber stuffed with prawn. 'This is a step up from a cheese and pickle sarnie,' I hear one police officer remark to his colleague as they pass our table, though from the look on his face I think he might have preferred a doorstep to the dainty offerings on his plate. The Met officer who came over earlier returned to say goodbye and add that he had given his details to my FLO so we could be in touch whenever I was ready. For now I must be content with that.

Not everyone has stayed for lunch and those who remain largely confine themselves to their own tables. I wouldn't know how to start 'mixing' today or asking about other people's stories. The FLOs listen while James and I mull over what we think has been positive about the morning and what has not gone down so well. We pretty much agree that the informative overview at the beginning was good. 'After that it would have been really valuable to have tailored site meetings with people who are directly involved in the ground work,' James is saying. I agree that surely it would have been perfectly reasonable to direct people to four distinct areas of the hall relevant to each of the specific bombing sites. That way we could have filled in many of each others' 'gaps' and at least have some discussion if not full enlightenment over specific questions, without the frustration of losing time discussing the other bomb sites. Well, hindsight is a wonderful thing and it is all too easy to criticize from a moral high ground but that doesn't stop us airing our frustrations between ourselves. By now I don't think either of us is in any sort of frame of mind to be acquiescent, though James calms down first.

'I guess this is a valuable day away from the investigation.' James's observation has quite a salutary effect. 'I expect they would rather be working on the case than here with all of us,' he adds.

Most of the panel have now left. One or two have stayed on to talk and have joined groups seated around tables. Some people have amalgamated to form larger groups, but the room is definitely emptying. Lunch is being cleared away and there is nothing here now to keep us from Edgware Road.

In the cloakroom on the way out I study my reflection in the mirror as I wash my hands. Make-up doesn't conceal the weariness in my face. If anything it makes it worse – a badly applied cover-up. I look as if all the life has seeped out of me. Maybe it's because I'm dressed in black, as though I'm at a funeral. The unbidden thought brings me up short. I'm going to have to think about it. I'm really going to have to think about my daughter's funeral. I stare at my reflection above the washbasin for a time, communing with my own image. My hands are grasping the edge of the basin as if drawing some kind of fortitude from the cold stone. The funeral must be filled with beautiful music and poetry and requiem; not celebration. Jenny's life is too soon ended, far too soon and brutally for celebration. Beyond that one determined thought I cannot or refuse to contemplate it at the moment. Instead I think of the off-hand jokey way I have passed on instructions for my own funeral. A piece of music heard on the radio, a poem or reading: 'I'll have this at my funeral.' My daughters raise their eyebrows and tell me to write it down! Children expect parents to say such things and laugh it off. Children tend not to say such things to parents. They are generally too young and too full of life, as Jenny was.

The door opens with a grind, breaking through these funereal thoughts. A woman in a green jacket barely glances at me before passing into a cubicle. I recognize the jacket from one of the tables in the hall. I recognize the jacket though not the wearer. The lock on the door clicks into place as I finish washing my hands and turn towards the hand-dryer. By the time my hands are dry and I've fiddled about with lipstick and a brush for a bit the woman has left the cubicle and joined me at the washbasin. We catch each other's eyes in the mirror and exchange a polite smile, nothing more. I leave as she is leaning slightly over the sink towards the mirror applying lipstick. Had this been a wedding I might have spoken; so might she. As it is, what can we say? *Have you lost someone? Were you there?*

The approach to Edgware Road tube station is cordoned off. Police are in attendance and as Colin attempts to turn the car into the street a uniformed arm is raised, clearly indicating that we should go no further. Wendy is out of the car and speaking to the officer before the car has come to a complete stop. The cordon is removed to enable the car to pass through. All the way here, from the Horticultural Halls to the traffic lights at the junction where we turned off from the main Edgware Road, the car has been abuzz with lively chatter as we sifted through the morning's briefing. Now all talk has stopped and we are alert to the change in atmosphere. Although we are still in the car I am aware of the need to be calm, to breathe deeply. Neither James nor I speak while we absorb information that the car will park in the street away from the entrance to the station. We will be escorted the short distance to the station. There are media and TV news cameras across the road from the entrance. They will not approach us unless we wish to speak with them. Are we OK with that?

'Yes.'

'Keep walking forward and keep your eyes on the entrance. We will walk one on either side of you both.'

I am afraid. Not of walking along the road to the tube station but of what I might find when I get there, or more to the point what I might find in myself when I get there, how I will be. I try not to show this. So far today, for the most part, I have been calm, reasoned and fairly articulate. Now I'm trembling. 'In fear and trembling stand . . .' words of a hymn that suddenly hit the spot and fill my being like an unbidden and unwanted prayer. I do not want to lose control, crumble or become a sobbing wreck. I want to get inside that tube station. See the place where Jenny's life ended. This is what I'm here for. I will not allow fear and trembling to get the better of me.

'The flowers.' The urgency in my voice is immediately stalled when I see Colin has retrieved them from the boot of the car.

So it may be with a vestige of fear and trembling but also determination that I prepare to move towards Jenny's place of death, side by side with her beloved James.

'Ready?' Colin has positioned himself on the outside of the pavement nearest the road.

'Yes.'

We're on our way, stepping out along the street; sunflowers, bold and gold and yellow leading the way. I see it as though I am outside my body or in a dream.

A black skirt with a floaty handkerchief hem is light and airy about my legs. On my feet are open black leather sandals; toenails are painted red. I'm wearing a black fitted stretch top with a v-neck and three-quarter length sleeves. Around my neck is Jenny's silver necklace, a figurative tear drop. On my right wrist are my silver comedy and tragedy mask bangle and Jenny's silver rope bangle. On my left wrist is a plain round watch on a brown leather strap. On the fourth finger of that hand is a silver ring with an oval moss agate stone which I bought with my first pay packet when I started nurse training over thirty years ago from an antique shop on Park Row in Bristol. If you hold the ring up to the light you can see the moss inside the stone, otherwise it just looks like a dark moonstone set in silver. On the fourth finger of my right hand is a silver ring of contemporary design with one large and two smaller topaz-type stones inset which I found on a stall in Covent Garden Market about two years ago. Greg was with me. We paid fifty pounds for it and I have worn it more or less ever since.

These are the details I focus on as we progress along the street neither hurrying nor lingering, merely putting one foot in front of the other. I try not to think about what might lie in wait beyond the entrance to the tube. Instead I fixate about rings on my fingers and bangles jangling about my wrist; until the rhythm of putting one foot in front of the other has had a grounding effect and I can take in more than my own façade.

There are buildings on either side of the road and other façades. As we walk I have a curious sense of being in both the past and the present. This was the scene on television. The approach to the station was chaotic then, loud with sirens, excited journalists and commuters. I can hear voices and voices over voices shouting. I can see dazed anonymous faces stumbling out from the entrance, the same entrance gaping wide and open at the end of the road, coming closer with each step we take. Marks and Spencer! Familiar M&S where the injured and dazed were tended, given water to drink. For a few hours this store became a place of sanctuary, an improvised field hospital. The scene is full of images, people leading and being led, people helping and being helped. This is the aftermath of disaster; spectres here for all time – all my time anyway.

The store is closed and shuttered. The images are left behind and the street is quiet again, with only our footsteps echoing along the empty pavement. Our small procession passes a large bronze sculpture of a man with a ladder. I don't understand the relevance and there isn't any time or reason to look more closely as we have arrived at the entrance to the station. A small collection of journalists and photographers are grouped just beyond the entrance, on the opposite side of the road. 'Take no notice,' I hear Colin say. But they're not bothering us.

And so we pass through the entrance into the station, nodding a greeting to the police officers in attendance. Here is a sense of déjà vu for this is the tube station I used on my daily commute for the three years I lived and worked in London in the 1970s. It is a bleak irony that has brought me back here now. A small group of people, underground staff I think, are standing in a formal line. Tentative smiles and sympathetic eyes greet us. A man introduces himself as a Transport for London representative and conducts us along the walkway, around a bend in the corridor and through the line of ticket barriers. Then we are on the main concourse, a wide flat area with flights of steps at either end leading down to the platforms.

'Would you like to lay your flowers?' Colin is asking.

'In a minute.' I want to look first.

In all the time I used this tube station I don't remember taking one second to look at my surroundings. They weren't important, merely the packaging around a means of getting from A to B. The steps on either side of the concourse are vaguely familiar. I would not have taken any notice of staff about their duties, or the tubs of greenery and plants – if indeed they were in place all those years ago. I remember stone and concrete and green paint and a ticket barrier, and rushing headlong up and down those steps with all the other commuters, pushing and jostling my way through. Which is how, I imagine, it would have been for Jenny.

There are already some flowers propped against the wall in the centre between the two flights of steps. James and I take our flowers and lay them alongside other bunches of flowers, red roses, white roses and sunflowers. Then a card for Jenny with all our love, so much love, is placed tenderly amongst the sunflowers. Straightening up and looking down at the card nestled amongst the sunflowers I see Jenny nestled in her cot, sleep-filled and her hair a tangled mass of golden curls.

We are escorted down to the platform by the station manager who was on duty on 7 July. As we walk down the twenty-odd steps he says very little, taking his lead from us. None of us needs to say very much at the moment.

At the bottom of the steps the stillness is arresting. There are no trains. Apart from benches and billboards the platform is empty. Down here all life and activity is at a standstill. Time and even air seems suspended. I am not aware of feeling any emotion; no anger, no passion, no rising tears. I am only aware of stillness; a grey stillness that reaches right into my bones. I don't want anyone to speak or say anything to disturb the balance and nobody does. The station manager has stepped back, enabling James and me to walk along the platform in our own time and at our own pace, which we do. At first we stand together but then move apart, each of us alone with our own thoughts. There is nothing for us to do here, except to stand and stare and build pictures in our minds.

Where would Jenny have been standing? Would she have been waiting on the platform as the train pulled in or would she have come running down the steps and jumped into the nearest carriage? After being diverted from the Bakerloo line, if indeed that is what happened, Jenny was already late. If her text 'Bakerloo line screwed', means what we believe it means, then she was most likely rushing. Guesswork and piecing together fragments and reasoning. With a heavy heart I accept it is unlikely I will ever get a full picture of the last minutes of her life, other than what I conjure up in my imagination. James has moved back to stand at the barrier close to the end of the platform nearest the steps. When I join him he brings up the subject of film footage, so I guess he's thinking along the same lines. 'The CCTV footage might show where Jen was standing.'

'We can ask.'

'The police won't have time to look but I could.'

This is not the first time that James has brought the subject up. He has an idea that if he could sit and wade through the tapes he would spot Jenny. 'They could put me in a secure room with a police officer.' James doesn't believe this will happen any more than I do but that's not the point. The point is that we are grasping at anything that will reveal Jenny's crucial last moments.

From the barrier we can look down along the track and into the tunnel. By leaning forward we can peer into the grey dustiness. There isn't much to see, only grime and cables and the brick wall of the tunnel. Tracks lead into the distance, around a bend and out of sight. This place holds the key; it holds Jenny's last breath, her final moments and has a story to tell. Yet I can see nothing, nothing at all to give me any clues. I have the framework of a jigsaw puzzle but not its centre. This realization is almost my undoing and I can no longer stand and stare.

I want information.

The point of impact was the second carriage, the station manager explains. Ten seconds into the tunnel the explosion occurred. As the bomb detonated a train was travelling in the opposite direction, coming into Edgware Road from Paddington.

'Where would the second carriage be?'

We're shown the position of the carriage in relation to the platform, before the tube moved off into the tunnel. I visualize the length of it and where Jenny might have been standing or sitting.

'Do you know how many people were in the carriage?'

'I'm afraid I don't.'

'Presumably it would have been quite full as it was still rush hour?'

'Yes.'

I wish I could see further into the tunnel, to the point at which the bomb was detonated and where Jenny's life was ended. 'Is it possible to go into the tunnel?' The question has tripped off my tongue before I can consider the logistics and it is no surprise to learn that of course the answer is 'no' due to health and safety and no one here having the authority to give that kind of permission.

At the top of the stairs is a large map of the underground. There are other staff members nearby.

'We don't understand why my daughter was even on this train. She was travelling in completely the wrong direction for work. She should have been travelling away from Paddington.'

'Where was your daughter heading?' Another man has come forward. A small group of us are now standing in front of the under-ground map.

'Tottenham Court Road.'

'She was probably heading back through Paddington to Notting Hill to pick up the Central line which would take her straight down to Tottenham Court Road.'

Here, at last, is a spark of illumination which emits a chorus of 'Ahs' from James, Colin and me. While we're grouped around the underground map I ask if anyone knows what the problem might have been that apparently caused Jenny to switch from the Bakerloo line to Circle and District. One member of staff believes there was a fault on the Piccadilly line, at Piccadilly Circus, affecting the Bakerloo route that morning. There's more explanation and pointing out on the map as we're shown where the Piccadilly line and Bakerloo line cross.

'Would there have been an announcement advising commuters to seek a secondary route?' We're told that it will be a simple matter to find out more exact details from central control.

Before we leave I want to have one last look into the tunnel that Jenny passed into en route to her death. If only I could see further inside. No matter how far I lean across the barrier, I can't see far enough. Tunnels, barriers, restricted views; right now they all stand as metaphors in this dark and horrible deed and my quest to find out more, know more, and see more. Perhaps now is not the time. This is quite a calming thought as I stare into the tunnel. Perhaps this is a time for merely 'being' in this place with Jenny. Leave the information-gathering for later, a little voice is saying inside my head. So I continue to gaze into the tunnel and think of Jenny with a heart full of love and sadness, longing to be in that place with her so she was not alone; fold my arms around her and take her back inside myself. These longings that I have had so many times in the last two weeks are stronger now that I am here, so near yet so far from the place where her life was snatched from her. I had thought there was no room in my heart for anger because I was too full of sadness. Yet, standing here, looking into the tunnel, the shadowy face of a stranger intrudes. A stranger who has come into our lives and did not know or did not care what beauty he was killing. And I am angry.

Another member of staff is speaking. 'If you come over to the other platform you can see further beyond the tunnel, to the point at which the two tubes passed.' As we follow him back up the steps and over to the platform on the other side, it does not occur to me that I will return here again and again in the weeks and months and years to come. Today we have the station to ourselves; in the future it will be full of people about their travel. Ironically, this is a luxury, to be able to stand quietly at the barrier on platform 4, lean over to peer into the tunnel, count ten seconds, pause and move away. We will not be so fortunate in the future when the station is back to normal. James and I walk back up the steps, cross the concourse, and down the second flight of steps on to platform 2. Here we stand at the barrier and are shown the tunnel beyond the bend to where the tracks criss-cross and straighten out. Our guide points into the distance to where the two tubes would have passed and where the bomb was detonated.

What does occur to me as we leave the tube station, politely declining to speak to the waiting media, is that this has become a special place. The mystery of life and death is contained within these walls. The abundant humanity of the people who work here, who witnessed so much of the aftermath of the dark and horrible deed, has impressed itself upon me greatly. In the space of an hour, Edgware Road Circle and District line has become a sacred place.

On the way home the car is quiet. James and I look out of opposite windows. *Finlandia* is playing in my head. I have no idea why, although

I've listened to it many times. There is something defiant and strengthening about the piece. Maybe that's why it's come to mind now. 'It's a symphonic poem,' I can hear Jenny saying. I never quite understood the difference between a symphony and a symphonic poem, though Jenny tried to explain. A symphony is made up of several movements and a symphonic poem is one continuous interpretive movement. *I think I'm beginning to get it, Jenny.* Today began as a symphony and ended as a symphonic poem. The day has contained many movements and much poetry, from awakening to turbulence to stillness and awe.

I wonder if the dead can send music to the living. If they can I think Jenny is sending all this music to me and I thank her for it because sometimes music is better than words. She would understand that.

Chapter 8

Lament

SLAUGHTER OF THE INNOCENTS

A voice was heard in Ramah, wailing and loud lamentation, Rachel weeping for her children; she refused to be consoled, because they are no more

MATTHEW 2:18

Ever since leaving Edgware Road yesterday I have felt as though a chunk of me was left at the entrance to the tunnel. My body has come back but my heart remains underground. Looking out of the bedroom window I am not seeing the garden but peering deep into the tunnel, imagining Jenny lying dead or dying, over and over like a video on continuous replay. The impulse to go inside the tunnel is strong, as if by doing so I could somehow reach her. Debating the issue last night over supper with Vanda, Stef and James, I was convinced there must be a way to achieve it. By the time I went to bed I was prepared to drop everything, delay plans to return to Bristol yet again and go back to the station before it re-opens. I would sign any amount of disclaimers, turn up at 3 a.m. or whatever time maintenance work is carried out, anything just to walk inside the tunnel to the spot where Jenny's life ended. Last night all my arguments sounded perfectly reasonable. Health and safety restrictions were ridiculously bureaucratic and inflexible. In the cold light of day I can accept a more balanced view. Even so, I find I am responding to this latest hurdle in much the same way I have responded to advice over viewing Jenny's body: like a compulsive terrier.

Such thoughts need to be shaken off for the time being. This morning I am going home, back to Bristol. There is nothing to keep me here now. Or perhaps it's more truthful to say I can no longer justify remaining. With Jenny's body already in Bristol and a funeral to plan, my time here is over. I am reconciled to going. This house has been my shelter but it is time for it to be restored to its family, just as I must be restored to mine. My bag is packed and the house scanned to ensure nothing is left behind, not even a toothbrush. Nothing, that is, except the story this house has to tell.

Before I leave there's just enough time for one last amble around the outside of the house which inevitably includes a final pause on the swing.

Today feels like a rite of passage. One stage is ending and the next stage about to begin. How will I do it? How will I make the transition? Since I've been here life has changed, life and me with it. That was determined the instant the bomb was detonated. Greg, Lizzie, Thomas, my parents, friends, are waiting for me to return. The trouble is I'm not sure who is returning. I doubt I can be the wife and companion that Greg needs and I'm frightened of not being the parent Lizzie and Thomas deserve. Jenny's death has ripped through us all and we are going to have to wait and see where grief takes us. The shape of our family has changed. There is a missing element that cannot be repaired or replaced. I am going back to a place that I can no longer locate as home in the same way as when I left it. I am returning to a vicarage, a dwelling place. Right now, home is somewhere between the family of my childhood and an underground tunnel. Everything in between is a muddle.

Lament

Backwards and forwards, backwards and forwards, my thoughts sway in motion with the swing. This house will be hard to leave. I will be back to visit but it will never be the same place it has been over these two and a half weeks. It has been not so much a household as a holding house. Waiting, fear, brokenness, shock, hope, despair, and a fountain of tears have been contained within this place in loving company and hospitality. Tucked away around the side of the house this swing has been the calm corner. With its rough-hewn seat and sturdy ropes it has provided a retreat for solitude and quiet, where battered spirits have been cradled and gently rocked in the shade of the overhanging tree. I am sad to leave it. The swing comes to an abrupt halt. I have brought it to a halt as I have brought my time here to a halt. It is time to go.

'Have you got everything?'

'Yes, I think so.'

Vanda picks my bag up and walks out to the car with it. My car, which she is driving us back in. On the back seat is a pile of newspapers chronicling the past seventeen days. Next to it, a carrier bag of sympathy cards.

'This is a bit different to when I arrived,' I say to Vanda as we get into the car.

'Yes, I'll never forget it.'

And I will never forget a moment of my time here. It's as if the first intense movement of a great symphony is drawing to a close, the last few notes fading away as we fade away from the house, away from the drive and settle in our seats for the journey ahead.

We're outside my parents' house. Vanda has wrenched the handbrake on. The sound is final. We have reached our destination.

Stepping out of the car and stretching I glance around at the familiar garden, unchanged from when I was last here. The noisy clunk of the metal gate as it is opened hasn't altered, nor has the well-tended lawn. The old hydrangea bush is still bursting with large pink and blue heads of lusciousness. Rose bushes lining the path from the gate to the door are their usual display of pink and red and gold. My mother's annual mass of sweet peas are growing profusely up the side of the garage. Shades of pink, purple, cream, white and rich deep red cover the wall with glorious colour. For a second I could believe that nothing has changed. Then the front door is opened. An ensemble of white hair fills the doorway. Mum, Dad, Auntie Karina, Uncle Jimmie.

There's relief in all their faces and warmth, real warmth in their embrace. The four of them are a welcome sight, looking fresh and summery, completely together. If I had expected any of them to have fallen apart I should have known better. My father's greeting extends to patting my back in a gesture I remember from childhood which translates as 'come on, come on' and 'it's going to be all right'. The combined scent of sweet peas, the aroma of roasting lamb and fresh mint wraps itself around us as we step into the hallway. A bunch of sweet peas stands in a vase on a cupboard just inside the front door. 'The sweet peas are lovely,' I say to my mother, lifting the vase to my nose to breathe in the scent.

'I picked them this morning; there are loads this year. You must take some home with you.'

They return seamlessly to what they were doing before we arrived. Karina is chopping mint, Dad is setting the table and Jimmie pouring drinks. As Mum makes her way back to the kitchen, leaving me to sniff away at the sweet peas, it occurs to me that she is putting her own grief on hold today, concealing it in order to look after her returning daughters.

Lament

Scenes of Bristol mingle with family pictures on walls around the house. A framed picture of Brunel's ship the SS *Great Britain* is hanging in the hallway at the foot of the stairs, a gift from my sister and brother-in-law following their wedding reception.

S.S. Great Britain
Off Bristol, being warped out of Avon Dock, 24.1.1845

The picture shows nothing of the struggle to get the ship there, of how it got stuck in the floating harbour between dry dock and the river, or how stones needed to be removed from the lock wall to ease the ship through into wider waters. It shows only the great ship floating in the river Avon a century and a half ago after being hauled like an oversized baby into the world.

I've always thought 'warped' to be an odd term. If it means hauled then why not say so? Looking at the picture now I'm changing my mind. 'Warped' suggests more than hauling. Distortion: a distortion of the framework needed to haul the ship through. I want to call my family, tell them to stop what they're doing and look at the picture with me. If I gathered them all around this picture now and said: Look at it with fresh eyes, can you see the connection? Can you see how we too have been 'warped' into this place? would they get it or think I was losing my senses? They would probably wonder why I was bothering with such triviality and part of me is wondering that myself. This is either a moment of madness or an epiphany, and it's probably unwise to try and decide which. There is just something in that picture that is niggling away at me and it has to do with the scene in this house at the moment, which shows nothing of the struggle of getting here, only the arrival.

Baby pictures follow on from the ship, evenly spaced frames on the wall leading upstairs, a portrait of each grandchild on their first birthday beginning with Jenny. Five chuckling faces, podgy fingers and bare feet waiting to be tickled belie the fact that anything could possibly be warped here.

The sitting room is the same as everywhere else: tidy, undisturbed. My father's current book is on the cabinet next to his chair and his paper opened at the crossword but neatly tucked away. In these surroundings there is no sign of the turbulence we are all experiencing. My mother's and my aunt's way is to be occupied; work, keep busy, control that which can be controlled. If the garden was neglected, dust an inch thick and cushions and papers scattered about there may be a sign of something amiss but then it would not be my parents' home and that would be even more disturbing. Salvation by order and routine has its merits.

Uncle Jimmie hands me a drink. 'Taste that and tell me if it needs more gin.' I can't help smiling at the unlikely prospect and after taking a sip assure him that the drink is poured to perfection.

I take my drink into the kitchen where Vanda is talking to Karina. Mum is occupied at the oven, carefully removing a large roasting tin containing the sizzling leg of lamb.

'Can I do anything?' I ask.

'No, it's all ready, just waiting for the potatoes.'

I feel sad watching her. Since leaving Anglesey I have unintentionally deprived her of a closeness and involvement in things. Of all people, I should have kept her close. Beyond Greg and me, this is the person most immersed in Jenny's young life. I can see Jenny now, sitting on a high stool at this kitchen unit, wrapped in Grandma's big apron helping make cupcakes and covered in cake mix, unlike her sister Lizzie who could apply herself to the same task and come away as clean as when she started. Even at four and two years old they were messy cook and tidy cook. Death is messy and I don't think any of us is going to get through tidily – if we get through.

Dad is opening some red wine. 'You can put this on the table,' he says, handing me the bottle.

Mum adds, 'There's white already opened in the fridge. You can take that in as well.'

In the dining room Dad has finished setting the table, which is spread for a delayed Sunday lunch, a homecoming lunch. Crystal glass, the best silver cutlery, place mats depicting old English pubs, and two wooden wine coasters are laid out methodically on a large white embroidered tablecloth. Above the table, hanging on the chimney-breast wall, is a print of Brunel's Clifton suspension bridge straddling the Avon gorge, one of Bristol's most famous landmarks and a stone's throw from the house I grew up in. Familiarity and foundation everywhere I look.

Everything is fine until we are all sitting around the table. Talk is safe. The only giveaway is the nervousness in all our voices. Everyone is walking and talking on eggshells. I am glad to be here yet I feel so out of place. Less than twenty-four hours ago I was standing with underground staff speaking of horrors and gazing into a dark tunnel picturing Jenny's last moments. Here we are now, an incomplete family gathered around a table remarking on how delicious the lamb is and exchanging news but not daring to go anywhere near the deep stuff. Despite this being one of my favourite meals, suddenly I am not hungry. I cannot bear to sit here for one moment longer and excuse myself.

Dad has followed me into the sitting room where I am curled up in an armchair next to the window. 'Aren't you eating your dinner?'

My reply to this most parental of questions is immediate and true. 'I'm not very hungry.'

As Dad settles into his armchair he doesn't pursue the subject or give any indication of wanting to. I don't need to watch my father to know that he has taken up his usual seated position of resting comfortably back in the chair, folding his arms across his chest, crossing his now quite spindly legs and looking over to the window, apparently deep in thought. His post-lunch behaviour is predictable. 'Leave the dishes, I'll see to them later, when I've had a rest,' is his routine announcement as he leaves the table after Sunday lunch. 'A rest' is sometimes to have forty winks but more often than not it is to sit in this way and finish his glass of wine which, as it happens, is nearly always full, in keeping with his attitude to life. It was once suggested to him that over the winter months it might be a good idea to move into the room at the back of the house as it was cosier. His response was that there was plenty of time to be cosy when he was in his coffin and that he liked being in the front where he could see people and watch the world go by. 'I don't have time to sit down anyway. Your mother keeps me too busy,' he frequently pretends.

There is none of this repartee between us now. Having my father near, not speaking, not even acknowledging my presence, is comforting. I don't give any indication that I am remembering him on a cold, crisp Boxing Day morning, pushing a shiny dark blue and chrome Silver Cross pram across the Clifton suspension bridge whilst reciting the bridge's history to his new baby granddaughter. Or remembering holidays when he would stride out wearing an ancient yellow sweater, filling his lungs with air, looking forward to a hearty pint of beer when he'd done. He'd be walking at such a pace that Vanda and I would need to half run to keep up with him. If age has diminished his stature, it has done nothing to dim his spirit. I would very much like to hug him and tell him how dear he is to me. Instead we both continue to look out through the window at the empty street.

I can only think back; I can't think forward. Perhaps this is what death does: opens up an album of images of things gone, lost to the past.

Being in this house is confusing. I can't stay here for much longer. I want to let go; crumble; be reassured by my parents. But I can't. I'm not five years old any longer. In good biblical manner I need to push away childish thoughts.

Just when I think I might leap up and run outside, Dad has decided to speak.

'How are you?' His voice is deceptively matter of fact.

'I'm OK.'

The carriage clock on the glass cabinet is suddenly loud and intrusive as if its insistent ticking is reminding us both to make the most of this time. 'OK' does not measure up to the question.

'I feel life is over. I can't imagine going on.'

'You will. You have the strength. Not today or tomorrow but you will rebuild your life.'

There's a pause before he continues and again his voice is matter of fact. 'But not me – I'll bide my time here now, until I join her. Jenny.'

Jenny. Dad can barely say her name. His voice is weak with emotion and his eyes full of tears. I could go over to him, sit on the arm of his chair and put my arm around his shoulders. I could tell him that we will all help each other get through this. I could but I don't. Instead I watch as he takes out a large white handkerchief to blow his nose. 'I should have gone first.'

Mum has put her head around the door. There's just a slight hesitation before she asks if either of us would like pudding.

'Not for me, love.'

'No thank you.'

The moment has passed but the exchange has left a truth in the room. As my father has assured me, I will go on. I will find a strength and a purpose; for myself and for my children, my surviving children. It is different for Dad. When he says that he will bide his time, I believe him. I don't mean, any more than he does, that he will lie down and die. He has too much spirit for that. He will bide his time pottering in his garden, doing small jobs around the house, occupying his mind and enjoying his daily tipples. But a spark of life has gone from him, been pounded out, a body blow from which ultimately he will not recover.

He doesn't realize it but my father, with his downy snow-white hair, thinning skin bruising easily with each new knock and graze, has given me a new strength and motivation to rise up out of this chair and press on, to much more than returning to the house I left three weeks and a lifetime ago.

My mother is outside, snipping away with a pair of scissors at the wall of sweet peas. I came upstairs to freshen up a little while ago and have been watching her from the window of my old bedroom. She's forming a little posy in her hand, turning the bunch round as she works, evenly distributing the colours as she picks each new stem. She packs as many as she can into her hand and has almost stripped the plants bare. In another day or two the wall will be covered in sweet peas and full of colour again. For now, this is her gift to her daughter, all the flowers she can carry.

Greg has opened the door. Any awkwardness is curtailed by a frantic little dog pushing in front of him and jumping up at me, crying excitedly and chasing round in circles. While I'm responding to the fuss Misty is making, Greg is wrapping Vanda in a bear hug and asking how the journey was. Greg and I hug in greeting but we do not enfold each other. Greg's embrace is tentative as mine is restrained. Then with the dog tearing around our feet we're over the threshold, almost tripping over the pile of shoes and trainers in the entrance lobby.

'Wait till you see the post,' Thomas warned me over the phone a few days ago. 'When we got back from Anglesey we couldn't get the front door open.' Surveying the load of post in the sitting room I see what he means.

Greg is behind me. 'I've opened some but there are so many. I thought we could open the rest when you came home. More arrive every day.'

'I didn't realize we knew so many people.'

'It's incredible, isn't it?'

If these cards are an indication of the reaching out and support of people beyond our immediate family and close friends then it is a wonderful expression of caring humanity and I know, even before they are opened, that I will treasure each and every one.

Standing in the middle of this room, I might have left it to go shopping a couple of hours ago. I do not feel that I have been away from it for three weeks. Yet the feeling of strangeness persists. Greg is trying to welcome me but I will not be welcomed. The wine-red and gold-coloured walls looked so rich and warm before I left. Now they just seem dark and oppressive, closing in on me.

The patio doors are wide open and the curtains pulled back. A radio stands on steps leading up to the garden with a few gardening hand tools scattered around and a trowel speared into the earth: a study of interruption. Greg will have heard the car in the drive, thrust the trowel into the ground, wiped his hands on his shorts and switched the radio off to come and open the door. This radio has followed Greg around the house and garden for as long as I can remember and it doesn't require much imagination to picture him sitting on the side of the patio wall with his hands weeding and his head tilted towards the radio, absorbed in the afternoon play or the test match.

'Where do you want these?' Greg is standing in the doorway with the pile of newspapers in his arms.

'They can go in the study for now. I'll sort them later.' I hadn't noticed that Greg and Vanda had gone back out to unpack the car, or that my case is in the hallway and the bag of cards propped next to it.

'Cup of tea?'

'Yes please. You've been gardening.'

'Pottering really; it passes the time.' His voice is flat and his shoulders slumped over as he turns in the doorway to go out to the kitchen. I am unable to do anything about it except watch his grief-stricken figure and wonder if either of us has the resources to help each other.

While Greg is making the tea, I have come upstairs to unpack my case. It doesn't take long. Once I've finished and opened the windows to let some air into the room I lie down on the bed for a minute or two looking around. We've only been in this house for twenty months and as the house was empty at the time we were able to decorate most of the rooms before we moved in.

The day we moved in, a few days before Christmas, it was pouring with rain. The churchwardens came to welcome us and offer help. The following day we went out and bought two large Christmas trees, one for the hallway and one for the front drive. One of the churchwardens organized an electrician so we could have outside lights on the tree. The parish welcomed us and I thought I could be a good priest-in-charge here; or vicar as most people like to think of parish priests. Jenny was not so sure. We drove over one day, soon after I'd been invited to consider moving here and before the appointment was made public.

'The house will be locked up but we can walk around the outside. It should be enough for you to get a feel for the place,' I say as we park the car.

Jenny is not saying very much. As we walk around the perimeter of the house, leaning over the fence to get a better view of the garden, I point out a pear tree.

'That's nice,' she says.

As I'm narrating the layout of the house to her and the fact that the back bedrooms look out onto a couple of lovely blossom trees she is climbing up to get a closer look at the garden.

'Do you want to walk over and have a look at the church?' I ask.

'Not really, unless you do.' I don't understand Jenny's reticence. It is so out of character.

'I've already seen it. We might as well go home then.'

On the way home we stop at traffic lights and when I turn to say something to her, she is looking out of the window with tears running down her face.

'Jenny, what on earth's the matter?'

'I don't know.' There a pause then, 'I don't want you to come here'.

'What do you mean?' I'm at a loss to understand where this upset has suddenly sprung from.

'I don't know. I just have a bad feeling about it. I know you won't be happy here.'

'What makes you think that?'

'I don't know. It's just a feeling. I'm being silly. Take no notice of me.'

It's impossible to take no notice of her. I don't like to see her upset. She looks so distraught. It doesn't matter how much I try to get to the bottom of her unease, she can't explain it. I don't

think she even understands the feeling herself. Tears trickle down
her face all the way home. If I catch her eye she smiles but it's a
sad smile and she doesn't say anything else. I am bewildered by
her overwrought response to what was quite a nice house.

However, on the subject of my happiness there, as it turns out, she was right.

The house was built in the 1970s and has lots of stained dark wood throughout, including window frames and skirting boards and the staircase. This room is the largest bedroom. I suppose estate agents might call it the master bedroom. The walls are painted a shade of creamy white, 'Calico' according to the label on the paint pot, with a feature wall behind the bed painted a deep lilac. The curtains are cream and the carpet is cream. The room is light and airy but the feeling of oppression has not lifted. There are fitted wardrobes on one wall in the same dark wood as the rest of the house. Pictures of the children hang on the walls, a first portrait picture of each of the children as babies, and a series of pictures taken in front of the Christmas tree year by year as they were growing up.

There will never be another picture of the three of them. The thought is like a dagger through my heart and I get off the bed, kneel on the floor and thump it with all my might. *Why, why, why?* Not expecting an answer; not getting one. I am too angry, too full of rage for tears. Greg has come upstairs, by which time I am standing again and straightening the covers on the bed. 'Tea's made.'

The ice is broken as we sit together with a cup of tea, opening cards, passing them backwards and forwards to each other to read. We are companionable in this at least and I guess that has to be enough for now.

Vanda is running a bath. I give her a bottle of bubble bath, a large bath towel and leave her to a long relaxing soak while I catch up on three weeks' worth of emails. Greg has gone to pick up Lizzie from a rehearsal so it's just the two of us in the house. The sound of water gushing from taps follows me downstairs, through the hallway and out into the lobby.

The study is a purpose-built extension on the side of the house. The door opens, as I open it now, on to a rectangular low-ceilinged room. Even on the sunniest of days it is necessary to switch a light on in here if I want to work. A single window at the far end of the room lets in limited light owing to trees outside, and there is only a very small window behind the door.

I don't move into the room immediately but remain in the doorway undergoing a kind of refamiliarization. Behind me is the lobby, stuffed with shoes, coats and umbrellas. Just inside the study door to my right is the piano, a dark-wood upright, set against the wall. A music stand is next to the piano and a collection of other instruments are scattered nearby. On the wall opposite the piano is a white sofa with a cream throw draped over the top and a small coffee table alongside. Children's artwork and posters of exhibitions and plays hang in clip-frames along the length of this wall. On the floor in front of the sofa is a large striped rug in bright primary colours with a chair at either end. This is what I think of as the meeting/music end of the study.

Fitted into the top left corner of the room is a computer unit. Next to this and centred under the window is a large old wooden desk. On top of the desk is all the paraphernalia of work: desk diary, a pot of pens and pencils, telephone and fax machine, and three-tier correspondence tray overstuffed with papers. A brown swivel office chair is in front of the desk. On the wall to the right of the window is the large parish photocopier, a blot on the landscape but there isn't anywhere else for it to go. This is the office end of the study. The wall linking the photocopier with the piano is filled with bookcases divided into sections on theology, drama, poetry and non-fiction. Filing waiting to be done, packs of photocopy paper and a box of files line the floor at the base of the bookcases at the office end.

Coming further into the room my steps don't take me immediately to the computer but to the piano. Jenny learned to play on this piano, so did I and so did my mother and aunt. Jenny's most recent graduation picture is propped against her metronome. The picture is still in its card frame with the insignia of the University of Bristol inscribed at the bottom. My fingers trace the letters before propping the picture back in its place and taking a step back. There she is, in her graduation robes at the symbolic gateway of her future. *This should not have happened, Jenny. It is wrong, so wrong.* The piano lid is open and ivory keys lie waiting to be played; a most unwelcome invitation that inspires nothing more than a hand reaching out to close the lid.

The water has stopped gushing which must mean that Vanda is in the bath. Outlook Express has sprung into action and emails are flooding into my inbox and I'm recognizing many of the senders' names without attempting to interrupt the flow of mail coming in. Then one stands out above all the rest and I can't open the box quickly enough.

Hiya,

How's your weekend been? Mine was really busy so I'm very tired now. Not such a good start to the week.

Friday night we went to James's department summer bbq which was really fun, except I hurt my back on the bouncy castle. They really aren't for big people! Then we went over to V & S which was also lovely but tiring because we hadn't fully

recovered from Friday. Managed to have a good catch-up
snooze when we got back on Sunday afternoon.

Bought The Magician's Nephew on Sat. £6.99 from W/stones.
I'll give you my feedback as soon as I finish it, I've got another
book on the go too. When's your next meeting about it and I'll
strive to have it done by then?

One of my friends sang in the choir at Sir John Mills' memorial
service last week and brought the order of service into work
with him the next day. It looked like quite a nice service, they
had a verse of a poem printed on the front cover which read:

> For life is a poem to leisurely read,
> And the joy of the journey lies not in its speed.
> Oh! Vain his achievement and petty his pride
> Who travels alone without love at his side.
> (The Traveller by Ella Wheeler Wilcox)

Nice sentiments!
What does your week bring you?
J xxx

Sent Monday 4 July, the morning I left for Anglesey. My hand is on the
mouse scrolling up and down the page to read and reread the email.
'What does your week bring you?' My other hand is clasped over my
mouth and my entire body is shaking and I can't stop reading the last
question. *'What does your week bring you?'*

I'm shouting while running from the study into the hallway and
then running back into the study because I don't want to leave the
email. My hands are shaking as I try to save it.

'What's the matter?' Vanda is calling out from upstairs.

'I've had an email from Jenny.' Still shouting.

'What?' She's rushed into the study.

'Look.'

'What am I looking at?'

'Here.' It's an email from Jenny. Read it.'

'Oh my God.' Vanda is standing behind me, reading over my shoulder.

'Do you know the poem?' she asks.

'No.'

Neither of us can stop reading the email.

'It's amazing.'

'I know.'

'When did she send it?'

'Monday, the day I left for Anglesey. She'd forgotten I wouldn't be here.'

'I thought you'd had an accident or seen a spider or something. I jumped out of the bath and ran downstairs.'

Now that I can tear my eyes away from the computer screen I see that Vanda is wrapped in a bath towel, dripping from head to toe with soapy suds around her ears and neck.

'I'm sorry. It was such a shock. You can go back to your bath now.'

'No, it's OK, I'll get dressed. I couldn't relax after that.'

While Vanda is heading off back upstairs I remain with the email. Jenny has sent me a poem; I so much want to believe that. It's like a final gift. She has conveyed something so beautiful and precious that I really want to believe that she is reaching out to me through it, caressing me. And then she asks, oh so casually, 'What does your week bring you?'

If only you knew Jenny, if only you knew.

Lament

My friend Fran has called in; she's going to give Vanda a lift to the station later. Meanwhile, the three of us are sitting on the floor drinking coffee, surrounded by cards and letters which we are trying to put into some kind of order. We are sorting into groups according to relatives, friends, colleagues, Jenny's friends, people I need to contact now with details of the funeral, and people I can write to later. There is a further smaller pile labelled 'particularly poignant'. The logic is that when I want to locate a specific card or sender, I will know which bundle to look in. Besides which, the activity is giving me something productive to do and I am more purposeful than I have been all day. Creating order out of the mountain of cards spread across the sitting room is oddly satisfying. It's a slow process as I keep stopping to reread messages. On top of the 'particularly poignant' pile is a card from an old university friend. He writes:

Dear Julie
You may struggle to remember me, so long it is since we last met ...

Of course it's obvious why I'm writing – and you must have a lorry load of these to get through/not get through. Given that I came from where I came from (Belfast) it is bitterly ironic that it is *I* who should be contacting *you* in such circumstances. Whilst I have known and been close to too many people maimed and killed in 'The Troubles', it never reached the appalling depth you're having to endure. For what it's worth, I'm so sorry.

It was a jolt to see Jenny's face on screen, listed as 'missing'. I met her only twice, years ago, but have never forgotten her. You'll just have to trust me when I say that I don't believe I've ever been in the presence of someone so positive and vibrant as her. Apart from the rest, your anger must be boundless.

There are those who say that a person never dies if there are people left behind who love them. If that's true, then, from what I remember and from all I've heard, Jenny will live forever.

Our thoughts and prayers are with you all – may God give you strength.

I do not struggle to remember the writer. I do struggle not to cry through every word.

Greg and Lizzie and I are together, on our own, for the first time since before 7 July. Earlier I phoned Thomas in France. I spoke to Sharon first who said they were all keeping an eye on Thomas and Mike was spending quite a bit of time with him. They were trying to keep busy and occupied and looking forward to driving to Italy for a few days at the weekend.

When I spoke to Thomas I thought he sounded a bit quiet.

'Are you all right?'

'Yeah, it's just really hot and I can't get cool.'

He was keen to know when we could go shopping for a suit to wear for the funeral. I assured him we would go and buy a suit the day after he came back from holiday. Then he brightened up a bit describing a water fight he and Mike and Martyn had after they'd erected a giant-sized paddling pool in the garden.

Lizzie is sitting next to me on one sofa. Greg is on the other sofa watching television. As soon as Lizzie and I sat down, the dog took it as her opportunity to nestle in between us, wriggling her little body until she was quite comfortable and quite sure of not being turfed off. She is sleeping soundly, gently snoring and making little yappy sounds now and then. 'She's dreaming of squirrels,' Lizzie says, stroking the dog's ears.

Lizzie has been quite low this evening. Rehearsals for the Edinburgh play are not going well. She is not happy with the play or preparations and, as a result, is having a few doubts about going. 'Everyone else seems to think the play is really funny but I think it's pants.'

I guess this is a measure of how Lizzie is feeling. Nothing is going to sit well with her at the moment, any more than it is with any of us. There is only one important aspect in our family in the here and now, one thing that matters. Everything else is insignificant. Trying to behave normally is impossible. We don't know what normal is any more. I say something along these lines to her, realizing the truth in it for me as well as for her. Normal for me has been dealing with the police or lying on a sofa in Hampshire watching the birds. I also know how I have reacted when someone has inadvertently said the wrong thing or when people are going about their daily lives as if nothing has happened. This prompts me to add, 'You mustn't blame people around you for how you are feeling. Jenny's death is not their fault.'

'Can I do something for the funeral?'

'Of course; do you want to read?'

'No. I want to do something that is just from me to Jenny.'

Neither of us can think of anything immediately. Painting the coffin, to symbolize Jenny, might have been an option but her coffin is made of the wrong sort of wood and for other reasons it's just not feasible at this stage.

'Did you choose the coffin?' Lizzie asks.

'No. It's the one Derek, the undertaker, took to London when he went to collect her from the mortuary. He took the best that he had. I wouldn't like to move her now.'

Thinking of Jenny in a coffin is really hard. It is not a place for the young. It is a place for people whose life has run its course and have exceeded their three-score years and ten. Even macabre conversations about coffins have become part of our new normality.

'Why don't you make a cover for her coffin?'

The idea seems to appeal to Lizzie and she begins weighing up how much time she would have to work on it before leaving for Edinburgh at the end of the week.

We end up talking about a picture Lizzie made for Jenny and James last Christmas, a collage of symbols and quotations from their joint disciplines of science, music and literature on an abstract sunflower background. Lizzie seems to have found her inspiration. As she says, 'It's a bit of a given.'

Greg has stood up; Misty is instantly alert, jumping off the sofa and up at Greg, sensing a walk in the offing. This is part of the nightly routine. Between 10.30 and 11 p.m. Greg will make a move, Misty's ears will perk up and as soon as Greg goes out into the hallway the dog scoots past him and waits impatiently by her lead. Tonight is no exception. I suppose there is a kind of normality in the house, even if it's restricted to the dog.

The dog is in her basket at the foot of the stairs. She's giving the illusion of being asleep but is really waiting for the house to be in darkness before creeping upstairs and trying her luck at finding an open bedroom door.

Greg is asleep and the bedroom in darkness when I go up so I think I will sleep in Jenny's room where I can have the light on and potter about for a while. It is not difficult to come into this room. I just wish there was more of Jenny in evidence. The room looks more like a spare room now, not the girlie, academic space it was when she lived at home last year. Manuscripts and scores of music would often be spread over the bed and scarves and necklaces draped over ends of furniture, and of course the ever-present stash of books and CDs overflowing from her small childhood bookcase.

Jenny has finished her master's dissertation and is preparing to go back to Reading.

Driving home after a funeral I think how much we will miss her around the place. After her initial unease over moving in here, she seemed to settle well, better than I have in a way. The reason for this may be her short-term occupancy. She has been here for less than a year, a demanding three terms of academic study with frequent visits back to James. I am greeted by shouts and activity as I open the front door. Upstairs the landing resembles a removal in progress. The loft hatch is open and Jenny is balancing on the ladder passing a box of children's books through the gap to Thomas. 'I thought you might appreciate having a spare room again,' Jenny calls down. 'Unless I'm home for a visit when I'll claim it back!' I laugh, reminding her that I'd used her room as the spare room since she left for university when she was eighteen. Even so, it is still distinctly Jenny's room to come back to with her choice of décor, her books and childhood relics about the room and her belongings filling cupboards and drawers. All afternoon, while I am working in the study she is crashing about and empty-ing her room of all excess baggage.

'Shall we have some music on?' I hear her say to Thomas. I can't hear his reply but a few minutes later Queen is blasting out from the CD player. Every now and then Jenny's voice joins in, loudly. Eventually I'm summoned upstairs and given a briefing of the afternoon's work.

Items that aren't returning to Reading with her are boxed up for storing in the loft, stowed under the bed or bagged up and taken to a charity shop. Apart from a couple of items of clothes she couldn't bear to part with, the wardrobe and chest of drawers were empty, as was the bookcase. Only her desk remains intact. 'I'll sort the desk drawers out another day,' she said, full of fun and pleased with her day's efforts. 'I've just left a couple of things around so you don't miss me too much and the room doesn't look too bare!'

The room looks as bereft as I feel. Although Jenny has been back for the odd night or weekend and the room has been in use as 'the spare room', it does not have an inhabited feel, more a sense of waiting for its next occupant. A bright yellow light shade is like a blob of sunlight draped from the ceiling. On the desk is a short stubby candle in a dish, the wick still white and unused. Next to that is a framed picture of Jenny taken on a sailing boat. Little wispy bits of blond hair have come loose from her ponytail and are curling around her smiling face. Dartmouth harbour is in the background and she's wearing a life jacket. Like a sudden shower of sea spray, tears have sprung from my eyes and are dripping all over the photograph. Because of the life jacket I have started to cry, because she didn't have a life jacket the day she needed one.

Inside the top drawer of Jenny's desk is a bundle of letters and cards. The uppermost card is a picture of a piano with a pair of girl's legs encased in keyboard patterned stockings. On the reverse of the card is printed 'Piano Legs'. I sent it to Jenny to cheer her on her way to a piano exam. A sticky Post-it label has come detached from it and slipped to the side of the drawer. On it Jenny has written: 'Special cards and letters etc. To keep!'

In the next drawer are pads of manuscript paper. The bottom drawer is filled with music magazines and theatre programmes. The drawers have been sorted and left tidy. It takes me quite a few moments to contemplate with a sad acceptance that Jenny has cleared out her own room and saved me the task of clearing it out after her death even had I wanted to.

I once took part in the Trinny and Susannah *What Not To Wear* style makeover television programme. In the early days when it was just getting going and I had barely heard of the now infamous duo or their programme, my daughters and my sister secretly nominated me to take part as a surprise for a landmark birthday. I knew nothing about their scheming or the furtive filming that was going on behind my back with my nearest and dearest and closest colleagues. The first I knew of what they had been hatching was one day in mid-summer when, at the end of a church service, as I stepped forward to give the blessing, the doors opened at the back of the church and coming down the aisle towards me were Trinny and Susannah and what appeared to be a host of people with cameras and other filming paraphernalia. It was a complete shock – though in hindsight I realized I had thought it was a bit odd for my entire family, including James, my sister and her family and my parents to all decide to come to my church that day. 'It's for Father's Day,' Lizzie had told me, who rarely darkened the doors of any church.

And when my colleague David made a big thing of referring to Trinity Sunday throughout his sermon, I just thought it was a joke I wasn't getting. Anyway, with my family and a surprised congregation smiling expectantly, Vicar David beaming and looking pleased with himself at having pulled off a coup, and Trinny and Susannah standing on either side of me waving a cheque for an entire new wardrobe, I agreed to take up the challenge of being 'made over'.

Within hours a television crew had taken over the house. Within days my new best friend was the director of the programme and within weeks I was a new person, inside and out, having had, despite moments of public humiliation, one of the most fun and rejuvenating experiences of my life.

Why am I remembering this now? Because standing here in Jenny's old room I am reminded of the day I left for London to begin filming for the programme. The previous day, members of the production team had bagged up my entire wardrobe to take it to London in readiness for filming the next day. I stepped out of the shower, wrapped one towel around my body and another around my hair and went into my bedroom to get dressed. I opened the cupboard door to decide what to wear and it was empty. The shelves and drawers were empty; my shoes were gone; even my underwear had disappeared. They had only left one set of clothes to wear that day. As I stood before the empty cupboard it was as if I had died. There was nothing of me there. Years and years of history in clothes wiped out. This would normally only happen when someone had died. When else would most people's wardrobes be completely cleared out? The sudden awareness gave me quite a jolt: it was an engagement with my own mortality.

I went on to have a great adventure. To use the language of my profession, I experienced a kind of rebirth into a part of me I had lost sight of. Jenny and Lizzie were wondrous through it all, delighting in seeing Julie, their mother, resurrected from beneath the proverbial black cassock.

I did not, could not imagine that two years later I would be forced to engage with my daughter's mortality. Until it happened it would have been inconceivable. It is still inconceivable to have arrived at this place. There are no thoughts of rebirth here. I am barely reconciled to her death. In a way I wish I could feel confident that she is even now embarked on a new adventure beyond this life as many of the cards downstairs affirm and assure. But I am not confident of that and I do not have any thoughts of the resurrection. Standing in her room amidst so much emptiness and absence I only have thoughts of Jenny's death and they are as dark as the sky outside. Lying in her bed, wearing an old pair of her pyjamas, I feel an absence of hope, an absence of anger, and an absence even of tears.

When I wake, the sky is still dark and the dog has crept on to the bed. I let her stay because her warm little body curled up at my feet is comforting.

Colin called first thing this morning. It's only my second day home but already I feel a bit cut off from our FLOs so it was reassuring to hear his voice on the phone. Colin explained that he had received a response from London Transport with regards to the problem on the Bakerloo line on the morning of 7 July. There was a defective train at Piccadilly Circus and the service was suspended between Paddington and Elephant and Castle in both directions between 8.15 a.m. and 8.30 a.m. He hopes to call again tomorrow with a response to the other questions James and I raised at the police briefing.

Fifteen minutes. A fifteen-minute technical problem led to Jenny rerouting her journey to the Circle and District line. Fifteen minutes changed her destiny. If it hadn't been for that defective train Jenny would not have been killed. After calling James to let him know and after telling Greg who shook his head in disbelief, I have come upstairs to get dressed. But I don't get dressed. I get back into bed and pull the covers over my head, wrapping them around my body and wrapping my arms around Jenny's bundle of clothes, holding them tight against my chest. Destiny! Well, Jenny certainly went out to meet hers.

Lizzie is calling me, wondering what fabric to use for the cover. She wants to make a start before leaving for rehearsal. I don't have a clue and suggest she calls my friend Bobby who is a textile artist. At least Lizzie has roused me from under the covers and by the time I've showered, dressed and come downstairs Lizzie has spoken to Bobby who has not only advised but offered to help her buy and dye the fabric.

'Bobby thinks natural calico might be best as it can be dyed or tie-dyed whatever shade I want.'

'What will you use for the design?'

'Fabric paint or pens.'

Thanks to Bobby, Lizzie has left for the day's rehearsal in better spirits than when she arrived home last night.

The tree outside Jenny's bedroom window is a beautiful almond blossom which looks so lovely and freshly alive when it blooms in early spring. Just as the tree is blossoming into its full gloriousness, a wind can come along and destroy it, stripping the branches bare. The white papery blossom covers the ground like confetti until it is blown away or turns brown and pulpy in the rain. Beyond the tree and garden are other gardens and rooftops. Across the way, not too far distant, is the church of which I am priest. I'm picking it out amongst the houses and second-hand car yard, trying to imagine the scene described to me when Jenny was missing: the flowers people took and left there; the vigils held night after night; prayers of hope uttered. I remember the moment, the final moment when all hope was stripped away with conclusive DNA and dental records. It is over. I cannot deny or pretend or languish any more. Turning from the window, I go through every bedroom, opening all the windows and propping doors open so the air can circulate; I repeat the ritual downstairs, working my way around the house until I get to the study. Here I take down my large Oxford Reference Dictionary and look up the word 'destiny'.

Do I believe in destiny? I don't think so, not in the clichéd romantic way it is often used. I do not believe that Jenny went out to 'meet' her destiny the day she was killed any more than I believe that her share of life was somehow appointed at birth. No, I will not subscribe to that and firmly dismiss destiny, fate, karma, kismet, or any other easy term that might suggest Jenny's death was somehow unavoidable when it happened. Destiny only becomes so when something happens in life to make it so. If Jenny had stayed in bed on the morning of 7 July, I do not believe that her life would have ended when it did. A defective train and defective humanity created Jenny's so-called destiny. I do not believe it was the destiny or fate of fifty-two people to die on the London transport system that day, nor do I believe that it was some kind of predetermined lot in life. To think in this way negates responsibility from human action and belongs in fiction. Four men chose to detonate bombs amongst a random company of travellers, having planned, plotted and rehearsed their action before killing, maiming and traumatizing their victims. That is not fate or destiny. That is premeditated slaughter. The deed must not be disguised. It must be named.

I've collected up a few books of poetry and a bible and have taken them into the sitting room. I also found an unused exercise book and have written in heavy underlined letters on the front: '*FUNERAL*'. Whilst in the study I telephoned Father John, our old parish priest, to talk about the requiem mass. He asked if I'd like to go and have coffee tomorrow. I said I would.

An hour later, I've done little except read poetry and the latest delivery of cards and letters. Turning my attention to the bible, trying to locate possible readings to incorporate into the funeral, I get caught up reading the story known as the Slaughter of the Innocents. In his anger King Herod orders every child under two years old to be killed. God, so the story goes, sends an angel to warn Joseph, the father of baby Jesus, to take his son and wife Mary and flee to Egypt. The baby Jesus is saved but all the others are massacred. This seems grossly unfair to me; if God could save one child, why not all? Or better still, why not just bump off Herod? I cannot think of God on this level. In fact, at the moment, I'm struggling to think of God at all.

While Mary and Joseph are counting their blessings in Egypt, 'a voice was heard in Ramah, wailing and loud lamentation, Rachel weeping for her children; she refused to be consoled, because they are no more.'

Cruel inhumanity, slaughtered innocence, the doomed and the inconsolable; the story writer did at least get that right.

I'm glad to break off and go into the kitchen and answer the phone. An old friend is calling to chat and see if there is anything she can do to help. We talk for quite a while, until I am assured 'at least she wouldn't have suffered'. I can't bring the call to an end quickly enough and afterwards noisily thrash around making a cup of coffee and feverishly dunking digestive biscuits. Even though I know the words were intended to offer comfort it doesn't stop me raging at the phone 'so that makes it all all right then!'

Music is soothing my crotchety spirits. I'm back on the sofa with Britten's folk songs playing, reading through the poem that Jenny quoted in her email and which I downloaded from the internet. After reading the poem a couple of times I put it to one side and look through the open patio doors on to the garden. 'Salley Gardens' is playing. I've lost count how many times I've listened to this over the last two weeks and it never fails to hit the mark. The punctuated phrase 'full of tears' seems to be more pronounced today.

The phone is ringing again. It's a bit of an effort to go and answer it but it might be important.

'Hello.'

'Hello. Is that Reverend Nicholson?'

'It is.'

'Reverend Nicholson, can I say how sorry I am for the loss of your daughter, um, um, Jennifer in the London bombings.'

'Who's speaking please?'

Somebody or other mumble, mumble, from the something or other news agency.

'This must be a very difficult time for you, Reverend Nicholson. Can you spare a few minutes to talk to me?'

'No. I'm sorry. Please can you go through the Bishop of Bristol's press office?' This is what the Bishop's press officer has advised us to say.

This time when I put the phone down, I don't yell at it but say quietly, 'We didn't "lose" Jennifer, she was stolen from us.'

I am in danger of losing something: a sense of beauty. I do not want this to happen. I do not want to be consumed by ugliness and angst and yet I cannot deny the feelings that rise up without warning and completely overwhelm anything else. There is such conflict raging inside me. I am besieged by feelings of absolute and impotent rage over what has happened to Jenny and I am afraid of the creeping shadow of darkness and disorder that is distorting all things. I do not want Jenny's loveliness that I hold inside to be contaminated by thoughts of her killer. He has already destroyed her body. I will not allow him to destroy her spirit. I do not want the grotesque shadow of the bomb to blot out the radiance of Jenny and the beauty in the world around. I cannot allow that to happen. I must not allow the monster to suffocate the angel and stop me from recognizing beauty and love when it is in front of my eyes. I must find a way of delighting in the squirrel scurrying up and down the tree outside and not see it as an intruder in the garden.

The doorbell is ringing. For a moment I'm unsure whether or not to go and answer it. Greg would have his key and Lizzie isn't due back until the end of the day. Curiosity gets the better of me and as soon as I see it is my friend Rosey on the doorstep all is well and I almost drag her inside the house with me.

It is therapeutic to sit in the sunshine talking and catching up. Rosey and I have shared such a lot of fun and laughter since we met on the first day of theological college. We have consumed much gin and undergone much heart-searching together. She came to visit two or three times when I was in Hampshire but this is the first time that we have talked on our own.

'It's been difficult to get close to you.'

'What do you mean?'

'I think you've put up a barrier.'

'I'm not aware of it but you're probably right.'

'Is there anything you need?'

'I can't think of anything.'

'Shall I bring a meal over for you all?'

'That would be lovely, thank you.'

'I expect it feels strange being home?'

'Yes, it does. I miss my sister's garden. I liked watching the birds. It was soothing.'

When Rosey has left I telephone my mother and ask if they would like to come over tomorrow afternoon and stay for something to eat. The music has stopped so I change the CD to Beethoven and settle back into the sofa, reflecting on the conversation with Rosey. I am aware that we were a very intense family unit, especially in the first week or so. Perhaps I did shut myself off from the rest of the world there. Perhaps I am still shut off, inside. People are offering comfort and I will not be comforted. I am trying to hold things together but maybe it would be easier for people around me if I was a crumbling heap. What Rosey has perceived as a barrier, I would describe as self-preservation.

I am suddenly very tired of battling with my conscience and feel I could sleep for a week. The doorbell is being rung again, piercing through the music and my drowsy state. When I open the door Rosey is standing in front of me bearing a large bird table and packet of bird feed. 'I thought it might attract some birds for you to watch.'

'THE TRAVELLER'

Reply to Rudyard Kipling's 'He travels the fastest who travels alone'

Who travels alone with his eyes on the heights,
Tho' he laughs in the day time oft weeps in the nights;

For courage goes down at the set of the sun,
When the toil of the journey is all borne by one.

He speeds but to grief tho' full gayly he ride
Who travels alone without love at his side.

Who travels alone without lover or friend
But hurries from nothing, to naught at the end.

Tho' great be his winnings and high be his goal,
He is bankrupt in wisdom and beggared in soul.

A Song For Jenny

Life's one gift of value to him is denied
Who travels alone without love at his side.

It is easy enough in this world to make haste
If one live for that purpose – but think of the waste;

For life is a poem to leisurely read
And the joy of the journey lies not in its speed.

Oh, vain his achievement, and petty his pride
Who travels alone without love at his side.

ELLA WHEELER WILCOX

CHAPTER 9

Funeral Song

Despite everything, life is full of beauty and meaning

One-thirty a.m., sitting up in bed surrounded by hymn books attempting to choose hymns for the funeral. A library of hymns and I can only identify five that even begin to work. Either the words are wrong or the tune is wrong. I want poetry and mystery but can only find doctrine and dogma. Hymns where an appropriate theology and humanity connect are proving difficult to find. One verse works and the next throws it all into disarray. There is a conflict between many of the hymns I have loved, that Jenny has loved, and the words on the page before me now. This is my problem. I am reading verses as I might read a poem; carefully absorbing, scrutinizing meaning. Phrases are becoming more and more unpalatable. There are only a few that I can contemplate for Jenny's funeral. If I was choosing hymns in antic-ipation of my own funeral, or my parents' or friends' I could find suit-able hymns, beautiful hymns. I have no doubt about that. If Jenny had died in my arms, gently, I might have been able to find a hymn – a gentle hymn for a gentle end. To put it bluntly, there isn't a hymn with a theology for my 24-year-old daughter blown up by terrorists.

Pushing the books away I lean over to switch the CD player on and select a disc from a small pile on the floor next to the player. The disc is in a plain plastic sleeve, a home-made compilation pushed through the letter box today. An attached note lists a selection of Russian orthodox music and Ukrainian folk music. The handwritten note ends with the message: 'with our fondest thoughts and prayers'. Switching off the light and pulling the covers up around my neck my body is cocooned as a single bass voice begins, low and deep. The sound is rich and full and could be rising from the earth instead of the electronic device on the floor. Other voices join in, so subtly I cannot tell them apart. The sound is beyond singing and invokes the smell of incense and holy icons and candlelight. A resonance wraps itself around my head, mass drone-like intoning filling my ears and drawing me into a deep place where I can close my eyes and not think beyond this gift of music.

The mechanical whirr of the CD having finished wakens me. Reaching an arm out from under the cover to switch off the machine, I am not sure if I have been sleeping or hypnotized by the music. At a guess I would say it was 3 a.m. or 3.30 but tiredness prevents me from turning over to check the time. My eyes blink open and closed against the shadows and shapes of the dark room. I'm jolted further awake by a thud which, as I soon realize, is a hymn book dropping off the bed on to the floor. It is difficult to move my legs. To one side is the hard lumpy feel of books and to the other the curled-up mound of a sleeping dog. My head is immediately full of hymns again and the subliminal echoes of sacred chant and restfulness give way to renewed anxiety and doubt.

Pushing the leaden canine weight to one side in order to turn over and in a more wakeful state, I question whether I am really up to organizing the funeral. If I can't even choose a hymn it might be better if I were to hand the preparation over to a colleague or two. This thought does not sit well, causing me to straighten up and switch the light on. No, handing the funeral over would require me to relinquish too much. This is my job, this is what I do and I will find the resources. Jenny's life was cut short and I will never be able to give her the wedding she was beginning to look forward to. All I can give her now is a funeral and I am determined it will be the best I can provide. I will surround her body with family and friends and all that she loved when she was alive. I will not allow the ugliness and brutality of her death to overwhelm the beauty and joy of her life. It will be more than a funeral. It will be a lament, a song for Jenny. How can I hand that over to someone else? With renewed purpose I plump up the pillows to begin work. The first hymn is chosen for its melody and a two-lined phrase in the last verse:

> And with a well-tuned heart
> Sing thou the songs of love ...

'Can only men carry coffins?'

Greg and I are in the sitting room, talking to a friend. Lizzie's voice has arrested conversation in mid-flow. All three of us turn to look at Lizzie standing in the doorway. 'Sorry, I didn't mean to interrupt.'

'No. Why?'

'I don't want strangers carrying Jenny. I would like to do it.'

I can't see why this wouldn't be possible. Derek the undertaker is coming later so I promise we will talk to him about it.

When our visitor has left there is more discussion as to who might carry the coffin. Greg doesn't think Thomas will want to do it but we will ask him. I wonder if any of the cousins might like to. Lizzie thinks her cousin Katie would like to do it and goes off to give her a call.

Almost immediately Lizzie is back saying that Katie would like to and so would her sister Joanne.

'Perhaps all the older cousins could do it, if they would like to.'

By the time Derek arrives I have made a list of what we have to discuss with him; how many cars we will need and the logistics of the requiem mass in our old parish church followed by the funeral the next day in the cathedral. None of us likes the idea of Jenny's body going back to the funeral home after the requiem mass so she is going to stay in the church and those who wish can stay with her. We will keep watch with her through the night. In the morning her coffin will be moved to my parents' home at my father's request and we will leave for the cathedral from there. Derek is wonderful over the sensitive issue of Lizzie and her cousins carrying the coffin. His only caution (at least the only one voiced to us) is that the girls should be secure in their footwear, i.e. avoid high heels. The thought of the girls teetering along on four-inch-high heels bearing Jenny on their shoulders amused us all, as it would doubtless have amused Jenny. I promise that on this occasion heels will be restricted to no more than an inch!

On the eve of Lizzie's departure for Edinburgh she has arrived home asking to visit the funeral home. She doesn't want to leave without seeing Jenny. The office is closed but I called Derek at home and he has generously offered to meet us there and open up.

'You do know the coffin is closed and you won't be able to see Jenny,' I remind Lizzie.

'I know but I want to say goodbye.'

Goodbye, that important rite denied Lizzie and denied us all. The privilege of speaking special words, sharing last thoughts, repairing hurts, holding hands and being together in stillness and love, now only possible beside a closed coffin.

There's a few minutes wait while Derek 'prepares the room'.

'Are you sure you want to go in on your own?'

'Yes.'

Derek accompanies Lizzie along the short corridor to the room Jenny has been placed in while I wait in the lounge. I hope she will be all right. I think she will.

The lounge has a new carpet smell: the same smell as every funeral home I've been in and I've visited a few in the course of my work as a parish priest. Light oak furniture and arrangements of flowers soften a space where staff deal carefully and professionally with newly bereaved families, ready to be of service and sensitive to emotions and needs. On a shelf under the table are catalogues of coffins, caskets and other trappings of the funeral director's trade. The catalogues are neatly arranged, their contents not immediately obvious to anyone entering the room. The carpet is burgundy red with small grey flecks, costly and hard-wearing. I know this because it is the same carpet we had in our last house before I was ordained and moved to a church house. The thought of having the same carpet at home as in a funeral home is a bit disconcerting. It is just as well we are no longer in that house for if we were I might have to go home and replace it for something less resonant.

This is not my first visit here since returning to Bristol. The place where Jenny's body resides is a frequent draw and within walking distance. 'Come whenever you want,' the staff assured me and I do. Some days there is nowhere else I want to be. Other days I can't bear to go near the place, days when Jenny's coffin is too bleak a sight to contemplate.

I wonder how Lizzie is getting on. I won't ask unless she tells me. It is an intimate time between two sisters. Derek will stay with her for a moment or two, until he is satisfied she is OK on her own, and then respectfully withdraw. An image forms in my mind of my two daughters. Sisters enclosed together in a room. Their bodies separated by a hard wooden sealed coffin. One lies inside broken and cold; the other looks on, full of life and passionate. It is so wrong, utterly wrong in every way and merciless. It is unbearable to me, their mother, that one should be lifeless inside the coffin and the other left to bear the burden of grief. These sisters with all their sibling love and rivalry are separated now by the awfulness of destruction and death. The perpetrators took away more than the lives of their victims and they would have had much to answer for had they lived. An increasingly familiar resentment is forming in the pit of my stomach and again I find it necessary to breathe deeply to overcome its nauseous effect.

Derek has joined me. Immediately the room is less funereal. His solid presence and kindly manner is humanizing the space. Derek's smile as he sits opposite me is warm and full of care. The fact that he has a daughter is reassuring. In one of our earlier conversations it was on the tip of my tongue to say, *Please treat my daughter as you would treat your own.* Just in time, before opening mouth and putting proverbial insensitive foot in it I realized this was both unfair and unnecessary.

Most of the conversations I have had with Derek have been over the phone and concerned with practicalities. Now we have a few minutes to spare whilst waiting for Lizzie I am able to ask how the dead would have been treated at the scene and in the temporary mortuary, what level of dignity and respect they would have been afforded. I believe that Derek will know, or if not that he will at least have an informed view.

'Who would have been caring for the dead?' I ask him.

Of course, Derek is only able to surmise whether there were undertakers and funeral directors involved in the operation, professionals like him who are part of a national rapid response team, whose function it is to look after the dead. Undertakers would normally be involved in such a team but, Derek explains, may not have been involved in the 7 July incident. Rapid response personnel will have been restricted due to the nature and high security level of the emergency.

'Part of this whole nightmare,' I say, looking down at the grey flecks in the carpet, 'is acknowledging the fact that the dead would not have been the top priority in the scheme of things.' With necessary emphasis on rescuing survivors and massive forensic examination of the four sites, I understand the reason why. Nevertheless, I would like to believe that in death, in the absence of anyone near and dear to her, Jenny was looked after by someone. My fear is that she spent hours, even days lying in a tunnel or on a mortuary trolley, ignored, unattended beyond the rigour of identification. These are questions I wanted to ask at the briefing but I couldn't, and I do not know now how to get to the truth of these things.

Derek is not able to comfort or reassure me, quite the contrary, but I am grateful, very grateful for the time he is taking with me. Response to a terrorist attack, it seems, like the act itself, has its own set of rules and protocol. This is something I'm going to have to learn to live with. In the absence of firm knowledge, Derek's willingness to engage with all my concerns over Jenny's body is the best I can ask for at the moment. Jenny's death is part of a wider picture; wider and, I am beginning to think, impenetrable.

When Lizzie is finished I pop in, run my hand over the name plaque, blow a kiss and say, 'Good night, God bless.' This is a bit of an irony in the circumstances as I don't feel any of us to be blessed by God at the moment, least of all Jenny. Neither do I know why I talk to Jenny as though she were still alive, as though she can hear me. I ask her what music she would like for her funeral. I tell her that I hope we are getting it right and that she would approve. I tell her we will look after James as long as he wants us to be part of his life. I tell her I am so sorry I couldn't protect her when she needed protection most. I have told her this many times.

On the way home Lizzie does not speak of what passed in the room, other than to say she is glad she was able to say goodbye to Jenny before leaving for Edinburgh tomorrow. Feisty Lizzie is nowhere to be seen, the Lizzie who insisted 'something's happened to Jenny' on the morning of 7 July, the Lizzie who with eyes blazing held a pen like a knife and obliterated the newspaper image of Jenny's killer, the Lizzie who stood her ground over carrying her sister's coffin and poured such love and passion into making a last gift. This Lizzie is quiet, looking pensively ahead with all the angry fire of recent weeks gone from her eyes. This is a temporary state and the fire will surely return. But for now, having so recently left her sister's side, there is an air of sobriety about her. Like mother, like daughter; both overcome by the ebb and flow of this unpredictable current of grief.

The days are mostly filled with preparations for the funeral now. It is this which is providing a purpose, a reason to get out of bed in the mornings and occupation for the endless nights. I have settled into a rhythm of working in bed at night. When tiredness creeps over me and I can no longer concentrate I switch off the light. With music playing softly in the background I settle into the pillows and watch the transition from shadowy moonlight seeping into the room to the changing light of dawn approaching. Around 4.15 the birds begin their morning song. It is only when this happens that I can close my eyes and slip quite readily into sleep. By nine or ten I am up and working at the funeral again. Pages and pages of lists are strewn around the dining table and about my desk with books of poetry, bibles and Shakespeare plays; CDs are scattered around the CD player, overflowing on to the floor as music fills the room where I work. Being immersed in every aspect as if it is a theatrical production is creative and energizing. The funeral is carrying me along and getting me through each day. I feel very close to Jenny in this. It is a labour of love. Structure, ritual, music, flowers, cars and readings, even a champagne reception afterwards; yes, the irony is that my beloved daughter's funeral has many of the elements of her anticipated wedding, even the processional music that she and James wanted and hymns she might have chosen.

Greg and I pass each other around the house, being kindly with each other but I do not think connected with each other's purpose or grief. We co-exist in the same space, eating together and going about the day-to-day stuff of domestic practicality. We talk about Lizzie and Thomas but we do not talk about that one thing that has brought us to this place. Pain is keeping us apart. We are withered spirits, unable to voice our deepest grief-filled thoughts to each other. I believe our pain is so deep and so different that it has no voice, only a demeanour and sometimes nothing more than a numbed expression. If I am finding a kind of solace in wrapping myself up in the funeral, then Greg is probably finding his solace in the garden or sitting in an armchair listening to the radio.

In the hallway, the centre of the house, a candle is kept alight for Jenny. The candle is in a silver tea-light holder, a gift from friends. There is a Hebrew inscription engraved on the side which, translated, means 'everlasting remembrance'. A fresh candle is lit every morning by whichever of us is first downstairs. We are together in this ritual at least. The candle is set on a glass cabinet next to a framed picture of Jenny. Taken on the day of her twenty-first birthday, it is the story behind the picture that holds so much for us both.

17 October 2001

Greg and I were driving to Reading to take Jenny and James out for a celebratory lunch. In the car we journeyed through the years as we journeyed through the miles, chatting about Jenny's birth, the joy she brought into our lives when she was born, her toddler antics and her courage when she had to undergo major surgery in her teens. After leaving the motorway we stopped off at a garden centre to buy some flowers, white blooms, bright yellow gold sunflowers and a funny cabbage thing in the middle. Greg raised his eyebrows at this, saying through a laughter-filled voice that 'at least she can eat it if she gets hungry.' The flowers were stowed on the back seat. Padded and packaged in the boot of the car was a surprise birthday present, a dulcimer made by a friend who specialized in playing and making the ancient instrument. We couldn't wait to see Jenny's face when she opened it. Over the summer she had bemoaned the fact that once she finished university she would no longer have a piano to hand, which gave us the idea for this gift. The attached card read 'Now you shall have music wherever you go', a pastiche of the childhood nursery rhyme.

At the sight of the flowers her face was a delight, transforming to wide-eyed surprise when a few minutes later she opened her present. James had given her red roses and booked a box for a Proms concert. She was happy, happy, happy, hair shining, face glowing and eyes sparkling. 'Do you like my new top?' she said, twirling around to show it off.

In the restaurant we drank champagne cocktails, raised our glasses and toasted her, wishing her a bright and glorious future. Later, after the meal, sitting around the table with coffee, we took photos, spontaneous and laughing.

It is this picture of Jenny that we love, her joyous face captured close-up on camera as she turned towards us at the end of the meal. This is the picture that we have placed next to the candle of everlasting remembrance, not because it is the best picture ever taken of her but because of the memory it holds, a sort of collective of twenty-one years. In the background of the picture, outside the window of the restaurant, is a set of traffic lights. The traffic lights are on red. When the film was developed, we laughed at the unfortunate background blip, a proverbial blot on the landscape of an otherwise lovely view. Now when I look at the picture the red light is more significant. It says stop, and stop we have. We have come to a standstill. Even so, it is Jenny's face, full of light and life, shining out in the foreground, which is the greater presence and unites her parents in memory if not in grief.

I look at this picture after each new fragment of news about the bombings and details of Jenny's death. It is becoming a restorative ritual. This evening Colin telephoned with the latest report. The carriage Jenny was conveyed in was number 6505. Her body was found between the hours of 15.05 and 18.30 on 7 July. Her body was removed at 1200 hours on Saturday 9 July and placed in a refrigerated lorry. She was taken to the temporary mortuary set up at the Honourable Artillery Barracks in City Road, London, near Moorgate Underground at 16.35 the same day. At 1700 hours on Tuesday 12 July Jenny was formally identified by dental records, an operational scar on her back and a bracelet watch she was wearing.

With the photograph fixed in front of my face where I can look right into Jenny's eyes I try to see her as she was on her twenty-first birthday, twirling around in bright magenta pink, not how she lay anonymously in the midst of destruction, dirt and devastation for fifty-one hours and ten minutes. But it is hard, very hard.

A Song For Jenny

Tonight, lying in bed, I am unable to distract my mind and spend hours listening to Faure's Requiem over and over again. As it begins its first stirring chord seems to say 'Listen', then the soft opening phrase 'Requiem aeternam' followed by two more strong chords, each one more insistent than the last: listen, listen. As the requiem goes round I see Jenny, broken, lifeless and abandoned in the darkness and in my darkness, I try to gather her up and hold her to me, but she is elusive. No matter how hard I try my mind's eye is unable to free her from the refrigerated lorry and a cold metal mortuary trolley. The nightmare images will not be redeemed by either music or memory. My last conscious thought is that if only I had been able to see her in those early hours I could have identified her myself. The scar on her back would have been enough. Then I could have held her to me. She might not have been alive but at least she would not have been alone.

Jenny is lying on a surgical trolley, dressed in a white gown. Four years of consultations, discussions, X-rays and medical recommendations have brought us to this point. It is two days after her last GCSE exam. She is sixteen and about to undergo surgery to correct a curvature of the spine. The curve is at the base of the spine and is pushing her hips out of alignment. The surgeon had wanted to carry out the surgery as soon as possible after Jenny finished her exams so she could recover during the long summer holidays. She is buoyant in anticipation of a straight spine and looking more composed than I am currently feeling at the prospect of several hours of corrective surgery. Last night we were taken into intensive care and shown the apparatus and machinery that would provide artificial ventilation for the days immediately following surgery. 'So you're not alarmed when you see her,' we were told. Jenny is on a surgical trolley now. 'One of you can go into the anaesthetic room with Jenny,' the nurse is saying.

Greg and I look at each other across the trolley. 'You go,' he says before bending over to kiss Jenny, assuring her, 'I'll be waiting, see you in a few hours.'

It is only as Jenny is being transported on a trolley along a corridor towards the lift that she shows any sign of nervousness and grips my hand tightly as I walk beside her. In the anaesthetic room Jenny is keeping hold of my hand (or perhaps I am keeping hold of hers) while staff joke with her about being an inch taller in a few hours. I'm allowed to stay with her while she drifts into drug-induced unconsciousness. Her grip on my hand relaxes. I watch my sleeping daughter taken from my care into that of anaesthetists, orthopaedic and neurosurgeons and as the doors into the operating theatre close behind her I whisper into the air, 'Please take care of her, she is very precious.' The plea might have been a prayer, my deepest hope, I don't know, but there's a hand on my shoulder, a brief touch, a voice replying, 'We will.' A gowned anaesthetist pushes his way through the doors towards Jenny as the nurse who brought us from the ward guides me out by the opposite door.

Greg and I hold our breath, waiting to hear that Jenny is through the operation safely. We are parents waiting for news, not speaking very much because there isn't much to say. We share the task of waiting by looking out of the window on to the hospital forecourt below, staring into space or at the floor, flicking through magazines uninterestedly, or pacing around the room. Every now and then one of us will go out of the waiting room and walk along the corridor to bring back coffee in plastic cups dispensed from a hot drinks machine. Finally, nearly eight hours later, the surgeon appears in the doorway to tell us the operation was a

*success, Jenny is in the recovery room and we will be able to go
down to ICU to see her very soon.*

*We are accompanied into ICU and find Jenny in her post-
operative state, unconscious and attached to a ventilator. It is
distressing but also a relief to see her. She looks vulnerable though
restful. For more than two days we take it in turns to keep watch
by her side, talk to her even though she is unable to respond.
During the night hours I look on as a man is brought into the
next bay. I hear words like aneurism and critical and sense the fear
of death close by. I stroke Jenny's hand while observing the noise-
less hurrying and scurrying of staff around the man's bed. I think
how fragile life is and how blessed I am to have my daughter safely
restored, despite her being unconscious and with an arduous recovery ahead of her. A staff nurse has persuaded me to go and get a
drink and something to eat while she attends to Jenny. Reluctantly
I leave Jenny's bedside to freshen up in the family room attached
to the unit. When I return, Nick, our parish priest, is sitting at
Jenny's bedside reading a newspaper. 'Thought I'd come and keep
you both company for a while,' he says. His presence is reassuring
and I feel that all will be well and Jenny will soon be restored. She
will have a resurgence to full health and full life.*

'All shall be well and all manner of things shall be well.'

Except all is not well! Last night, after listening to the music of requiem
I dreamt I was sitting beside Jenny's bed again, waiting for her to wake
up. The dream was muddled. Jenny wasn't sixteen, she was twenty-
four, and her head was bandaged. It was a strange dream with fragments
of the past and the present mixed up together. This morning the bedcov-
ers are all over the place. I'm hot and sticky and once more tormented
by thoughts of what might have been. If Jenny had not died, if she had
survived, even if she had been badly injured, maimed, she would have

had the courage and determination to deal with it. I know she would because I saw a glimpse of it when she was sixteen. But ifs don't get you anywhere and lying in bed wishing it were otherwise is useless. With a determined effort I get out of bed and, driven by anger and frustration, strip the covers and throw them over the banisters to land in a heap in the hallway below. Then I stand under the shower while memories, dreams and 'what ifs' once again wash away with night sweats down the plug hole, leaving me more refreshed to face the day.

'Good morning, Julie. How are you today?'

'I'm OK, thanks, Colin.' I'm wondering what the next update is going to be.

'I've had a call from the detective who spoke to you at the briefing. He's asked if you would like to meet with him so he can address some of your questions in person. He's willing to travel to Bristol to meet with you. Is that something you'd like to happen?'

'It is, yes.' My mind is running ahead. 'I'm happy to meet him in London though. I'd like to visit Edgware Road again. Also, would it be possible for me to see the carriage?'

Immediately I put the phone down it rings again and there are two or three more calls before I manage to put a slice of bread in the toaster. One call is from my sister-in-law Chris confirming she has cancelled our planned annual trip to Edinburgh, to the Fringe Festival. We discuss flying up on spec for a couple of days after the funeral, to support Lizzie. 'We don't need to book any shows,' Chris says, 'we could go with the flow or wander down to the book festival where it's less crowded.' I agree we could.

There is a long list of things I wanted to do this morning. Instead I'm sitting at the computer with my elbows resting on the edge of the desk, face cupped in hands and staring out at the garden at nothing in particular. Bach's Preludes are playing but they are in the background to my thoughts. Sometimes the cello predominates, which is when I think less and listen more. My mood is pensive, which is just as well after last night's turbulence. Ups and downs, highs and lows, I never know what to expect next. The emotional rollercoaster is exhausting. So many people have asked: 'What can we do?' 'I don't know,' I tell them. I don't seem to know what I want or how I'll feel one day to the next. If that's difficult for me it must be doubly difficult for people around me. When I'm alone I feel abandoned; when I have people with me I want to be alone.

A colleague asked, 'What helps?'

'Music and poetry,' I responded rather flippantly. But it's true. I do not know where I would be without Beethoven or Faure or a line of verse which speaks of love and longing and is able to say so much of what I am feeling myself. This does not negate family and friends whose constancy and support is the daily bread of getting through each day, the people who share the grief of what has happened to Jenny. When I talk about music and poetry I believe I am talking about heart and soul and whatever part of the psyche controls emotion. In music and poetry I have found a way of working through conflicts and confusions, dark, awful and heart-rending encounters. In listening to a certain piece of music or reading a poem there can be a soothing sort of comfort, yes, but it is more than this. It is the means by which I can rest my mind, pull the proverbial blanket over my head and give vent to the pain and turbulence that I feel inside. Music especially, is able to draw something out of me. I have found in it a healing quality. When I fear I am most in danger of losing a grasp on life, when I am at my lowest ebb, it is music and poetry that has the ability get into the darkest recesses of my being to restore some equilibrium.

Like last night before I went to bed. I threw a bottle of wine across the length of my study. It was about half full. One moment I was thinking about pouring a glass, the next I had thrown the bottle at the wall. There was no conscious thought involved; the bottle left my hand like projectile vomit from a child. Red rained down everywhere, splattering papers, books, furniture and floor. I watched, horrified, as the bottle bounced against the wall and rolled on to the floor. It did not break. My spirit did. I was frightened by the loss of control and there was nobody to say *it's all right, it's understandable, calm down.* I longed for someone to be with me, to rub my back as my cousin did on the day I broke down at my sister's. There was no one. I was sorry and I was glad. Sorry there was no comfort to be had; glad there was no witness to the appalling loss of control. I cleaned up the mess; spread papers to dry, fanned out books and propped them on any available surface so the air could circulate between the pages. By the time I had mopped the floor, scrubbed the wall so only a faint pink splodge was visible, and checked that the computer still worked, I was spent and didn't have the energy to lift a glass let alone throw a bottle.

At times I find it difficult to grieve authentically; it's not that I can't, but I believe I must put a brave face on, show that I'm coping. There are times when I look at the world and convince myself that I have no right to grieve as deeply as I am. My child, my precious Jenny, has been killed and killed violently and without mercy; selfishly I feel that my grief is the only grief, my loss is the only loss. But I can't express that outwardly as fully as I feel it in the pit of my stomach, because a little voice inside is saying, *You are not the only mother to have lost a child; in some parts of the world grief is a luxury; at least you have two other children whom you love, be grateful.* Thoughts such as these play on my mind and I feel, well, guilty, I suppose. But whatever my conscience is telling me, the truth is I am grieving with a longing that is insatiable and completely self-centred. I am so battered by what has happened to Jenny that I have nothing left to feel for anyone else. It is during these periods, when I am in the darkest pit of despair and self-absorption, unable to believe that any other living person could possibly understand the awfulness of what has happened, that I turn to the likes of Beethoven or Bach, Shakespeare and the poets. And Job. I have not found too much in the Bible at these times, but I have found a kind of meeting place in the Book of Job, from memory and dipping in if not from daily application.

The colleague who asked 'what helps?' has himself helped in a way, by encouraging me to think about these things.

The random and often unexpected acts of kindness have also helped; in fact they have more than helped: they have been a life blood. The milk of human kindness has flowed like a river, surging through the mire of wickedness that has brought us to this place; a taxi driver, a platter of fruit, peeled, sliced and arranged beautifully, a jam jar crammed with garden flowers left on the doorstep, a child's drawing pushed through the letter box, a bay tree in a garden tub, a bird table, all the people who have taken the trouble to write with poems, music and special memories of Jennifer, Jenny or Jen. All these things help, and the birds that sing me to sleep, and the sun that keeps shining even when I shout at it to stop.

It is necessary to blow my nose and wipe my eyes but now I feel more able to get on with the day. Time to put Bach into the wings for the time being and give Nina Simone the stage. I turn the volume up and Nina's fantastic voice fills the room and probably the rest of the house, lifting me out of a daydreaming soliloquy and setting me more readily to work.

Funeral Song

It seems that nothing is too much trouble for anyone. The response to requests for the funeral is overwhelming. Brendan, the cathedral canon responsible for music and liturgy, understood when I said, 'I want Jenny's funeral to be an immersion in music, mystery, poetry and ritual.' David, an actor friend, is working with a group of thespians who will read Shakespeare, poetry and readings from the Bible. Friends of Jenny's from university; colleagues from the music publishing office where she worked; and choirs she has sung with are going to form a massed choir to sing in the cathedral, and our friend Alison is playing the organ. Jenny's friend Charlie is advising and helping with the music. Together, via email and telephone conversations, we are compiling and editing a list of music until we have a programme which reflects Jenny's life and expresses her death. Through Charlie I am discovering music Jenny enjoyed that I never knew of. On good days I like to think that Jenny is continuing my musical education through her death and through her friends.

Today Charlie has emailed details of three solo pieces for me to consider: 'Fear no more the heat of the sun' by Sondheim; 'Now that the sun hath veil'd his light', Purcell and Fuller's Evening Hymn; and 'Because I knew you, I have been changed for good' by Schwartz.

Of these three pieces only the first is familiar. The words are from Shakespeare's play *Cymbeline* but I need to look up the play to recall any more than the well known first line. It is a dirge, the saddest of songs, sung over the grave of Fidele. For a while I am distracted reading the text and then some notes. The fact that Fidele is not really Fidele but Imogen who is not really dead but drugged is, at the moment, irrelevant. It is the song that has me captivated and I read it as I have never read it before ...

A Song For Jenny

'SONG'

Fear no more the heat o' th' sun
Nor the furious winter's rages;
Thou thy worldly task hast done,
Home are gone, and ta'en thy wages.
Golden lads and girls all must,
As chimney-sweepers, come to dust.

Fear no more the frown o' the great;
Thou art past the tyrant's stroke.
Care no more to clothe and eat;
To thee the reed is as the oak.
The sceptre, learning, physic, must
All follow this and come to dust.

Fear no more the lightning flash,
Nor th' all-dreaded thunder-stone;
Fear not slander, censure rash;
Thou has finish'd joy and moan.
All lovers young, all lovers must
Consign to thee and come to dust.

No exorciser harm thee!
Nor witchcraft charm thee!
Ghost unlaid forbear thee!
Nothing ill come near thee!
Quiet consummation have,
And renowned be thy grave!

… and read it again, going over single lines. For a split second, the tiniest fragment of time, I forget where I am and what I am doing and reach for my mobile phone instinctively to text Jenny – 'Wow, I've just had a moment of epiphany!' – then there's immediate realization and tears, more tears from the endless well of tears.

After washing my face for the second time this morning I decide fresh air and company might be a good antidote to solitary soulful weeping.

Greg is in the front garden, stooped over and snipping away at the bushes under the window, which are growing a bit rampant. He's listening to the radio, a cricket match from the sounds of it. He straightens up when he sees me and smiles.

'I'm going to the flower shop to see Fiona.' And then as an after-thought: 'Would you like a coffee before I go?'

'No, it's OK thanks, I'll go in and make one when I've finished this. Will you be long?'

'Probably not, depends how busy Fiona is in the shop and if she has time to chat.'

Leaving Greg to the peace of the garden and radio, I flip-flop my way around the block to the flower shop, hoping not to meet anyone on the way.

The familiar Pick of the Bunch shop doorway is a welcome sight. Bay trees, plants and pots stuffed with cut flowers form a carpet of summer colours in front of the window. The door is propped open and I can see the stand of hand-made beads and bangles just inside. Fiona is out from behind the counter as soon as she sees me, with a hug and a pleased and surprised, 'Hello, stranger.'

'I want some sunflowers,' I say, looking around and finding a tub of large sunny blooms and a tub of smaller varieties.

'Are they for you?'

'Yes, for my study.'

While Fiona wraps the flowers she tells me all about the media chaos in my absence. 'Journalists and reporters were all over the place, asking all about you … if I knew where you were … if I knew Jenny … I didn't know what to say. I tried to play dumb.'

'I'm sure whatever you said was fine. Fortunately, my sister's house is so remote even the police had trouble finding us.' We both laugh at this. Fiona always makes me laugh, always has a smile and a welcome and a funny story to tell. From the day I moved into the vicarage she has been one of my best friends here. I love her artistic and hippy approach to life and her bohemian, slightly quirky style. Almost every subject under the sun gets covered in this shop: love, death, religion, relationships; often outrageously irreverent and always fun. Fiona's shop is an oasis and I always leave it feeling more uplifted than when I went in.

'This is the real church in the community,' I said to her once.

And Fiona once said to me, 'Could I get married in your church?'

'Of course you could.'

'Could I wear a black dress instead of white?'

'Wear what you want!'

'A black lacy dress and deep red roses?'

'You old goth, you!'

An hour ago I did not believe anything could lift my spirits today, but Fiona has worked her magic and as I make my way home I can lift my head from the ground and feel the sun on my face, like the sunflowers I carry in my arms.

Fiona's Pick of the Bunch delivery van is pulling away from the house when I get back. Her partner John stops to say a brief hello before driving off again, waving. Inside, Greg is in the kitchen making coffee.

'More flowers,' he says, indicating the newest arrangement standing in the sink.

It was not really necessary to buy sunflowers, I suppose, though I'm glad I did.

I am surprised and pleased to receive a card from the priest James and I met in St Paul's Cathedral on the day of the two-minute silence, the priest who stood with us in silence, holding our hands. The card is dated 15 July so took a while to reach me. The image on the front is Henry Moore's 'Mother and Child'. On the back of the postcard is written:

> I am the priest you met in the cathedral yesterday. I am retired
> and do a half-day once a month there. I am glad I met you and
> James and I shall not forget you. I find Moore's carving a very
> powerful evocation of mother and child – he did not want it to
> be seen simply as a Madonna and child.

It was our good fortune that the priest's half-day coincided with our time in the cathedral – an encounter I carry in my heart.

Day after day I am overwhelmed with sadness yet when I look at this simple carving, an outline form devoid of face or features, I think of all mothers who have lost children. I am reminded that I am not the only mother to have experienced the death of a child and that each death is a death too many. The carving could be any mother and any child and all mothers and all children. Looking at the picture now, I am grateful to Henry Moore for naming his carving 'Mother and Child'; Madonna is specific; motherhood is universal.

I need moments like these, moments when I can find meaning beyond my own bleak feelings. This is my fear, that a seed of hatred could so easily be sown in my heart. For what has happened to Jenny

I do believe I could grow to hate. If that happened I do not think I could bear it.

'Despite everything, life is full of beauty and meaning.' This is a quotation sent to me by a friend. It arrived handwritten on a plain white card. At the time I did not know the source but I have since been given a book putting the quotation in context. It is from the letters and journals of Etty Hillesum. Etty was trying not to hate all Germans for what was happening to the Jews. Over and over again she wrote these words: 'Despite everything, life is full of beauty and meaning.' I suppose it was a kind of mantra, as it has become mine. Etty eventually died in Auschwitz Concentration Camp, a place whence the horrors of inhumanity still reverberate around the world. It is also a place made synonymous with great courage and dignity through the people incarcerated there. This seems a remarkable accomplishment, that someone witnessing so much cruelty and slaughter could keep affirming a vital blessedness of life.

Every day that passes I think I understand more and more Etty's determination not to hate. There is something deeply and poetically truthful in what is expressed that resonates strongly with my own inner struggles. Some days it is so difficult not to see all Muslim people as colluding with the same corrupt ideology that became implanted in the hearts and minds of the 7 July bombers. The first time someone felt it necessary to tell me that not all Muslims are bad I was rather put out. Of course I know not all Muslims are bad. My head can reason this out every day – and it does. Yet, if I'm honest, there is conflict and confusion in my heart. I do not want to hate; I do not want to see all Muslim people as I see Mohammed Sidique Khan and his co-conspirators. Yet I am aware of a questioning fear that if those four, why not others? As I walk along the street in the multi-cultural area close to where I live and work, where so much community spirit and inclusivity exists, I cannot help that fearful little voice pricking at my conscience. I pass someone who might be a Muslim and I wonder: Who are you? Do you believe terrorism is justified? Are you planning and plotting your own act of terrorism?

I cannot begin to articulate the pain this causes, that I have come to think in this way. Even though in my intellect I know such generalizations to be untrue, in the light of my recent experience I have to own my fear. There is nowhere to take it, this fear, to say: 'This is my fear, what is your fear and what can we do about it?'

Terrorism unleashes monsters, monsters that conspire, plan and carry out atrocities. But there is another monster, the monster of suspicion, prejudice and distrust that can plant its seed in the hearts and minds of good people. This is my fear, that such a monster plants its seed in my heart or the hearts of my children.

Despite everything, life is full of beauty and meaning.

The more I say these words, the more I feel the poetry and music within them. The mantra, for that is what it has become, reflects the pain and wonder, the despair and hope of my own struggle and experience. Within it, there is a determination to keep the glass of life half full that I find utterly compelling.

My niece Joanne has arrived; she has come to stay for a week to be a helpmate. James is also here for a day or two. I have been playing music to them in an attempt to find a piece of music to accompany Jenny's coffin into the cathedral. I do not want to use the traditional sentences from scripture to lead her in. Phrases such as 'I am the resurrection and the light says the Lord' do not evoke a sense of holiness or mystery for me. I cannot find any imagination in them. I am not comforted by the words nor do I wish to be. I have not arrived at a point of comfort; to use the metaphor, I am still at the crucifixion stage. No, a series of sentences does not fulfil the need. So here I am on my knees at the altar of the sound system searching through CD after CD looking for that elusive piece of music which has the ability to inspire awe, capture the fearfulness of death and have the strength to draw us into the place where we would rather not go. I've been thinking about it for days, off and on. I know the piece exists; I just don't know what it is. Then I spot a disc I bought a few months ago after hearing a track played on the radio.

'Listen to this, tell me what you think.'

Five minutes twenty-eight seconds later, looking at Joanne and James, noting the expression on their faces and the stillness in the room, I think we have found the perfect piece.

'It's beautiful.' Joanne says. 'What is it?'

'"Mortal Flesh" by Christian Forshaw.'

The funeral was difficult to conduct. One of the worst I've taken. Even funerals that end in fisticuffs have atmosphere. This one had nothing. It was the dreariest of days, dull, drizzly and cold. The family wanted it over and done with quickly. No fuss! No flowers, no music, no readings, no eulogies and definitely no hymns. Not even a few verses of 'All things bright and beautiful' for people to mumble along to. I tried my best and even slipped in a couple of sentences of 'My father's house has many rooms' just to give it a sense of occasion. When I glanced up during the prayers, requested to be kept 'to a minimum', I was met by a row of staring faces. In the middle of the prayer of commendation, the prayer when the deceased is entrusted to the grace and mercy of God, a mobile phone blared out. There was none of the usual embarrassed fumbling to turn the phone off or creeping outside to take the call. The culprit hunched forward in his seat as though he was a child eating an illicit sweet in the classroom.

'Yeah mate.'

'Sorry mate.'

'Call yer later.'

'Old boy's funeral.'

'Vicar's talking.'

'No.'

'Yeah.'

'About ten minutes.'

'OK.'

It was a relief to press the button of dispatch and watch the curtain glide across the coffin. At the door there were a few nice-service-vicar, you-did-him-proud-type comments and one, 'Are there many lady vicars now then?' to which I replied, 'Yes, we're becoming quite prolific,' but on the whole people just wanted to get out.

On the way home I felt out of sorts and unusually sad – there must be more than this at the end of someone's life. Giving up on pointless musings I switched the radio on just as a new piece of music was being introduced. The music was compelling, beautiful, ethereal and full of longing. I began crying, I couldn't help it, my eyes misted up and out came the tears, streaming down my face as I drove along a stretch of busy road. Vision blurred, I pulled the car over and parked up for the duration of the piece. For several minutes I listened as the haunting sounds grew stronger and more compelling while tears ran down my cheeks in perfect symmetry with the rain running down the car windscreen. When the music ended there was a moment of complete quiet before the presenter's voice cut in. That was Christian Forshaw with 'Mortal Flesh' from his Sanctuary album – or words to that effect. I grabbed a pen to write down the details. When I looked up, before switching the engine back on, I saw I *was parked outside the Co-operative funeral home which, in the circumstances, was somewhat ironic.*

I continued home and parked in the drive, but didn't get out of the car. Instead I turned the car round and drove back into town to buy the CD. If I didn't do this now, the moment would be gone.

James has come with me to the cathedral to meet with the canon who is overseeing the funeral. We've come with an outline for Brendan to approve and I am slightly anxious that I am going against the grain of the cathedral way of doing things.

'I'd like to create an atmosphere of a concert into which we bring Jenny and then have it flow seamlessly into a funeral rite.'

'Wonderful.'

'And I don't want the usual sentences to lead the coffin in.'

'Good.'

'There's a particular piece of music that we're hoping to use. I've only got it on disc at the moment, which wouldn't work. It needs to be a live performance so I expect we'd need to get permission.'

'What is it?'

'It's an arrangement of "Let all mortal flesh keep silence" by Christian Forshaw.'

Brendan has almost leapt out of his seat, proclaiming, 'I know Christian – I've booked him for a concert in the cathedral in January. It's a wonderful piece of music. I'll send him an email now and ask if we can use his arrangement.'

Christian not only gave permission but said he would send a copy of the score, requesting only that it should be destroyed once we had finished with it.

Ellie and William have asked if they can see Jenny's coffin. When Vanda asked I didn't see why not if it was something they wanted to do. It might help them.

'Auntie Julie?'

'Yes, William.'

'What does the inside of Jenny's coffin look like?'

We are in the funeral home waiting in the reception lounge. Vanda and the children are here; Joanne has also come and Ellie is sitting very close to her, snuggling up.

'A bit like a bed.'

'Is there a pillow and covers?'

'Not exactly.' From the catalogues under the table I take one out and open it to show William a picture of a coffin similar to Jenny's. The inside is lined with white satin. His curiosity is insatiable, one question leads to another and I am struggling to find answers that are truthful but not disturbing.

'Why can't anyone see her?'

'Because she was hurt and now she's wrapped up in her coffin, a little bit like being tucked up in bed and asleep, so I don't want to disturb her.'

Thankfully, I am saved any more questions by a member of staff coming to tell us they are ready. We are all quiet in the room at first, and tearful, but it isn't long before William's curiosity gets the better of him and he ventures closer to the coffin.

'What are those screws for?' He's pointing to the bolts that secure the top of the coffin.

'To seal the lid so it doesn't come off.'

'Can I see?'

'No!' Vanda and I speak in unison.

Vanda says she would like to spend some time on her own with the coffin, to say goodbye.

'Auntie Julie, please can I say goodbye to Jenny on my own?'

'Of course you can, sweetheart.'

'Can I go in with Ellie?' says Wills.

'No, William, I want to go on my own,' Ellie tells him.

'Can I go on my own then?'

'Yes, all right, but don't argue, you'll upset Mummy.'

William seems to be taking quite a long time to say his goodbyes.

'I'll go and see if he's all right,' Joanne offers.

Seconds later the door is opening and Joanne has hold of William firmly by the hand, giving us a horrified look and saying, 'I caught him on a chair trying to unscrew the bolts.'

'William?'

'I just wanted to see inside!'

'I hate leaving her there; I wish we could take her back with us,' Vanda is saying as we walk to the car.

Back at the house William asks if he can borrow some of Thomas's tools and did I have some wood and glue. Quite a while later, as the rest of us are in the kitchen chatting and drinking tea, William appears in the doorway with his hands behind his back and looking pleased with himself.

'I've got a present for you, Mummy,' he says, presenting Vanda with a small, roughly made wooden box on which he has written RIP in black felt-tip pen. 'It's to remind you of Jenny because you didn't want to leave her; you can keep it in your car.'

The detective I first met at the police briefing said it is not possible to view the carriage as it is still undergoing forensic examination. I understand this. Between Thursday and Saturday Jenny was covered in a blanket – which is at least something, some dignity in death.

Patiently he answered all my questions with as much information as he had and that he had been able to gather from other sources.

We talked about the bombers and the bomb, but I think my mind has blocked that out.

He showed me a diagram explaining where Jenny's body was found in relation to the whole carriage and to the suicide bomber.

He confirmed four hundred body parts had been recovered and sent to a specialized laboratory in Bosnia for ID, which could take several weeks.

I asked if there were photographs of the carriage and of Jenny's body.

He said there were.

I said I would like to see them, please.

He said I could see the photographs but he would advise me not to. He is concerned they might traumatize me for life and that was quite a responsibility.

I said I would take responsibility.

He will arrange for me to see the photographs at Reading Police Station and will bring them in person to show me.

I said I would like to see them before the funeral.

He agreed.

He has two young sons.

He told me he went home late after working round the clock.

They were sleeping.

He just wanted to hug them.

After the meeting I went shopping, to buy an outfit to wear to the funeral.

I'm on the train now, writing notes about the meeting but trying to remember all the details is taxing and my mind seems to have gone blank. Perhaps it will come back to me later. I feel light-headed. Low blood sugar probably, as I haven't eaten. I wonder how far it is to the buffet car. A bar of chocolate would go down well.

The train is pulling into Swindon station. A woman is hurrying along the platform in line with the train. She's carrying a baby in one arm, balancing a bottle to its mouth, and holding on to a small child with the other hand. She's smiling. The child, a boy of about three years old, is waving excitedly at the train as it comes to a stop. He's wearing pyjamas, a red and blue checked dressing gown and red wellington boots. I can see from his mouth he's shouting 'Daddy, Daddy.' A man comes towards them, letting his case fall to the ground and opening his arms wide for the child to run into and be lifted high in the air and swung round. The man leans over to kiss the woman and then the baby, cupping its head in his hand. They are all laughing delightedly, confidently and joyously as they turn away from the train and walk back along the platform, the little boy with his arms around his father's neck, not bothering at all about the disappearing train. This is how it should be, laughing parents, small children in welling-ton boots and dressing gowns, babies being fed, oozing joy and confidence and safe in their world.

I want to cry out: *Grasp it, hold on to it, for any moment it could be wrenched away.*

It is August and the days are hastening on to Jenny's funeral. Waves of panic flood over me as I contemplate not having her here. I know she is dead, I know it but I cannot always fully believe in the fact. I have heard the truth in my head but have not embraced it in my heart. The fact is too incomprehensible. I think Shakespeare must have known this when he wrote: 'So have I heard, and do in part believe it.'

Denial is part of the grieving process and quite normal. It is one of about seven stages of grief. Passing through the various stages is not necessarily a tidy process and the different features of the various stages can come and go. You might think you have passed through a stage, anger for instance, but then it can come back and you have to pass through it again. I have a shelf of books on the subject. Theoretical perspectives! I can't bear reading these things. Yesterday I threw two books in the recycling bin – probably in a fit of pique – because of the terminology: words and phrases such as 'acceptance', 'moving on', 'reaching a point of …'

I am yet to find a really helpful book on the subject of grief. Maybe one day someone will write a 'Rough Guide'. The Victorians might have overdone the sombreness but I'm beginning to think they had the right approach: retreat from the world for a year, spend a lot of time in cool, darkened rooms and gradually emerge through black, purple and grey: outward signs that send out warnings for people to 'beware, there's mourning about'.

This angst on the matter was not helped by a phone call when someone enquired kindly and in soft tones if I thought the funeral would provide some 'conclusion'. I replied in less soft tones, 'Conclusion from what?' I did not find that question helpful and I might even go so far as to say offensive.

I will grieve with all my heart, mind and soul for all the days of my life. How can I not?

At the moment I recognize grief as a separation from a familiar world, feeling everything to be changed, a frightening unpredictability of emotions, and a deep and overwhelming sorrow for Jenny and for the absence of compassion and humanity that caused her death. The mere fact of a funeral will not change these things. Conclusion, like denial, is a simplistic term; I have not found the last month to be the least bit simplistic.

James and I are in London to visit Jenny's work colleagues and pick up her personal belongings. We had lunch in a restaurant in a road off Shaftesbury Avenue before coming into the office. It's tough being here. Jenny's desk is not yet occupied. Very soon a replacement member of staff will be sitting there, stamping his or her personality on to the desk and on to the job. Someone had gathered up Jenny's things for us, but the desk looks as if she has just popped out to make coffee. I really can't say what's worse, the fact that Jenny is absent or the fact that someone will soon take her place. We're not going to stay long. It feels uncomfortable. People have paused for our visit but need to get back to work. There was an interval of time between Jenny failing to turn up for work on 7 July, the telephone contact throughout that day and the next few days, and the extraordinary concert following the two-minute silence, when all our lives were interrupted and we were brought close through Jenny and the terrible event. But now, despite the fact that some of Jenny's work friends are singing at her funeral and most others are attending, this office has returned to business as usual. I would not have expected anything else. Nevertheless it has brought into sharp focus the contrast between those whose lives were interrupted and have been resumed, and those whose lives were interrupted and cannot be resumed. When the suicide bombers struck, all life in London was interrupted. For some it was just that, an interruption, and people and workplaces have picked up where they left off. For others that interruption was far-reaching and wide-ranging, even unto death.

My immediate thought as I stepped through the doorway of Foxhill Road this afternoon is that the house feels lifeless. The life that Jenny and James together breathed into this house has gone. It is emptied of energy. Our spirits are low after returning from London with Jenny's belongings. On the train I kept seeing the empty desk and chair and imagining Jenny's laughing presence bursting into the room with a mug of tea in her hand.

James is taking items out of a brown cardboard box and showing them to me. They are Jenny's personal effects retrieved from Edgware Road. Amongst the items are £3.82 cash, Jenny's travel pass, umbrella and watch. There is no mobile phone and no silver cross and chain. The umbrella is or was a gold fabric telescope type which Jenny kept rolled up in the bottom of her bag. It is now singed black and full of holes. James has opened it out to show the extent of damage caused by the blast. Then, without speaking, he hands me Jenny's watch. The glass has been blown out and the hands have stopped at 08.50.

Time stopped for Jenny and it is running out for us. There is so little time left to hold her here, keep her with us. The watch, as I hold it in the palm of my hand, is to me a sign and symbol of a happy past, a painful present, and an uncertain future. If the hands, stopped abruptly at 08.50, could but tell their own story of an abrupt end.

I am shown into an interview room in Reading Police Station. The DCI whom I met in London is already there, waiting with his assistant. Pauline, the family liaison officer, is accompanying me. Both men have stood up as we enter the room. On a table in front of the DCI is a blue folder. I'm given a glass of water as I sit down. The chairs are arranged so the DCI is at right angles to me at one end of the table. His DS is sitting further back.

'Are you sure you want to go ahead with this?' the DCI asks.

'Yes, absolutely sure.'

He explains, 'We'll go through the photographs one at a time. I'll turn over when you are ready to move on from each photo. If you want to take a break, rest, or stop at any time, just say. There is no hurry; we can take as much time as you need.'

Pauline is sitting just behind my right shoulder: my guardian angel.

The DCI turns the folder round and pushes it closer towards me. 'The photographs are in chronological order, beginning with the carriage. I will tell you which picture is coming next, before turning it over.' His hand is resting on top of the folder. He has a wide gold band on his wedding finger which looks a bit incongruous against the folder. Beside the folder I have placed a photograph sleeve, for afterwards.

'I'll start when you're ready.'

'I'm ready.'

One by one, slowly and steadily, I am taken through the photographs. I have no sense of time or place, only the images before me. No one speaks, other than the DCI occasionally to ask if I want to go on.

Pictures of the carriage.

Pictures of Jenny covered by a blanket – these could be anyone.

'The next picture is Jennifer's body without the blanket. Would you like me to carry on?'

'Yes.'

The DCI is taking me on a journey through the aftermath of the bombings, the stages of Jenny's progress from tube to mortuary, more than twenty pictures, each one more harrowing than the last, but I must see them all. I must see what Jenny went through and how she ended up.

I am not aware of tears trickling down my face until Pauline places a tissue in my lap. Even then I don't take it up. I don't want to move, I only want to look and not take my eyes away from Jenny or any stage or station of that journey where each image strips her of more dignity than the last. Yes, to me these are very much the stations of my daughter's cross as Christ's were to his mother and I cannot rest until I have travelled with her to the final station.

The folder is closed. Pauline is stroking the back of my hand. The DCI has offered me the glass of water. Only then can I move to wipe my eyes and dry the tears.

Inside the photograph sleeve I placed on the table earlier is a picture of Jenny and Lizzie, taken at a summer garden party, standing close together with their arms about each other, slightly tipsy and toasting the camera with a cocktail glass. 'I brought this with me for restorative therapy,' I said to the DCI.

I did not want the last image I saw before I left the room to be the last image in the folder. I brought this picture to look on at the end to restore Jenny to her rightful place.

Despite everything, life is full of beauty and meaning.

Chapter 10

Stabat Mater

Let all mortal flesh keep silence

Time has run out. Today I am at the funeral home to look upon Jenny for the last time, after which her coffin will be sealed. I have brought with me gifts to be placed with her, from James and members of Jenny's family. I am giving her my much-loved, old and well-read copy of *Jane Eyre* with passages marked out including the extract that Jenny had in a frame: 'I am no bird and no net ensnares me, I am a free human being with an independent will.'

As I stand beside her coffin I wonder if this moment would have been less painful if I had been able to care for her at the end of her life, or if I had been able to go to her immediately after her death instead of waiting days and days for news, then more days before her body was released. In this moment, I gather up all the moments that have gone before, through every moment of the last five weeks to this final moment of longing, to gather her to me and cradle her in my arms.

The image I hold in my heart now is beyond the mother and child. The image I hold is the Pietà, the suffering mother whose heart has been pierced, the image of Mary cradling the broken and lifeless body of her son Jesus. When I look on the Pietà or see it in my mind, I think it is me cradling my daughter; or it could be any parent cradling their own broken and lifeless child.

I gaze on my daughter with such love. For one last time I touch her toes, run my hand along her covered body, stroke her hand and kiss her alabaster lips. She is far away now. I long to cradle her in my arms but know that is no longer possible. Instead I cradle her in my heart and in my memory and there she will abide for as long as I have life.

Silently I stand, weeping, then kiss the tips of my fingers dampened with tears and touch them, one last time to her mouth.

The road ahead is closed, cordoned off by police. The cortege has come to a standstill and the cars have pulled into the side. Derek is speaking to a police officer in attendance while we wait anxiously inside the car for information, assuming there has been an accident and hoping there are no fatalities. When he returns, Derek confirms that there has been an accident. There are no serious injuries but there is a lot of debris and it will be half an hour or so before the road is reopened.

'The police want us to divert,' Derek is saying, explaining which way we are being redirected.

'But that's miles out of our way. We'll be late.' My cousin Martyn is out of the car and following Derek to try and find out what kind of accident has occurred. I'm appealing to a police officer standing at the barrier. 'We're on our way to my daughter's requiem mass; please, is there any way you could let us through?' The policeman looks at me and speaks into his radio.

A few minutes later, the road block is removed to let us pass. There's a motorbike overturned on the opposite side of the road and an ambulance parked alongside. As we drive by I am relieved to see that the motorcyclist is sitting on the edge of the ambulance, looking stunned rather than injured. I am glad nobody is badly hurt. Once away from the scene of the accident the cars pick up speed. Martyn is looking over his shoulder at the debris. 'I can't believe this, every time we get into a car there's a police drama!'

As the funeral cars pull into the lane which runs alongside the church, the hearse is already there, ahead of us. Father John, our old parish priest, is waiting with a collective of acolytes. I would not have wanted to be met by any other than these whom I have known, who Jenny has known and who have been part of the rhythm of this place for as long as she had life. Here they are, waiting to lead us into the church where Greg and I were married, where Jenny sang in the choir and where we came as a family Sunday after Sunday until I took us away when I was ordained.

The acolytes stand in a solemn group and Jenny's family look on while her coffin is taken from the hearse. Greg is next to me, looking down at the ground. I believe he cannot lift his eyes to greet the awful sight of his daughter's coffin being raised onto the shoulders of the pall bearers. A hand is in mine. I look into Lizzie's eyes. She is giving me strength. I recognize the familiar nod between funeral director and priest which communicates readiness to proceed.

Slowly we move forward, through the gate into the churchyard, along the path and past the ageless dead. The setting evening sun catches the cross as it is borne high, glinting gold on gold. The sun's glow is spreading like a mantle, part beam, part shadow, covering the tombstones of the ancient dead and the living who accompany the newly dead. Time has no meaning here. We are out of time. There is only this moment of sun caught on polished brass before it goes down. The light will soon be gone. I can feel tears in my eyes and grip Lizzie's hand more tightly as Father John's voice begins to recite the liturgy.

Jenny is being received into church, moving forward out of the sunlight and as we move forward with her it is as if all the people inside are gathering us in, enfolding us. This is what I feel as we enter this place, where my family has known laughter, music, tears, lit candles, formed friendships, said prayers, that walking steadily behind Jenny's coffin we are being enfolded and carried through the church to our places. Jenny's requiem mass, her funeral song that I began, is now in the hands of trusted priests and friends. Father John is speaking from the pulpit. He is speaking of rage against the dying of Jenny's day, of her sweet life and brutal end. He is speaking of the disciple Thomas who refused to believe in the death of his beloved friend until he could see for himself the wounds and ravages of his body. He is not speaking to us. He is speaking from the heart, his heart. We are all in this together; this shock, this trauma which has affected every single person in this place. After over forty years of ministry, this man of God is giving us his struggle, his rage, his belief, his emotion and his care. I could not ask for more.

Afterwards, during an ancient ritual where Jenny's coffin is censed and sprinkled with holy water and the choir are singing a Russian Kontakion for the dead, Father John interrupts what he is doing and moves along Jenny's family, embracing each one of us in turn. 'Give rest O Christ, to thy servant with thy saints … and weeping o'er the grave we make our song.'

And then silence.

Gradually people move. At the back of the church there is wine. Many people leave, many people stay. Some people arrive. Jenny's coffin feels remote, it was in its place for the requiem but now it feels as if it should be down amongst us. Four men lift Jenny's coffin from the catafalque onto two rows of chairs. I make my way to the back of the church and pick up a glass of wine and take it outside. It is dark now but people are not in a hurry to leave. When I go back inside I can't, at first, see Jenny's coffin. It is surrounded by friends, Jenny's and James's friends, Lizzie's and Thomas's. Everyone has a glass of wine in their hand and they are all talking. Some have arms around each other. Lizzie is talking to one of Jenny's primary school friends and she is being comforted. Thomas is talking animatedly to three friends he started infant school with. At the centre of them all is Jenny's coffin with bottles of wine and glasses resting on it. Jenny's coffin, at the moment, resembles a bar. She would love this, all her friends and family gathered around her at the centre having a great big party. Music is played and poems are read informally, not for an audience but to Jenny. At some point during the evening I hear a dulcimer. John, the carpenter and musician who made Jenny's coffin, has set up his own dulcimer and is playing quietly in a corner.

It is not a party but it is wonderful and people are enjoying being together. Laughter and tears weave their way through the next couple of hours. Friends ask if they can leave gifts and notes to go inside the coffin. I collect them up to give to the funeral director in the morning. None of this is planned. I had thought we might have a quiet vigil after the requiem and people could have a glass of wine to meet and greet each other before leaving. It has always been my intention to spend this last night with Jenny but this has taken on a life of its own. I pick up snatches of conversation: university friends are recounting memories of Jenny; nights of fun and drunkenness; dressing up in gorilla suits; singing with a madrigal group at dawn on a hill above Reading; her disbelief and delight when she achieved a 1st for composition in her first year; keeping fit by running daily across the campus between music and English departments, inevitably bursting into one or other class late. Yes, as I move around the church it is full of, 'Do you remember when …'

One friend is here with her mother. Fiona was one of Jenny's best friends at university. They developed a bond in the first year. In looks they are very different: Jenny tall, bouncy blond and Fiona small, petite and dark. Fiona is feeling Jenny's death very deeply and is speaking in a gently earnest voice about the time she was ill in their first year in Halls and how Jenny was a constant companion, looking after her. I think Fiona loved Jenny as a sister. Jenny was to have been bridesmaid at Fiona's wedding next year. Jenny used to tease Fiona about her fetish for pink so, 'There's no doubt about what the colour was to be.' But that is not to be and Fiona's joy in talking quickly turns to sadness. This is how it is: friends talk, laugh, remember and then they cry. It is the order of the evening and it is good, appropriate and warm.

As the night draws on the atmosphere becomes seamlessly quieter. A few people go home and come back with blankets and airbeds; others come back with flasks of tea and coffee, pizza and sandwiches. So it goes on through the night. Jenny's mass has undergone a transition through vigil to wake and now to watch. I am staying through the night and so are James and Vanda. We will not leave Jenny's side. We have placed airbeds around the coffin in case we need to sleep. Through the course of the night others come and sit silently in the church for a while and leave again. Dendy has come back to stay the night. We are never alone. James is stretched out on kneelers placed along a pew. He looks very uncomfortable. He says he's OK.

James does not stay stretched out on the pew. When the rest of us are lying down on airbeds, under blankets trying to get some rest, James has pulled a chair up to the head of the coffin. He has folded his arms as if to encircle the place above Jenny's head and rested his own head on top. It is a sight so full of tenderness and the most heartrending aspect of loss. He is sleeping and as I look at him I really believe that if James could get inside Jenny's coffin with her he would.

I watch the dawn through the doorway. It is Wednesday 17 August. One day short of six weeks since Jenny was killed. It is very nearly over. When Derek arrives soon after 9 a.m. I hand him the last remaining items to go inside Jenny's coffin.

'Is it possible or is the lid sealed too firmly?'

He smiles. 'I expect we can do that for you Julie.'

'Thank you.' I know he can, otherwise I wouldn't have asked.

I see Jenny's coffin into the hearse and watch as it is driven down the road towards my parents' house before I get into Vanda's car to drive home and get ready for the next and final stage.

The atmosphere at home is quietly busy with everyone getting ready and trying to get into bathrooms. The house is a mess, bags and clothes everywhere, mugs scattered and beds unmade. It doesn't matter as everything, all the hurly burly and chaos and nervousness of the morning, is for one end, to get us to the cathedral looking our best for 1 p.m. Outside in the drive flowers are being delivered, sprays, arrangements, no funereal-looking wreaths, but a mass of colour to reflect Jenny's sunny personality. And the sun is shining today; already it is high in the sky. The day has come with a gentle breeze. It is as perfect as it could be – weather wise. I'm glad, I hate rainy-day funerals.

Upstairs, I'm ready, sitting on the side of the bed and dressed in a deep purple skirt, long and soft with tiny silver sequins, topped with a fitted purple jacket. 'If it was her wedding, this is what I would wear.' I said to the person with me when I went shopping to buy the outfit. I had picked up the skirt in the shop. The light caught the sequins. 'They remind me of stars in a dark sky.' I had said at the time. They seem like silly romantic notions now but I bought the skirt anyway. I bought two skirts to wear with the same jacket, in case I chickened out of wearing something so sparkly and luxurious when it came to the day. Well, we have come to the day and I am wearing the skirt. I want to feel luxurious. James's parents have arrived. I can hear them downstairs. Even now I might take the skirt off and replace it with the plainer one. 'Wear it. There isn't going to be a wedding for Jenny so you might as well wear it for her funeral. It's the best you can do.' The voice of conscience in my ear is ringing loud and clear.

'You look fabulous mum!' Lizzie has come into the room behind me. Her timing couldn't be better.

'So do you.' She is wearing a strapless, gold corset top and is holding out a necklace for me to fasten around her neck.

'Are you OK? Everyone is downstairs, ready.'

'I know, I'm coming now.'

She gives me a hug. 'I need to get my jacket,' she says, and leaves the room. Neither of us can afford to cry at the moment.

Outside the bedroom, on the landing, Elizabeth, James's mother, is waiting to use the bathroom. She is wearing a long, deep blue skirt and jacket, looking very smart and elegant. Like James, his mother is tall and slim.

'How is James?' I ask

'Quiet but …'

The rest of Elizabeth's reply is lost as Graham comes upstairs saying, 'Cars are here … you've had your hair cut.'

'Yes, it's a bit short though.'

'Everyone looks very smart. We're not used to seeing James in a suit.'

Emotion is bubbling away at all our surfaces. We share a great grief between us. They are grieving for Jenny and for their son and I am reminded of James's words weeks ago, 'They have killed more than Jenny. They have killed our future.'

The cars do not hang about on the drive across Bristol to my parents' home where Jenny has been since this morning. When we arrive, my mother has a tray of drinks out for everyone, shots of sherry or brandy. My father is sitting in his chair in the front room with Jenny's coffin. He is looking at it, deep in thought. He looks smart in his dark suit and dignified but so frail and sad. He sees me and stands up, patting the end of the coffin as he does so, as if he has been in conversation with Jenny and now has to bring their talk to a close. My father's way of communicating love is to pat a shoulder, twice.

The police have provided an escort. Jenny would have been amused and touched by that. There is a fleet of cars. I did not want any of the family to worry about driving today. Greg and I are in the front car with James, Lizzie, Thomas and Martyn. Ahead of us is the hearse. The cover Lizzie has made hangs over the coffin, a bright abstract sunflower at the centre surrounded by smaller sunflower patterns with musical and literary quotations weaving in between. On top is a simple spray of white roses from Greg and me with a similar spray of deep red roses from James. Other flowers, sunflowers, sweet peas, all the colours of summer, surround the base of the coffin.

We have made this day as beautiful as possible.

Jenny's final journey takes her through all her favourite Bristol locations: past the church and common, over the Downs, under Brunel's suspension bridge and past the SS Great Britain. As the cortege approaches the cathedral, the bell is tolling low and slow and sombre. Every toll of the bell brings us closer to the place where we would rather not go. To the left of the cathedral is a mass of media, cameras, big lenses and sound booms. To the right is the gathered clergy taking part in the service, white and gold robes moving in the breeze. Inside, the choir made up of Jenny's friends will have been performing a programme of music while the congregation waited. I will never get to hear it, but I know the music will have been beautiful.

I do not know how to leave the car. 'Stay where you are for the time being,' Derek advises. None of us attempts to move but we all watch as the back of the hearse is opened and flowers are removed. Cameras are flashing but at a distance. Derek is leading Lizzie from the car and the cousins from the car behind to take up their places beside the coffin. The girls look beautiful, all dressed in dark trouser suits with gold corset tops underneath. The boys are in dark suits, white shirts and black ties. As they line up in pairs, they link arms around waists. Solidarity and support in every possible sense.

This ought to have been Jenny's wedding not her funeral. These girls should have been her bridesmaids not her pallbearers. I must not keep thinking these things, not today, but it is so difficult to rid my mind of what might have been.

Two bishops have come over to the car. They are leaning inside. Bishop Mike is conducting the service and will be doing the sermon. Not a happy task. I have not met the new Bishop, Lee. It was his service I slipped out from early to meet Jenny in June. He's introducing himself, saying he wanted to be here today. Is that OK?

'Of course,' we all say in chorus, 'Thank you'.

'It's time to go,' Derek is saying, standing aside for the bishops to move out of the way. Lizzie and her cousins are lined up with Jenny on their shoulders. They are standing tall and proud, their faces fixed and looking straight ahead. It is all happening too quickly. I am standing between Greg and James. I look behind to check that Thomas is all right. He does not look at me and like his sister and cousins he is looking straight ahead, only he is looking at his sister's coffin. Martyn is standing next to him, giving me a brief 'OK' nod as I turn. My parents are just behind. I'm not sure who is holding on to whom, Mum to Dad or Dad to Mum.

The procession is in place. Duncan, tall and distinctive with his eccentric moustache and Jenny's director of music from her church choir days is at the helm carrying the cross. All these people have come to be with Jenny.

'Listen to this Mum, "I want everyone to know we all need each other and each one of us makes a difference."' It's as if Jenny is whispering in my ear, 'Look after James.'

I lean forward and touch Jenny's coffin, 'We're here Jenny, we're all with you.' All her family are lined up except Lucy who is inside waiting with her husband and Jenny's friends to lead her cousin in to Christian Forshaw's music.

The procession moves forward, slowly and with dignity, pausing at the west door. I can hear the saxophone; improvising, soaring and then the bodhrán drum, earthy, solid measured beats and finally the solo voice, 'Let all mortal flesh keep silence and with fear and trembling stand.' We are walking through the cathedral to our places. My ears are trained on the drum and my eyes on Jenny's coffin to keep me moving forward. Greg and James and I are walking together but not touching.

There is an order of service on each of our seats. I see Jenny at every turn. The picture on the front cover is of her sipping from a glass of overflowing champagne. The two pictures on the back cover are set against a background of manuscript music: Jenny and James at a black-tie formal and a picture of Jenny as a little girl, big blue eyes and untidy golden curls looking directly at the camera.

Resonant voices fill the cathedral: 'For everything there is a season … a time for every matter under heaven; a time to be born, and a time to die'. But this was not a time for Jenny to die. I will never be reconciled to that; 'A time to kill, and a time to heal … A time to weep, and a time to laugh; a time to mourn, and a time to dance'. I think it will be a long time before any of us dances again, in the real sense.

A time to seek, and a time to lose;
a time to keep silence, and a time to speak;
a time to love, and a time to hate;
a time for war, and a time for peace.

I chose this reading with great care; for its rhythm and because it covers just about everything, even the matters I don't care for and the matters that have marked my family for ever.

The first hymn I chose for these lines:

For the joy of human love,
brother, sister, parent, child,
friends on earth and friends above,
pleasures pure and undefiled.

I open and close my mouth but no sound comes out. It is the same for all the hymns. All my sounds are in my heart today.

I am here, with it, composed and calm but I feel far away, in a place of disbelief and unreality.

There are wonderful voices singing and reading Jenny's favourite pieces or pieces that held special significance. 'Let me not to the marriage of true minds admit impediments.'

'The Temptation of Eve', read with all the feisty spirit that Jenny would approve of. Britten's 'Hymn to the Virgin' is exquisitely beautiful and I can almost imagine Jenny not in her coffin but in the midst of her friends singing and loving it. An academic tribute by her tutor is heart-warming and real, speaking of her vulnerability as well as her achievement. Mike talked about Jenny's early years, her 'biting' phase as a toddler when she would frequently nip her cousin Katie which made everyone listening laugh. He talked about her big, blue, almond-shaped eyes, at which point a quiet descended on the cathedral as people remembered. Stefan talked about Jenny's later years, her weekends at their home with James and a particular gin-tasting session. This is what I strived for, a funeral of beauty and gutsy reality with Jenny at the centre.

When James speaks, it is not to give an address but to read from Shakespeare's *The Two Gentlemen of Verona*. There has been some teasing over this, over James's reticence to read in public. 'James never reads in public,' his mother laughed. 'I read at school, once,' he said. The point is that James didn't want to read anything; he wanted to read this piece. He goes forward to read as the last lines of a hymn are sung out 'With a well-tuned heart sing thou the songs of love; let all thy days till life shall end, what'er he send, be filled with praise'. James is at the front, paper in hand, speaking with strength and courage and telling fifteen hundred people everything they need to know about his grief and love for Jenny.

To die is to be banished from myself.
And Silvia is myself; banished from her
Is self from self, a deadly banishment
What light is light, if Silvia be not seen?
What joy is joy, if Silvia be not by?
Unless it be to think that she is by,
And feed upon the shadow of perfection.
Except I be by Silvia in the night,
There is no music in the nightingale;
Unless I look on Silvia in the day,
There is no day for me to look upon.
She is my essence, and I leave to be
If I be not by her fair influence
Fostered, illuminated, cherished, kept alive.
I fly not death, to fly his deadly doom:

Tarry I here, I but attend on death;
But fly I hence, I fly away from life.

As he walks back, you could hear a pin drop.

I pity the person that has to read next. Jenny's godmother, Dendy, as it happens.

If every dramatic event has a climax, it is 'Hallelujah' from the film *Shrek* sung by Jenny's friends, which I first heard on the day of the two-minute silence in London, sitting in the church of St Mary-Le-Bow with James and Charlie and friends and colleagues from Jenny's work.

I am aware all around me of exquisite beauty and exquisite pain, in the faces of the people, in the atmosphere of the place, in the vibrant gold and blue of sunflowers and delphiniums, in the carved stone scene of the Crucifixion on the pulpit caught in a beam of sunlight through a stained-glass window and resting on Jenny's coffin.

Jenny's funeral is almost over. I don't want it to end because the end of the funeral is the end of so much more. I hear 'Steal Away' sung and prayers said and 'The Traveller' read, and through it all I have a sense of panic, of things slipping away and time nearly out. And time is nearly out. I watch my colleague David move around the coffin, sprinkling it with holy water as a sign of baptism and censing it as a sign of the indwelling of the Holy Spirit and I look across to Lizzie who has tears streaming down her face and along the line of cousins next to her, and think, arbitrarily or maybe because Jenny's funny spirit is about the place, that they resemble a water feature, a wall of beauty and trickling water trails. And then finally Jenny's friends sing the lament of 'The Silver Swan,' who opened her throat in song as death approached and in dying sung no more.

Silence.

'Guide me, O thou great Redeemer, pilgrim through this barren land', 'Always end on a good sing Mum,' I can hear Jenny saying from a time past.

We are leaving the Cathedral and for the first time I see people's faces, watching Jenny being carried back out into the sunshine to Widor's Toccata.

Lizzie and Thomas and the cousins are having a group hug. The funeral directors are politely anxious, the service has overrun and we need to get to the crematorium for our slot. Cameras are flashing and people are pouring out of the Cathedral: this is my last image as the cars pull away, moving faster than when we arrived.

There is confusion when we arrive at the crematorium. Another family are there before us. I don't know what happened, Derek sorted it out but we are ushered in, just the family and close friends for this final, final part. Short: we'll be here long enough to do the deed and no longer. There is nothing else left to say, readings to be read or music to be sung.

'Loud?' Derek is holding up a CD.

'Yes, loud.'

I have not told anyone about this. It is my gift to Lizzie and Thomas, one last piece of music.

As Jenny is lifted high on the shoulders of the pallbearers, not Lizzie and her cousins for this part, the song which Jenny and Lizzie and Thomas used to play incessantly, especially if they needed to cheer each other up, blasts out of the building. 'Build me up Buttercup' takes us into the chapel and up to the place where there is only time for one more look at Jenny's coffin, one more touch of its wood and the shutters open and it is gone from sight, leaving an empty space, bleak beyond words. We do not linger here, but return to join our friends and family at Bristol's Victoria Rooms, now the university music department, where Jenny spent some of the last glorious year of her life. There is champagne; lots of it. My glass is never empty.

I'm in bed, everyone has left. Many came back to the house after we had finished drinking champagne but nobody stayed long. This evening has been an anti-climax. It could not have been anything else. I don't think I can bear to wake up tomorrow morning but I must. In the darkness, I can hear Thomas's voice, something he said to me one morning this week, 'You still have me you know Mum, and Lizzie. We're still here'.

This is the thought I hold to my heart as the darkness takes me into the oblivion of sleep.

'ANOINTED'

Anointed of her womb
Holy and maternal
Chrisom of water milk and blood
Mystic food
Life-endowed birth
Flowing gushing free and pure
Blessed with mother's tears
Timeless ritual of touch and
Ceremonial kiss
Body consecrated with olive and balm
Vows whispered abundant divine

Wrapped in white cloth and placed in a warm bed

Protected
Anointed
In danger from wild animals
In preparation for battle
In the hour of death
Outward signs
Baptism of life
Sacred ritual.

JULIE NICHOLSON

Acknowledgements

It is four years since I began thinking about writing this book. At the time I was immersed in a rehearsal with about forty teenagers. It was almost a year after my daughter Jennifer was killed in what has become known as the 7/7 London Bombings. I was trying to find meaning and purpose in my working life and my role as an ordained priest in the community. I was keeping busy and keeping going in the best way that I could. Working with this group of vibrant and energetic young people, it was impossible to deny life. Typically, the rehearsal was full of noise and creative challenges. My phone buzzed in my pocket. A few minutes later, in the relative quiet of the office, I had my first tentative conversation with Mark Lucas, a literary agent. 'I would like to see you write a book,' he said. It was a moment of déjà vu. Some years earlier, Jennifer had said, 'What I'd really like to see you do, Mum, is write a book.' At the end of the phone call, when I returned to the adrenaline-filled hall, a new seed had been sown; coaxing it to life took a little longer.

There have been times when the hand that held the pen found it difficult to function and I am extremely grateful to Mark Lucas for his encouragement and wise advice; to Carole Tonkinson and Belinda

Budge of HarperCollins for their support and commitment; and to Helen Hawksfield, Richenda Todd and the team at HarperCollins who have wrestled this book from me to bring it into production.

My thanks to Stephen and Ann Martin for an open invitation and uninterrupted space to write in Wales; Bob and Claire Green for keeping my computer going, paperwork down and spirits up; Elizabeth McClune for the blessing of her home in beautiful Port na Blagh; Len and Sue North for a place to retreat and rejuvenate; Judy Lee for proof reading; and Miranda Peters and Roger Childs for asking the right questions four years ago. I am indebted to friends, some who appear in the pages of this book and many who do not but who have been no less essential to the progress of the book and as good and valued companions in life. I would like to acknowledge my deep gratitude to Christian Forshaw for his gift of music and his friendship; and to Kevin Crossley-Holland for his kind permission and gift of words.

In writing this book I have been aware of the families of the fifty-one beloved people killed with Jenny and who carry their own sorrow and grief. I would like to make a special acknowledgment to them, to their humanity and dignity and to friendships and respect that have emerged out of the traumatic events of 7 July 2005.

The author and publisher would like to thank Faber & Faber for permission to reprint a quotation from 'Burnt Norton' by T. S. Eliot, from *Four Quartets*.

While every effort has been made to trace the owners of copyright material reproduced herein and secure permissions, the publishers would like to apologise for any omissions and will be pleased to incorporate missing acknowledgements in any future edition of this book.